Original Sin Is A Lie

Peck

How Spirituality Defies Dogma and Reveals Our True Self

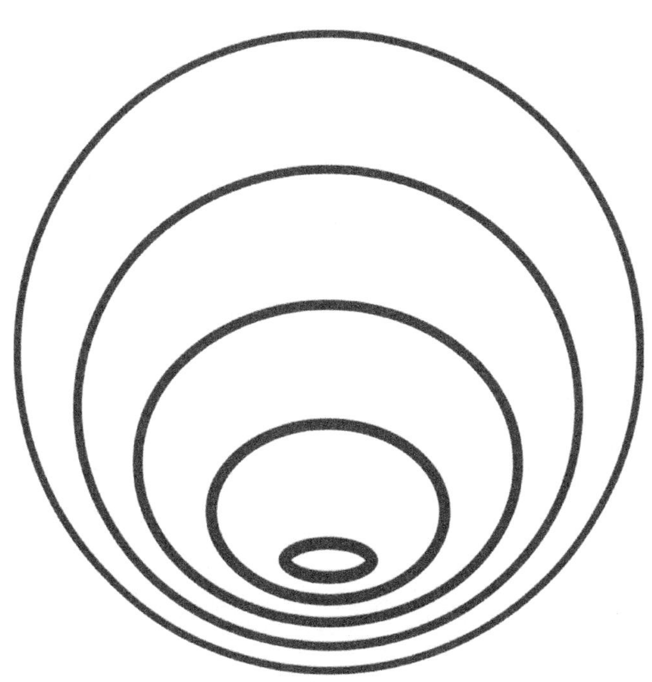

Original Sin Is A Lie: How Spirituality Defies Dogma and Reveals Our True Self

Written by Bob Peck.

Edited by Bob Peck & Scott Standley.

Book design by Elizabeth Nelson, Sarah Thomas & Daryna Shyliuk.

First printing edition 2022.

originalsinisalie.com

ISBN-13: 979-8-218-06583-6

Contents

Introduction ix

PART ONE: DEBUNKING FEARFUL INSTITUTIONS 11

CHAPTER 1 Christianity Misinterpreted Christ 13
- Augustine vs. Pelagius 13
- Paul: The Convert and Inauthentic Attribution 18
- Early Questions in Texas 23
- Why It's Okay to Pick and Choose 24
- "Have You Considered?" 33
- The 'Foolish' Pharisees as a Later Emphasis 34

CHAPTER 2 His True, Radical Teaching of Love 37
- The Good Samaritan Unveils Religious Hypocrisy 37
- Sermon on the Mount: The Essence 40
- A Piano Player and the Klan 46
- "They Know Not What They Do" 47
- Tío 52
- Layers of the Teaching 53

CHAPTER 3 Who Is He? Who Am I? 59
- From Christ to Kriya 59
- The Kingdom Within, "Inside" not "Among"! 62
- The Spiritual Gospel of John, Its Beauty and Its Issues 64
- Gospel of Thomas: The Fifth Gospel, or The Book That Changes Everything 70

PART TWO: THE PERENNIAL PHILOSOPHY: IT'S ALL TRUE 79

CHAPTER 4 Many Paths Up the Mountain 81
- The Apache Medicine Man 81
- Other Names for God 84

CHAPTER 5 Parallels Among the Central Religious Figures 91
The Avatars 91
Krishna 94
Gautama Buddha 95
Jesus of Nazareth 97
What Did They Teach Us? 98
Other Masks of the One 108

CHAPTER 6 The Inclusive East 111
The Kingdom Within, the Movie 111
Hinduism as a Spiritual Foundation 116
Yogas: Bhakti & Jnana, the Heart & the Mind 123
Ramakrishna Validates Them All 127
Cosmic Connections 132

CHAPTER 7 Ancient Religions and New Sciences 139
No Human System is Flawless 139
Transcending Ego 141
Scientists are the Modern Shamans 144

PART THREE: AWARENESS IS THE FOUNDATION 155

CHAPTER 8 Demystifying Mysticism 157
From the Outer to the Inner 157
Gnosticism 161
Sufism 163
Kabbalah 166
Zen 169
Advaita Vedanta 172
New Age 174

CHAPTER 9 The Present Has Everything 179
The Present Never Runs Out 179
Bobby the Zen Master: Emptiness & Presence 182
The Unpleasantness as an Anchor 184
Unraveling “PRAY. REPENT. OBEY.” 185

CHAPTER 10 Noticing Is The First Step 189
Sri Ramana, Self-Inquiry, and the Bull in the Stable 189

Going to 'the thing' 192
Byron Katie and the Work 193
Proving My Spiritual-ness 197

PART FOUR: THE COMPASSIONATE HEART . 201

CHAPTER 11 Turning Them into Us 203
How Can I Help? 203
The Blazing Heart 208
The Bodhisattva Vow 210
A Monk at Think & Drink 215
Solidarity with the Persecuted 216
Befriending a Nazi 218

CHAPTER 12 Jesus Despised Greed 221
St. Francis and the Wealthy Church Service 221
"My Son Won't Be Catholic" 222
Worship One: God or Mammon 225

CHAPTER 13 Self-Love is Not Ego 231
The Chakras in Brief 231
Richie Flores, the Ex-Convict Turned Yoga Master 236
Love Yourself, with Humility, without Ego 237

CHAPTER 14 Maharajji 241
"Meditate like Christ." 241
"Spleen." 243
"Don't You See It's All Perfect?" 247

PART FIVE: WE ARE NOT THE BODY: WE ARE SPIRIT 251

CHAPTER 15 What Happens To Us Is For Us 253
The Wheel of Samsara 253
Nil and Sam Harris 260
Katyayana's Laughter 261
A dear friend asked me, "Why? Why are you so certain of all this?" 262

CHAPTER 16 Psychedelia: A Glimpse but Impossible to Stay Up 265
Shamans Melting Boundaries 265

The Concord Prison Experiment 270
Maharajji's LSD Story 273

CHAPTER 17 Transcending What the World Offers 277
We Are Tourists 277
Cremation Luncheon 280
The Middle Way and The Narrow Gate 280

PART SIX: THE LOVE OF OUR CREATOR IS INESCAPABLE 283

CHAPTER 18 Piercing the Illusory Veil 285
Experience Rather Than Theology 285
"This Is A Table." 292
Flipping Desire Is All It Takes 297

CHAPTER 19 Hell Is A State of Mind 301
The Samurai and The Monk 301
"Gehenna" and the "Gnashing of Teeth" 302
Plato's Cave Points to Transcendence 308

CHAPTER 20 Our True Nature Is Love 311
Who Are We, Really? 311
A Father and Son: Human and Divine 318
An Emptying of the False, A Stilling of the Mind, A Transforming of the Self 319
Unconditional Love Is Fearlessness 323
Liberation Is True Forgiveness 326

EPILOGUE 331

THE EXPERIENCING: THE PARABLE OF THE POISONED ARROW 332

CITATIONS 337

GRATITUDE 364

STAY CONNECTED (TO YOUR INNER BEING, BUT ALSO TO ME) 366

This book is dedicated to Paramahansa Yogananda,

that extraordinary heart who dedicated his 20th century incarnation to the upliftment of his brothers and sisters in the West.

May his radiant smile continue to awaken millions more!

Introduction

This book was inspired by the mystical threads that are present in all the world's religions. My academic study and my personal experience with these religions have led me to conclude that some truths are universal.

In many cases, however, these truths—the original, elevated messages of Love & Transcendence—have been buried beneath layers of religious dogma, institutional control, and practices that have become incompatible with the intent of the great spiritual masters whose teachings provided the foundations in the first place. Lesser men saw these monumental ideologies as opportunities to increase their own power. Religion, it seems, has tried to cover up the very spirituality that birthed it.

Thankfully, the fuller spiritual understanding is not only still available to us, but shining luminously, encouraging our awakening. Within every spiritual tradition, there are those often referred to as "mystics". They are compassionate, highly spiritual beings who have appeared throughout history to share their wisdom and serve as examples of how to live in connection with the Divine, with our fellow humans, and with all of creation. As we begin to uncover the essence of one tradition, we can appreciate others. There is wisdom in every corner of the globe—how can the Source of All be restricted to one cul-de-sac?

But me? The current incarnation of the author is just a boy from Texas, who read the East in the West and started to glimpse 'through the veil' over a decade ago. My spiritually passionate early years led me to study Comparative Religion—from the shamans to the Sufis—and formative Christianity at the University of Texas at Austin. My studies led me to Yogananda and Kriya Yoga. My practice led me to becoming a certified mindfulness meditation teacher and a commentator on these texts, concepts, and methodologies.

It's worth mentioning that I use several names for God—as I'll discuss thoroughly in Chapter 4—because "God" is just a word. "God" is such a loaded term for so many of us that to capture what I (& the mystics) mean by "God" it takes a variety of terms to even start to point to its fullness, such as: The One, The Source, Divine, Truth, Love, Unity, The True Reality, Our Loving Creator, Infinite Intelligence, and The Rootless Root of All. There are many instances of poetic capitalization that might offend grammarians so beware! Whenever I break the rules, know that it is purposeful. I'm disconnecting us from concepts. From form altogether.

It is almost laughable that I should write this but I'd rather err on the side of clarity: I am not a guru.

I have zero desire to obtain a "following". It is not my intention to tell anyone how to live.

I do believe, like the Hindus, the Buddhists, and many world mystics, that every being is on a path to awakening. And I am working through my own stuff just like everyone else.

This book is a sincere act of service in pointing to the deepest instances of wisdom I've come across in spiritual philosophy: a collection of beliefs that can be utterly transformational. It is a great joy of my life to work with this material. And I am not a completed project. Trust me, I am still quite busy polishing my own mirror.

This book is a mashup of my favorite things, stories and teachers. My hope is that by looking through the mystics' lens we can re-examine the beauty of the masters' intentions and discover the truths our religious traditions still offer us today. All I'm doing is pointing to the best of us.

May it offer you understanding. May it offer you peace. May the words from these pages travel from my heart to yours.

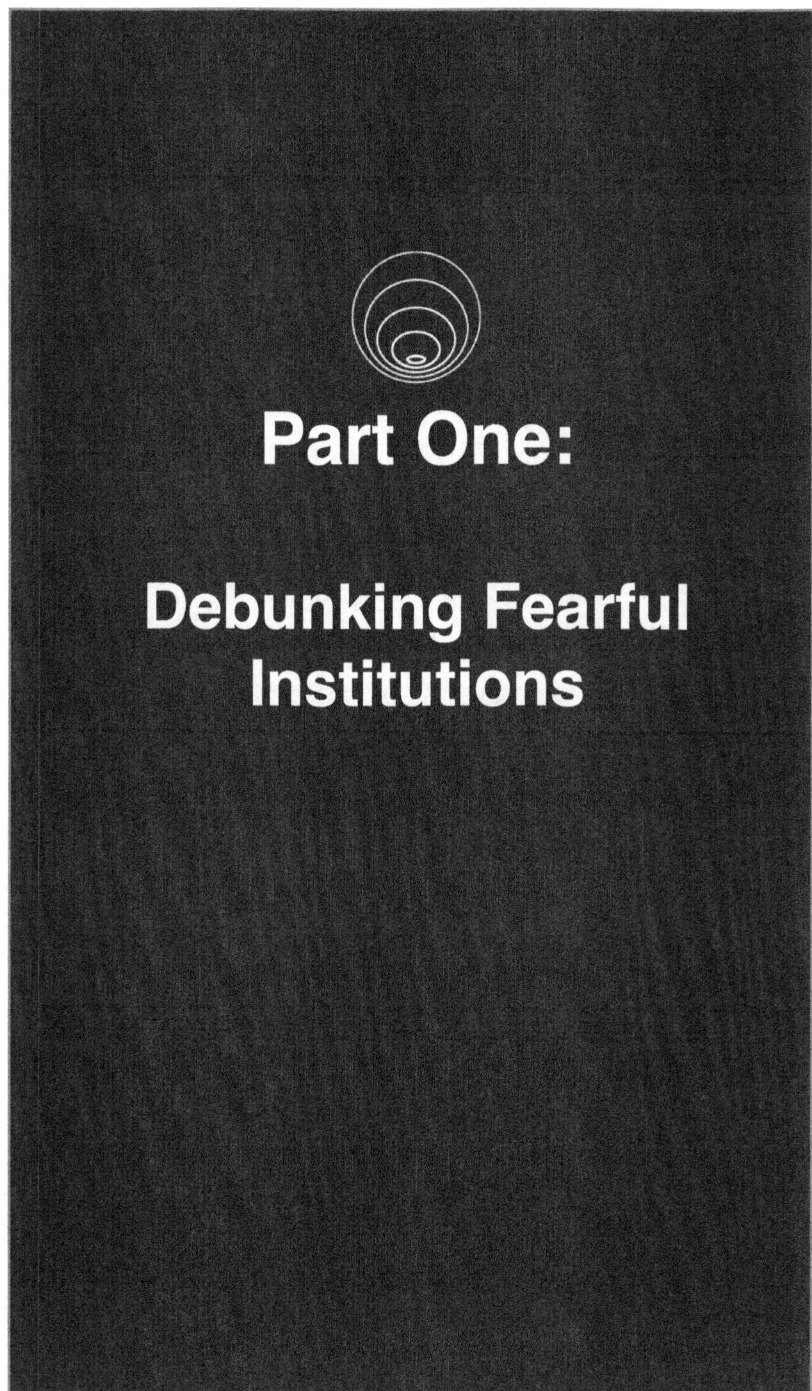

Part One:

Debunking Fearful Institutions

Original sin is a lie,

because deep within,

miles underneath
our self-imposed,
psychological blocks
and habitual hardenings,

is a shared truth,

a shared existence
among all beings:

at the very core of who we are,

Is Love.

CHAPTER 1

Christianity Misinterpreted Christ

Augustine vs. Pelagius

Nearly four hundred years after the death of Jesus, two monks were arguing.

Augustine considered human beings originally sinful.

Pelagius considered human beings as neutral: neither inherently divine nor inherently sinful.

Augustine had more political power, a larger movement of supporters, and a political savviness within the church authority that eluded Pelagius. Pelagius was eventually condemned to be a heretic and was removed from the Christian faith.[1]

Augustine became a saint.

Pelagius died in exile.

Augustine went on to become a gargantuan influence on not just Christian theology but Western philosophy as a whole.

Jesus himself never said a thing about "original sin".[2]

Most people are unaware of this. In fact, many Christians believe that "original sin" is an undeniable fact of human nature. They think it's some unquestionable truth about Christian doctrine, and therefore, ourselves.

And it is one of the most powerfully damning lies in the

modern lexicon.

To be clear this book is not exclusively about Bible scholarship and formative Christianity—I'll be happily covering a broad range of spiritual principles—but I am writing for those of us who were brought up in Christian families. We were programmed with a lot of awful falsehoods about how there is only one true religion, that Our Creator is a patriarchal god demanding obedience, and that disobedience to Him condemns us to a fiery eternity. These are all misinterpretations of the teachings of Jesus that took hold in order to scare believers into subservience.

After we learn about the context around these lies more deeply, we can begin to appreciate the real message of Jesus, of other spiritual systems, and ultimately who we truly are.

If we believe we are originally sinful, we have no love for ourselves.

When we have no love for ourselves, we have no love for others.

The fundamental belief in who we are has radical implications for civilization. If we believe we are inherently evil, then we (consciously or subconsciously) assume the worst about one another. Family members assume the worst about other family members, communities assume the worst about other communities, and governments assume the worst about other governments... We're stumbling down the path towards annihilation.

Pelagius suggested that it is on us to choose to listen to our Divine Creator, but Augustine preached that we are even incapable of *choosing,* suggesting that the very choice requires God's grace. From the Augustinian perspective, that's how dirty we are.

Their bitter rivalry actually began as distant admiration. After first reading Pelagius' *Commentary on Romans,* Augustine wrote that Pelagius was a "distinguished Christian man" and a "highly advanced Christian". Later on in their lives however, Augustine referred to Pelagius as "the enemy of God's grace", consumed by his mission to win out over his contemporary. In those same books against Pelagius, he spent a considerable amount of time discussing why infants needed to be baptized immediately in order to avoid damnation.[3]

Augustine's false belief of original sin comes from the primordial Adam and Eve story, but it's primarily a misread of the apostle Paul, not Jesus. If original sin supposedly comes from the *Book of Genesis* story, why doesn't the Jewish religion have it?

It doesn't.

The texts that Paul and Augustine are referencing are from the first book of the Hebrew Bible and Christian Old Testament. It was a Jewish text first, and yet there is no original sin in Judaism—the foundational religion upon which Christianity is built.

You're probably familiar with the Adam and Eve story. It's a creation tale, just like every civilization has their own creation tale. They were in the Garden of Eden, this extremely ideal situation, and God, our Endlessly-Loving Eternal Creator, played a trick on them. He said 'do whatever you like, but don't eat this one thing, this Fruit of Knowledge.' (*Genesis* 2:16-17) In this particular creation tale, we did that. We were tempted by an evil, persuasive reptile, and then they ate that damn fruit. This got them—and by extension all of their line, including us—kicked out of the garden.

Augustine added that moment as bullet point number one on why we're inherently evil.

But there are other reads on the creation tale of Judaism.

The Gnostics were a highly spiritual, esoteric branch of early Jesus followers who were eventually considered heretical by early Church Fathers, as I'll discuss later. They suggested that the Loving Creator to which Jesus refers—whose love falls on all of us, like the rain (*Matthew* 5:45)—was an entirely different entity than the god who created this plane of existence.[4] Marcion was an early Gnostic Christian (although some scholars consider him proto-Gnostic), who organized the first canon of gospels into what would become the New Testament. He called this entity "Yaldaboath", a false creator god who played that dirty trick on humanity in the garden. According to the Gnostics, Yaldaboath is the same one they call

"Jehovah" in the Old Testament. You know, the one who encourages the killing of babies? (*1 Samuel* 15:2-3)

Marcion wrote extensively about the idea that while there is a lower false creator from the Old Testament, thankfully there is also a Higher, Transcendent, Forever-Loving Divine Being of Oneness, beyond this lower plane of duality. Christ was referring to a True God of Love and Oneness, and these views are what got the Gnostics in trouble.

Marcion's theological view is fascinating because not only does it sound like a more transcendental, sophisticated view of existence, it helps us break away from the firm authority held by that demanding god who requires absolute obedience in the Abrahamic traditions. This is a vital step. It's a departure from patriarchal anger, into an opening-up. We can now begin to contemplate a wider worldview and appreciation for many spiritual systems. Institutional Christianity has been so successful at programming so many billions (!) of people to not question scripture. To not question that angry, jealous god (*Exodus* 20:15). But once you do, what you find is beautiful, enduring, and powerfully transformative. Let's go from fear to Love together, shall we?

Interestingly, at one point in his life Augustine of Hippo was a Gnostic. He practiced Manichaeism, which had influences from Plato, Plotinus and other Hellenistic philosophers. Because of this, some contemporary Christians have implied that Augustine 'infiltrated' the church with Gnostic doctrine. This is, however, an incomplete reading of history. What he did keep from his Gnostic days was the emphasis on the absolute non-materiality of God, writing:

> *"I was made certain that you exist, that you are infinite... that you are truly he who is always the same, with nor varied parts and changing movements, and that all other things are from you."*
>
> *—Augustine, Confessions 7.20.26*

Augustine's striking and bitter contrast against the Gnostics and the Neoplatonists was due to his insistence on Adam's sin corrupting the formerly innate perfection. He later diatribed against Manichaen Gnostics, calling their doctrines "insane".[5]

Like Pelagius and Marcion, Jesus didn't believe in original sin either.

Even Pope Benedict XVI, the gawdy golden Pope who embodies the material ostentation of traditional Catholicism, referred to "original sin" as "misleading and unprecise".[6]

There are exactly zero references to "original sin" in the gospels, the collections of stories of the life of Jesus. He's more focused on teaching compassion, forgiveness, and how to be truly spiritual. He teaches us how to pray. And attributes of his Father, the Father of All. He tells us to feed the poor. He tells us to visit those in prison. He tells us that what you do for the lowest of society, you do for him. (*Matthew* 25:40) This is because he understood that he was inherently One with All, even the most downtrodden, as someone who accessed that place of understanding which binds all beings together.

When you read the world mystics, you see this awareness emerge in other non-Christian traditions. Though the world tells us we are sinful, sages throughout the ages have insisted that we are One—all parts of a magnificent whole.

Unraveling fear-based institutional falsehoods is one of the most useful processes I have undergone in my humble experience on this planet. The evaporation of fear makes way for the True. And even beyond the analytical scholarship itself, the inspiration of those mystic seekers who have accessed these heights has unquestionably created who I am today. The highest gratitude I can express is owed to those brothers and sisters throughout our civilization who have contributed to reminding all of us of our True Essence. Our Oneness. Our Deepest Reality of Love.

So that's what we'll be exploring in this book. A bit of undoing, and a bit of rediscovery. We will untangle the exoteric to better understand the esoteric. By trimming back the thorns of the fearful ego can we see more clearly the radiant bloom of Self.

Paul: The Convert and Inauthentic Attribution

Beyond the Garden of Eden, Augustine's "original sin" comes from a few lines from Paul, who was an incredible teacher in his own right, but even Paul never knew Jesus in person.

Briefly, Paul was a member of another sect of Judaism called the Pharisees—which we'll get into more shortly. The Pharisees were in conflict with the early Jesus-following Jews in those first decades after the death of Jesus in 30-34 C.E. In those days, most practitioners of the Jewish religion worshipped in the Temple in Jerusalem. When the Temple was sacked by the Romans in 70 C.E, suddenly most of the religion was now without their center of worship. This opportunity made the Pharisees and the Jesus-following Jews competitive for a large population of temple-abiding Jews, newly shaken into a temple-less existential crisis.[7]

So Paul, initially Saul the Pharisee, was heading from Jerusalem to Damascus to stamp out some rowdy Jesus-following Jews (*Galatians* 1:13) when suddenly, in the middle of the road, he was graced by a divine vision. Saul was spellbound. Bathed in perfect, white light, he saw an image of a man. Saul asked the spirit, "Who are you?"

The spirit replied, *"I am Jesus, whom you are persecuting."* (*Acts* 9:5)

He couldn't see for three days, and finally came to after being healed in Damascus by a follower of Jesus... at a community gathering which he would have very likely been breaking up, if he hadn't gone through his life-altering experience.

Even though his conversion experience took place after the crucifixion, Paul became as influential as any apostle in spreading the teachings of Jesus. He traveled extensively throughout the Roman Empire establishing house-churches and corresponding with early church leaders on matters of theology and spiritual living. His letters comprise the Pauline Epistles, which account for 14 of the 27 books of the New Testament.

There is real beauty to Paul's conversion, primarily because it emphasizes that the Creator's Love is so powerful that it can even touch the heart of the hostile persecutor. It is unconditional, inescapable. And for any skeptics questioning the legitimacy of such an experience, after you read the Hindu guru stories of the 19th and 20th centuries, some of which I'll share in this book, as well as new scientific theories on the nature of consciousness, you start to approach mystical experiences like Paul's with considerably less scrutiny.

However, two points to emphasize in this early chapter are that: 1) Paul never knew Jesus in person. The attributed author of more than half of the books of the New Testament never met the guy on whom the whole religion is based. And 2) that the legitimate authorship of many of Paul's letters is disputed by both scholars and Christian theologians alike.[8]

I do want to be clear that Paul did write some real gems, like:

> *"Love is patient; love is kind; love is not envious or boastful or arrogant or rude. It does not insist on its own way; it is not irritable or resentful; it does not rejoice in wrongdoing, but rejoices in the truth."*
>
> *—Paul of Tarsus, 1 Corinthians, 13:4-6 (NRSV)*

And I particularly want to honor:

> *"There is no longer Jew or Greek, there is no longer slave or free, there is no longer male and female; for all of you are one in Christ Jesus."*
>
> *—Paul of Tarsus, Galatians, 3:28 (NRSV)*

Even Augustine has his moments... they don't just make anybody a saint.

But again, the second-most influential person in the creation of the entire religion (Paul) never met the first-most (Jesus).

What I'm getting at here is that the teaching we have today is two thousand years' worth of "Telephone". A Fully-Awakened Being taught Unity to disciples, who shared those stories for decades (called the 'oral tradition'), Paul heard these stories and wrote his own takes about them, then they entered the gospels in their own assorted interpretations, and then centuries later Augustine makes his own declaration that we must all be inherently evil. This is a faulty conceptual regression here, friends.

The second point on this foundational figure is that Paul's Epistles (letters) are placed into two categories: disputed and undisputed. We are nearly certain that seven letters were written by Paul himself:

- *First Epistle to the Thessalonians*
- *Epistle to the Galatians*
- *First Epistle to the Corinthians*
- *Second Epistle to the Corinthians*
- *Epistle to the Philippians*
- *Epistle to Philemon*
- *Epistle to the Romans*

But the other seven are unlikely Paul's at all:

- *Epistle to the Ephesians* (debated)
- *Epistle to the Colossians* (debated)
- *Second Epistle to the Thessalonians* (debated)
- *First Epistle to Timothy* ("Pastoral", highly unlikely)
- *Second Epistle to Timothy* ("Pastoral", highly unlikely)
- *Epistle to Titus* ("Pastoral", highly unlikely)
- *Epistle to the Hebrews* (inauthentic)

How are we able to make such a claim?

We can question who actually wrote each letter by using both internal and external evidence.

What do I mean by that?

Internal evidence means the text inside the document, and external means we have early church fathers writing other letters to each other with hot takes on the nature of these documents back in those days.

Internally, the structure and composition of the disputed letters are wildly different than the authentic letters.

The vocabulary is very different: terms like *"piety," "heretical,"* and *"the Savior"* as a name for Jesus, are only in the Pastorals; they do not occur at all in authentic Paul or anywhere else in the New Testament. The author(s) of *Colossians* and *Ephesians* understands redemption as the "forgiveness of sins" (*Colossians* 1:14), which also does not occur in Paul's other letters.[9] Many of the religious terms from these letters falsely attributed to Paul play heavily into modern American Christianity.

The authentic letters are personal, with Paul solving specific problems faced by these early communities, whereas the Pastoral letters are broad, far-reaching philosophical treatises that tend to reflect larger theological questions, including guidance on 'traits of a deacon', a role that didn't exist during Paul's lifetime.

Timothy himself in *1 Timothy* is my favorite example of the extreme contrast.

In the genuine letters, Paul considers Timothy extremely trustworthy and of an incredible character. Paul has "no one else" like him, who truly cares (*Philippians* 2:20), and he calls Timothy his "beloved and faithful child" (*1 Corinthians* 4:17). But in the Pastorals, Timothy is considered immature (*1 Timothy* 4:12), lacking in strength (*2 Timothy* 2:3-6), and prone to "youthful lusts" (*1 Timothy* 5:2, *2 Timothy* 2:22).[10]

The invalidation of *1 Timothy* is particularly important because of all this fun stuff:

Religious exclusivism!

> *"For there is one God, and one mediator between God and men, the man Christ Jesus."*
>
> *—1 Timothy, 2:5*

Patriarchal chauvinism!

> *"Let a woman learn in quietness with full submission.*

> *But I don't permit a woman to teach, nor to exercise authority over a man, but to be in quietness. For Adam was formed first, then Eve. Adam wasn't deceived, but the woman, being deceived, has fallen into disobedience; but she will be saved through her childbearing."*
>
> —*1 Timothy, 2:11-15 (NRSV)*

And of course, advice for slaves to better obey their masters!

> *"Let all who are under the yoke of slavery regard their masters as worthy of all honor, so that the name of God and the teaching may not be blasphemed. Those who have believing masters must not be disrespectful to them on the ground that they are members of the church; rather they must serve them all the more, since those who benefit by their service are believers and beloved."*
>
> —*1 Timothy, 6:1-2 (NRSV)*

Paul didn't write this.

Jesus didn't say this.

And Our Infinitely Loving Creator had absolutely nothing to do with such awful, Iron Age garbage mentalities.

There are a couple of adorable articles online written by amateur Christian apologists explaining why all of Paul's letters are indeed written by him. But that is not scholarship. Hardly any serious Bible scholar (Christian or non-Christian) accepts all of Paul's letters as authentic.

Blogger Christians are defending those letters' authenticity because they know what I know: the realization that the Bible is not infallible has massive implications for breaking out of unquestioning religious obedience. The infallibility doctrine is the preposterous idea that *every word in the Bible is literally true*. And it's a massive hurdle to overcome in the beginning of the spiritual awakening process.

Early Questions in Texas

My family and I are proud to be from Texas.

Although there are certain unfortunate connotations with the American South, I take pride in the fact that my grandparents on both sides supported the Civil Rights Movement and equality for all people. I never met either of my grandfathers, but my dad's father, Bob, played saxophone in the 40s, 50s, and 60s surrounded by musician friends of every race and background. My mom's father, Tommy, was a radio DJ in East Texas. He played soul & funk music, and one favorite family story is that he showed up to DJ a high school dance at a predominantly black high school. The emcee announced "Dr. Rock!" to great excitement, and upon his entrance, the dancers were stunned to see a lanky white guy with big glasses walk up onstage. Their concerns quickly subsided though, because as soon as he grabbed the mic he brought the same vibrant energy that they knew intimately over the airwaves.

There are a lot of churches in Texas. Living with my mom, we really were "Easter-Christmas Christians". Church was actually a great time to me, because we only went twice a year! We were Episcopalians who didn't know the words to most of the songs, but we sang them anyway, with the wholeness of our hearts. We had a great pastor, Father Patrick Gahan at St. Stephen's, a gifted orator capable of generating joyful laughter with a lighthearted observation and a moment later bringing you to a sincere testimony about grace and love. As our bi-annual pastor, he baptized me when I was eight.

Due to my personal experience of a much less forceful Christianity, I found some peace in it all. Some potential.

But as soon as I started to see the church's ego, my questioning began. Even good Christian people with noble intentions began saying things that made little sense.

Around that time, I can vividly remember going with my best friend's more pious Baptist family to a local "Vacation Bible School"—where the children go during the summer to soak up

Bible stories, and have Christian teachings reinforced in a more digestible way than the pastor's sermons on Sundays. An older woman came up to me and asked me, a nine-year-old boy, "Do you want to go to heaven?" Before I had a chance to reply, she said, "If you do, you must accept Jesus as your Lord and Savior. Just say these words and you're guaranteed to get into heaven."

Based on what I'd heard from Father Gahan heaven sounded like a better place than the alternative, but I didn't understand the concepts of Lord or Savior. What I did understand was that even to my nine-year-old brain earning something so important merely by mouthing some magic words seemed illogical. Many of the other kids went along with it, but it didn't make sense to me, so I couldn't.

Most American Christians have had similar experiences of this type of proselytization at an early age. Until that moment I had never questioned anything religious, but after that I began to question everything.

Why It's Okay to Pick and Choose

Only a few more Biblical bones to pick and we'll get beyond ancient Judaea. I realize it can be tough for some, but these points are crucial to undoing the fear. And regenerating the Love.

Whenever I talk about these ideas, I lose so many fellow Christian-upbringing adults who left the religion. Perhaps rightfully so. We couldn't grapple with the hypocrisies of modern-day Christian leadership, from the private jet televangelists to the child abuse from Catholic priests. From homophobia to the Inquisition, there are a few thousand reasons that church leadership has failed us over the millennia.

Honestly, I think so many of us came to the same questions Marcion and the Gnostics brought up in the second century, mainly: "how can a God of Love condemn us to a fiery eternity?" So we left Christianity.

But I didn't leave Christ.

And I don't mean Judeo-Christian-messianic-Bible-Christ, but rather Christ-Consciousness, or sometimes called the Cosmic Christ, really whatever you feel comfortable calling the state of awareness, of Unity, of Love, attained by that Jewish teacher from Galilee ambling across the Judaean countryside.

The Gospels, and even Paul's letters, do have value. They have some absolutely beautiful, transformative teachings for humanity, you just have to get archaeological with the text and do some digging. And once you see the real teaching *underneath* the false layers of controlling institutional rhetoric, the scriptures will start to come alive. You'll see their parallels in other faith traditions, and how they can contribute to a way of being that is harmonious, compassionate, and self-actualized.

But sadly, many secular-minded non-Christians don't get this.

For example, there is no shortage of atheists joking about Jesus cursing the fig tree. It is a complete lack of understanding of metaphor and the historical context regarding the destruction of the Temple in Jerusalem.

> *"The next day, when they had come out from Bethany, he was hungry. Seeing a fig tree afar off having leaves, he came to see if perhaps he might find anything on it. When he came to it, he found nothing but leaves, for it was not the season for figs. Jesus told it, 'May no one ever eat fruit from you again!" and his disciples heard it.'"*
>
> —*Gospel of Mark, 11:12-14*

Very simply, the fig tree represents the old ways of ancient Judaism, which is symbolic to the Temple in Jerusalem.

It was destroyed by the Roman army a few decades after the death of Jesus. The *Gospel of Mark,* in which this scene takes place, was written around 70 C.E., in the immediate time during and after the fall of the temple, so the Markan author is writing to Jews still reeling from the temple's destruction.[11] He's having Jesus prophesy its fall.

The fig tree, cursed by Jesus, is a literary device. It is a political, cultural, religious, and even sectarian symbol for mainstream religion.

If you don't understand this, then yes it's a pretty bizarre nonsensical moment. Hating on a tree.

If you do understand the historical context and the symbolic meaning, you can understand that Jesus is bringing about a new interpretation of Judaism—focusing on inclusion, love, transcendence, as opposed to exclusion, dogma, judgment—and that the old ways of ancient Judaism will soon crumble, along with the primary temple of their faith… which falls about forty years later.

While secular readers typically don't make this interpretation, churchgoers aren't too far ahead.

But it's not entirely their fault.

Contemporary church leadership doesn't want to go into great detail about *1 Timothy* being a forgery.

Or that out of the 5,700 manuscripts (copies) of the New Testament that we have today, there are more discrepancies (~400,000) in those manuscripts than there are words in the New Testament (~140,000).[12] Granted, that number might be a bit sensationalistic considering that not every variant changes the meaning of the text, but it helps paint a picture of how human this process has been over the millennia. There are differences between these accounts, stories, and teachings, and they are worth understanding more deeply.

Your local pastor only has his congregation for twenty minutes a week, really, and even in longer services the sermon usually doesn't exceed half an hour. Instead of spending time on these complex historical issues with heavy theological implications, most pastors are going to read a few inspiring verses and hammer home a point that applies to contemporary society: They emphasize that "Jesus is the greatest", throw in a Lord's Prayer or two, and let everybody rush out of there to beat that horrible after-church traffic. Okay obviously there are beautiful moments on some Sunday mornings, but in-depth biblical scholarship typically isn't happening.

My dear Catholic brother-in-law whom I cherish, was forced

to endure my endless (buzzed) spiritual-guy-proselytizing one evening, and he bravely, sincerely responded to one of my points by saying,

"I do appreciate what you're saying, but I just don't think it's okay to pick and choose."

This is a fairly common argument I hear from Christians. It's a friendlier framing of the "infallibility doctrine", without the pride.

And I am absolutely thrilled to share that—yes, it is okay to agree with and practice certain teachings in the Bible, while rejecting and taking issue with other teachings in the Bible.

For context, the New Testament was written by over a dozen different authors, for different communities, in different decades. And that's just the New Testament: the Old Testament was also written by dozens of authors, spread out across centuries. In the formation of the New Testament—the stories and teachings of Jesus—the initial events that took place were spoken of in Aramaic. Then we have decades of oral tradition before they were written down in another language, Greek. Then over the following centuries there were thousands of copies made, by hand, of those originals. To quote UNC Chapel Hill professor Bart Ehrman, today "we have copies of copies of copies of copies of copies of copies."[13]

There is historical reliability and historical unreliability. There is certainty and there is an overwhelming abyss of mystery.

Was there divine inspiration?

From the mystical point of view which I share, absolutely! The Sermon on the Mount is *sublime*. There are verses from Paul that are unifying, transcendent. There are moments in the recorded life of Jesus that will move the depths of your heart. But there are too many textual inconsistencies across our spectrum of authors to try to justify *infallibility*: there is no way around the *hundreds* of differences in plot points, let alone ideologies!

> *"What has been presented as Christianity during these nineteen centuries is only a beginning, full of mistakes, not full-blown Christianity springing from the spirit of Jesus."*

—Albert Schweitzer, Nobel Peace Prize winner and a father of modern New Testament scholarship

Initially we need a basic understanding of the timetable of this literature.

[As I have referenced previously, "Before Common Era (BCE.)" and "Common Era (CE.)" have become the standard in historical scholarship, replacing BC "Before Christ", and AD "*Anno Domini*" or (Year of Our Lord). Despite my overt admiration for the teachings of Jesus, as an author I'll be using secular historical markers. I'd like to clarify that my following brief summary is, again, a regretfully thin depiction of a subject that takes years to fully understand.

It took me five years to get a glimpse. Thousands of books have been written on the formation of the New Testament, entire careers are devoted to understanding its complexities. Start here but a few good scholars on the topic are Albert Schweitzer, Ferdinand Christian Baur, Bruce Metzger, David Flusser, Dominic Crossan, John P. Meier, Wayne Meeks, L. Michael White, Elaine Pagels, Bart Ehrman, James D.G. Dunn, Richard B. Hays, N. Thomas Wright. And then read the famous Christians' commentaries: St. Thomas Aquinas, Martin Luther, J.B. Lightfoot, St. Bonaventure, John Wycliffe, St. Hildegard of Bingen, St. Augustine, Origen.]

The brief outline is as follows:

- Jesus of Nazareth was born in Palestine under the rule of the Roman Empire, roughly the first decade BCE, during the reign of Herod the Great. Divine conception hypotheses aside, his parents, Joseph and Mary, were working class Jews in Nazareth, a small unremarkable town in the province of Galilee.[14] We have recently discovered the remains of the nearby town of Sepphoris, a larger metropolitan area—the very likely urban center where he and Joseph worked as craftsmen. Jesus began his ministry at age thirty upon being baptized in the Jordan River by a wandering Jewish apocalyptic preacher called John the Baptist. (*Matthew* 3:13-17; *Mark* 1:9-11; *Luke* 3:21-23) Jesus then travels around Judaea teaching radical, universal love within a new interpretation of Jewish scripture to a group of close friends, as well as larger crowds. His meteoric rise in popularity concerns both powerful Jewish leaders and the Roman provincial government. After a ministry of 1-3 years, he was tried by the Sanhedrin, and sentenced by Pontius Pilate to be scourged and finally killed by the state through crucifixion (an event present in all four Synoptic Gospels) in roughly 26-33 CE. His immediate followers claimed to have experienced his resurrected body days after his death. An oral tradition of stories, teachings, and parables began spreading throughout Judaea soon after.

- In the mid-to-late 30s CE, enter Paul of Tarsus, formerly Saul, who famously had that conversion experience on the road to Damascus. (Again,) Saul was a Pharisee (oppositional Jewish sect) who viciously opposed the Jesus-following-Jews (as they weren't quite "Christians" at that point). After his conversion experience, Saul became Paul. He spent the rest of his life traveling the larger Mediterranean world, meeting with surviving disciples, and helping to establish many "house churches", the earliest Christian communities. Paul's correspondence to these congregations (*Epistle to the Corinthians, Epistle to the Galatians, Romans,* etc) are the documents included in the New Testament along with the gospels themselves. The dates for most of his letters are estimated to be in the 50s CE.[15]

- According to the widely-accepted "Two-Source Hypothesis"[16], we have what is considered to be the first gospel, the *Gospel of Mark,* written around 66-70 CE, almost immediately after the destruction of the Jewish Temple in Jerusalem by the Roman army. (To be clear, that places the first gospel to be written thirty to forty years after the death of Jesus.) The *Gospel of Matthew* likely came next in 80-90 CE in the Jewish homeland, most likely Galilee. The *Gospel of Luke* was written next, typically agreed upon in 85-95 CE, along with a book by the same author, *The Acts of the Apostles,* which tells the story of what happened to the apostles after the death of Jesus. The Two-Source Hypothesis suggests that *Matthew* and *Luke* used *Mark* as a source, as well as another unknown document that scholars refer to as *"Q"*—thanks to around 250-300 verses of similar material in *Matthew* and *Luke* that is absent from *Mark.*[17] Last is the fourth canonical gospel, the *Gospel of John,* in 100-120 CE, which is so different than the other three canonical gospels (the "Synoptics" meaning "read together"), that already by the end of the second century Clement of Alexandria referred to *John* as the "Spiritual Gospel"[18]; less rooted in historicity, more focused on the divine elements of Christ that bring about a more 'kingly' Jesus.

- There are non-Christian references to the life and death of Jesus as early as 93 CE, by the Jewish historian Josephus in *Antiquities of the Jews,* and in 116 CE by the Roman historian Tacitus in *The Annals.*
- By the second century, there are hundreds of gospels about the life and teachings of Jesus. Early church leaders are forced to become critically selective of which ones are authentic, and which are forgeries written in the name of Jesus's apostles. Marcion of Sinope, who wrote about the false creator god, proposes the first Christian canon in 140 CE. Bishop Irenaeus is the first to give us the list with the four gospels of today's canon as the second century comes to a close. Origen of Alexandria contributed extensively to the canonical selection and its methodologies, and Bishop Athanasius of Alexandria gives us today's list of 27 books in his Easter letter of 367 CE.[19]

A summary about the sometimes strikingly different portrayals of Jesus in the four gospels is that "the Jesus of *Mark* would not recognize the Jesus of *John.*"

Although *Matthew* is placed first sequentially thanks to the birth narrative, historically we start with *Mark,* where Jesus is an outlandish desert wisdom teacher unappreciated by his hometown, who even has a faulty miracle (*Mark* 8:22-26). In *Matthew* we have a distinctly Jewish rabbi obsessed with fulfilling the apocalyptic message of the ancient Israelite prophets in the Old Testament. The Jesus of *Luke* is more concerned with preaching to the Gentiles (non-Jews) as it was likely written outside of the Jewish homeland, and then by the time we get to *John*, Jesus is an authoritative kingly figure, the direct descendant of God Himself.

> *"The Bible has noble poetry in it... and some good morals and a wealth of obscenity, and upwards of a thousand lies."*
>
> *—Mark Twain*

There is no shortage of resources listing the vast textual inconsistencies. The differences are discussed in books written by Bible scholars and on websites created by militant atheists proud to show the contradictions.

It would be easier to overlook the inconsistencies if they weren't so numerous and striking.

When the vast majority of people read the Bible, they start with the birth narrative in *Matthew*, read all the way through it, then to *Mark*, etc, onto the end of *John*. They all sound relatively similar. This is called "horizontal reading", how we read a book from start to finish.

Bible scholarship, however, begins to get quite interesting very quickly through "vertical reading", a scholarly method of analyzing a single plot point of one gospel in comparison to another. Then you begin to see just how distinct these accounts truly are.

There are entire volumes dedicated to these discrepancies—I have come to greatly appreciate Burton Throckmorton's *Gospel Parallels* as a reference guide in this method. (Throckmorton's *Parallels* only includes *Mark, Matthew* and *Luke*, not *John*, as *John*'s plot points are wildly different than the earlier three.) A cursory list is as follows:

- The genealogy of Jesus listed in *Matthew* has different ancestors than the genealogy listed in *Luke*. *Matthew* goes back to Abraham (*Matthew* 1:1-16), while *Luke* goes back to Adam (*Luke* 3:23-38).

- The nativity story only appears in *Matthew* & *Luke; Matthew's* is brief and simple while Luke's account goes into great detail.
- In *Mark,* flipping the moneychangers' tables in the temple in Jerusalem (*Mark* 11:15-18) causes his arrest and trial, while in *John* it's at beginning of his ministry (*John* 2:13-16).
- In the Synoptics (*Mark, Matthew,* & *Luke*), Jesus tells short teaching parables that illustrate a moral message, speaking very little about himself; in *John,* he often speaks at length about himself, with only two short parable teaching moments.
- In *Matthew,* the elders ask for a sign to prove he is the Son of God. He refuses and curses them. (*Matthew* 12:38-39) In *John,* the primary reason for him performing miracles is to prove his divine authority.
- The rejection at Nazareth is the first episode of his ministry in *Luke* (*Luke* 4:14-29); in *Mark* and *Matthew* it comes near the end of the narrative. (*Mark* 6:1-6) (*Matthew* 13:54-58)
- Passion week has differences across all gospels, but the contrast is particularly stark between *John* and the Synoptics. Unlike in the Synoptics, *John's* Last Supper is not Passover but rather the day before, making the following day, his crucifixion, the Passover Seder. This adjustment has theological implications—replacing the Passover lamb with Jesus, the "Lamb of God", for sacrifice.[20]
- While all the gospels agree that he was crucified and resurrected after three days, each account has differences: there are guards at the tomb in *Matthew* (*Matthew* 28:4), there's no guard but rather two angels in *Luke* and *John.* (*Luke* 24:23; *John* 20:12-13) The women come in the morning in *Mark,* but in *John* it's only Mary Magdalene at night. (*Mark* 16:1-2; *John* 20:1)
- There's even a "longer ending" of the *Gospel of Mark* that does not exist in our earliest versions. In this addition (*Mark* 16:9-20), Jesus tells the disciples they will "speak in new

tongues," and be invulnerable to snake bites—a clear (mis)inspiration to the Appalachian snake handlers of today.

What do all these differences mean?

How do they affect Christianity?

Most importantly, it means that these stories were not chiseled in stone by a divine hand. They were several different story collections being told orally, that were written down decades later by different authors in different parts of the Greco-Roman world. It's actually quite reasonable that they have so many discrepancies. It wouldn't make any sense to end up being a flawless, unified document.

To point to the mystical view, Jesus was fully realized. He made an impact on those around him, and after his death and perceived resurrection, the Judaean countryside was quite understandably ablaze with stories about this mysterious, impressive teacher for decades.

While certain discrepancies between the gospel accounts are minor plot points, others have extremely impactful differences theologically and culturally.

"Have You Considered?"

Ram Dass had a friend in Washington whose name was Milton Friedman.[21] There was another Milton Friedman who was a famous economist. Ram Dass' friend Milton Friedman was a speechwriter working in the White House.

One day he received a telephone call. The caller said, "Is this Milton Friedman?" And he said, "Yes." The caller said, "I represent a church in California, and we have a large surplus of money in our accounts, and we wonder if you could suggest how we should invest it."

To which his friend replied,

"Have you considered giving it to the poor?"

To which the man on the phone replied,

"Is this the real Milton Friedman?"

To which his friend replied,

"Is this the real church?"

The 'Foolish' Pharisees as a Later Emphasis

In the ancient Jewish homeland, the main Temple in Jerusalem was the center of Jewish life in many aspects: spiritually, culturally, economically. And as the historian Josephus records, the Temple priests, known as the Sadducees, were the most powerful Jewish sect in the first century. They had greater influence over the wealthier populace, while the Pharisees had more influence over the rest of Jewish society.[22] So when the Jewish Temple was destroyed by the Romans in 70 CE, there was a significant vacuum both existentially as well as politically.

The Temple-centered Sadducees were no more, leaving the other prominent groups: the Pharisees, the Jesus-following Jews, and the Essenes. The Essenes lived off in the wilderness and were not vying for power. So that left the Pharisees and Jesus-followers to grapple with how to live in a post-Temple Romanized world.

The Pharisees and the Jesus-followers were at war for new believers.

Among the four Gospels, *Matthew* uses especially Jewish rhetoric: the "Matthean author" is more concerned about the prophets, the Law, etc, than the other three New Testament Gospels, which is one of the main reasons scholars place the *Gospel of Matthew* to have been written in the Jewish homeland. Unlike *Luke* for example which is more concerned about preaching the message of Jesus to non-Jews (AKA "Gentiles"), placing the writing of *Luke* in another geographic area of the Roman Empire that was not the Jewish homeland.

This Jewish homeland context is significant because immediately after the Temple's destruction, the Pharisaical sect becomes the primary threat to the growing power and influence of the Jesus followers. It is no surprise then, that Jesus is particularly brutal in his condemnation of the Pharisees in *Matthew*.[23]

In the three "Synoptic Gospels" (*Mark, Matthew*, and *Luke*), Jesus calls the Pharisees out for being hypocritical. They were preaching purity and practicing impurity. They were concerned with how they were being perceived by others on the outside, without living truthfully from the inside.

He lists their woes in three gospels, but in *Matthew*, he really lets them have it.

In *Mark* their hypocrisy only gets a few lines, and in *Luke* a few more, but in *Matthew*, the Prince of Peace rails against them, calling them hypocrites to their face and ultimately referring to the Pharisees as "blind fools" and "you snakes, you brood of vipers!" (*Matthew* 23:13-35)

To be absolutely clear here, the excessive, uncharacteristically harsh tone of his condemnation in *Matthew*, is a later addition on top of the portrayal of Jesus, created by the author of *Matthew* who was reflecting the tense political divisions of his time, decades after Jesus' death.

The author used this scene as an opportunity to denigrate his political opponents beyond the original event, as the two other gospel accounts are considerably more mild-mannered, and not written in that tense political climate.

Sadly, Jesus's lengthy admonishment of the Pharisees in *Matthew* has been used throughout history as a justification for anti-semitism in a variety of different cultures in different time periods. According to scholars, this passage led to everything from the heartless medieval persecution of Jews by Christians, to even contributing to the Holocaust itself.[24]

This is what happens when the ego tries to dilute the truth.

The historical context provided does not completely invalidate *Matthew*, but it does strongly de-emphasize his criticism of the

Pharisees as awful hypocrites, and it paints a far less divisive, more loving Jesus. Ultimately it's a clear example that there have been political and cultural influences upon Jesus's original teachings. And that even before its formation as a separate religion, Christianity was quickly starting to misinterpret Christ.

CHAPTER 2

His True, Radical Teaching of Love

The Good Samaritan Unveils Religious Hypocrisy

When you begin to see all the contradictions in the Bible, you might wonder, "Why bother?" It's caused so much pain. It's been influenced by later political climates of authors trying to impose their own narratives and implications. Why should we continue to read it and try to understand these ancient teachings?

Because underneath the layers of falsehoods and exclusivism and discrepancies, there is a mesmerizing, transformative message of Oneness, Self-Realization, and Love.

There are several stunningly good passages and teaching moments in the New Testament. One of my favorites is the Parable of the Good Samaritan. (*Luke* 10:25-37)

"The Good Samaritan" is a cliche in the modern lexicon. It's a stereotypical term for a 'do-gooder'. It's associated with hospitals and nonprofits. But that's because it has permeated our societal consciousness for two thousand years. The story itself has a considerably deeper meaning and interpretation during the days of Jesus.

The story goes like this.

An 'expert in the law' asked Jesus,

> *"Teacher, what shall I do to inherit eternal life?"*

In several moments throughout the gospels, members of the priestly class give Jesus pop quizzes on Jewish scripture, AKA the Old Testament, for a variety of reasons: in many cases they're trying to see if he is a truly wise man who understands spiritual truths, but during this moment in *Luke*, the questioner seems sincere.

Jesus gives a Socratic reply with a question,

> *"What is written in the law? How do you read it?"*

The man paraphrases the true ethical teachings of the Jewish religion saying,

> *"'You shall love the Lord your God with all your heart, with all your soul, with all your strength and with all your mind; and your neighbor as yourself."*

Jesus agrees and affirms,

> *"You have answered correctly. Do this, and you will live."*

Seeking further clarification, the man asks,

> *"Who is my neighbor?"*

To define being 'a loving neighbor', Jesus tells the following story:

> *"A certain man was going down from Jerusalem to Jericho, and he fell among robbers, who both stripped him and beat him, and departed, leaving him half dead.*
>
> *By chance a certain priest was going down that way. When he saw him, he passed by on the other side.*
>
> *In the same way a Levite also, when he came to the place, and saw him, passed by on the other side...."*

The first two moments in his story are already hugely significant.

In ancient Judaism there was an emphasis on the clean and the unclean, specifically corpse impurity as stated by the god of the Old Testament in the *Book of Numbers*: *"Whoever touches a human corpse will be unclean for seven days."* (*Numbers* 19:11) The questioner, along with the audience hearing Jesus' teaching, would have certainly been familiar with this creed. So in the view of the two Jewish priestly characters in the story, if the injured man was actually dead, then assisting him could have repercussions for themselves and their community.[25]

They believe they're following the law, by not helping the injured man.

Not only do they not help him, they "pass by on the other side". They cross over to the other side of the road to avoid the situation altogether!

Jesus continues:

> *"But a certain Samaritan, as he traveled, came where he was. When he saw him, he was moved with compassion, came to him, and bound up his wounds, pouring on oil and wine. He set him on his own animal, brought him to an inn, and took care of him.*
>
> *On the next day, when he departed, he took out two denarii, gave them to the host, and said to him, 'Take care of him. Whatever you spend beyond that, I will repay you when I return.'"*

The Samaritan does the right thing, right?

The historical context of this story is incredible because Jews and Samaritans were bitter enemies. There were several recent violent conflicts between Judaea and Samaria and so the Jewish audience listening to Jesus tell this story would have despised Samaritans.[26] Members of the priestly class actually accuse Jesus himself of being a demon-possessed Samaritan in the *Gospel of John*. (*John* 8:48)

This parable is radically anti-institutional.

He's putting down his own religion's priests, who are following the letter of their law, while making a cultural rival into the ethical hero. Jesus then asks,

> *"Now which of these three do you think seemed to be a*

neighbor to him who fell among the robbers?"

He said, "He who showed mercy on him."

Then Jesus said to him, "Go and do likewise."

One of my professors suggested that the distaste for the Samaritan and for Jesus' telling of the story is even present in the reaction. The man can't bring himself to name "the Samaritan". He defines the 'true neighbor' by his actions ("he who showed mercy"), not his identity, which rhetorically might suggest his reluctance to admit that a Samaritan would do the right thing, especially in comparison to the priests.[27]

Despite my absolute adoration of this story, I can't avoid the fact that this parable has also been used by anti-Semites. The irony is that not only was Jesus a Jewish teacher, he was criticizing his own religion's hypocrisy in that time period. In no way does it justify racism against the Jewish people. Rather, it is a call to see beyond racial and cultural differences. The story is a sincere teaching of unity across disputed peoples.

Jesus gets across a lot in this short story.

The main point is that following the explicit, literal doctrine of religion can result in forgetting our common humanity.

And that the true way to live in this world is through self-less compassion to others, particularly those in need.

"The first question which the priest and the Levite asked was: 'If I stop to help this man, what will happen to me?'

But...the good Samaritan reversed the question: 'If I do not stop to help this man, what will happen to him?'"

—Rev. Dr. Martin Luther King Jr.

Sermon on the Mount: The Essence

The "Sermon on the Mount" is Jesus' longest series of teachings in the Bible. Its importance cannot be overstated. Not only has it been called the essence of true Christianity, but the essence of religion itself… a message for all of humanity:

> *"Gandhi and Lord Irwin, former Viceroy to India, were friends. On their return from the Round Table Conference at London, Lord Irwin paid a visit to the Mahatma in his ashram. During the conversation Lord Irwin put this question to his host: 'Mahatma, as man to man, tell me what you consider to be the solution to the problems of your country and mine.' Taking up a little book from the nearby lampstand, Gandhi opened it to the fifth chapter of Matthew and replied, 'When your country and mine shall get together on the teachings laid down by Christ in this Sermon on the Mount, we shall have solved the problems not only of our countries but those of the whole world.'"* [28]

It is a series of ethical teachings that hold up unbelievably well throughout the millennia.

To quickly reiterate the discrepancies piece, it's the "Sermon on the Mount" in *Matthew,* and the "Sermon on the Plain" in *Luke.* Different place entirely, but Jesus likely preached similar themes in a variety of places. *Matthew*'s is a bit longer, thanks to his issues with the Pharisees, and the line is "blessed are the poor" in *Luke* vs. "blessed are the poor in spirit" in *Matthew.* Ultimately though, the essence shines through.

A key moment is the Beatitudes ("Blessings"):

> *"Blessed are the poor in spirit,*
>
> *for theirs is the kingdom of heaven.*
>
> *Blessed are those who mourn,*
>
> *for they will be comforted.*
>
> *Blessed are the meek,*
>
> *for they will inherit the earth.*
>
> *Blessed are those who hunger and thirst for righteousness,*
>
> *for they will be filled.*

Blessed are the merciful,

for they will be shown mercy.

Blessed are the pure in heart,

for they will see God.

Blessed are the peacemakers,

for they will be called children of God.

Blessed are those who are persecuted because of righteousness,

for theirs is the kingdom of heaven."

—Jesus, Gospel of Matthew 5:3-10 (NRSV)

Blessed are the... "meek"? It was practically still the Iron Age. A lot of heads are getting cut off, even more than they are now, so encouraging the trait of gentleness and softness, calmness... is exceptional. Extraordinary for that time period.

Jesus says,

"You have heard that it was said, 'An eye for an eye, and a tooth for a tooth.'

But I tell you, <u>don't resist him who is evil;</u>

But whoever strikes you on your right cheek, turn to him the other also.

If anyone sues you to take away your coat, let him have your cloak also.

Whoever compels you to go one mile, go with him two.

Give to him who asks you, and don't turn away him who desires to borrow from you."

—Jesus, Gospel of Matthew 5:38-42

An "eye for an eye" was from the ways of old. And today, too, really. It's the pronouncement from that false creator god according to Marcion—from *Exodus* 21:24; *Lev.* 24:20; *Deut.* 19:21—and Jesus explicitly calls this out. Instead of being reactive, ego-based, punishing, guilty. Let's transcend. Let's go beyond reciprocal violence. And the way to do this is through love.

"Turn the other cheek" has been ignored by Christians for two thousand years.

The legendary Russian novelist Leo Tolstoy wrote that if you're truly reading the gospel message, a 'Christian military' is an oxymoron.[29] Tolstoy's collection of essays on the true message of Christianity, *The Kingdom of God is Within You*, inspired 19th century minds from Gandhi to the American Quakers—those oatmeal-cooking pacifists are worth exploring more deeply! The point is, violence has no basis in the original teaching whatsoever. And not only is it unrelated, it is an explicit contradiction.

Jesus continues:

> *"Be careful that you don't do your charitable giving before men, to be seen by them, or else you have no reward from your Father who is in heaven.*
>
> *Therefore, when you do merciful deeds, don't sound a trumpet before yourself, as the hypocrites do in the synagogues and in the streets, that they may get glory from men. Most certainly I tell you, they have received their reward.*
>
> *But when you do merciful deeds, don't let your left hand know what your right hand does, so that your merciful deeds may be in secret, then your Father who sees in secret will reward you openly."*
>
> *—Jesus, Gospel of Matthew 6:1-4*

"Reward" is what the 'hypocrites' get, in full, by being so visible with their giving. 'Look at me everybody, I am such a generous person!'

That external praise is empty.

It's surface-level.

What Jesus is saying is do the good deed *to do the good deed*. Then you'll get a true "reward" from the Father, from Our Infinite

Creator, from the Source of All, by connecting deeply with the love within all, and feeling that connection on the inside. It's nearly identical to Krishna's concept of *karma yoga,* which we'll be exploring later.

I love this one so much too:

> *"Don't judge, so that you won't be judged. For with whatever judgment you judge, you will be judged; and with whatever measure you measure, it will be measured to you.*
>
> *Why do you see the speck that is in your brother's eye, but don't consider the beam that is in your own eye? Or how will you tell your brother, 'Let me remove the speck from your eye,' and behold, the beam is in your own eye?*
>
> *You hypocrite! First remove the beam out of your own eye, and then you can see clearly to remove the speck out of your brother's eye."*
>
> *—Jesus, Gospel of Matthew 7:3-6*

We've all done this.

Humanity is doing this every second of every day.

We're so concerned with minor, even pointless mistakes that others make, while avoiding our own heavily judgmental thoughts, words, and actions.

The line itself is not condemning, it's humorous—a speck of sawdust in their eye while we've got a plank in ours. I like to think that when he says "you hypocrite…" it was a gentle ribbing that provoked laughter from the crowd… this is a pure message. He wasn't a fiery doom-and-gloom kind of person. He was light. There is real humor in this juxtaposition.

> *"..Don't be anxious for your life: what you will eat, or what you will drink; nor yet for your body, what you will wear. Isn't life more than food, and the body more than clothing? See the birds of the sky, that they don't sow, neither do they reap, nor gather into barns. Your heavenly Father feeds them. Aren't you of much more value than*

> *they?*
>
> *Which of you by being anxious, can add one moment to his lifespan?*
>
> *Why are you anxious about clothing? Consider the lilies of the field, how they grow. They don't toil, neither do they spin, yet I tell you that even Solomon in all his glory was not dressed like one of these."*
>
> —*Jesus, Gospel of Matthew 6:25-29*

Timeless! We're all concerned about everything outside of us. What we eat or drink. Our bodies! Our clothes! The perceptions of others about how we live our lives! He says stop worrying about everything. This man could easily be speaking to any person in the 21st century.

And perhaps most impactfully:

> *"You have heard that it was said, 'You shall love your neighbor and hate your enemy.' But I tell you, love your enemies, bless those who curse you, do good to those who hate you, and pray for those who mistreat you and persecute you, that you may be children of your Father who is in heaven.*
>
> *For he makes his sun to rise on the evil and the good, and sends rain on the just and the unjust.*
>
> *For if you love those who love you, what reward do you have? Don't even the tax collectors do the same?"*
>
> —*Jesus, Gospel of Matthew 5:43-46*

I can't mention this moment enough. Love your enemies. (And he even throws in a joke about tax collectors…)

Really sit with this one… praying for an enemy.

Do you have friends or co-workers with whom you're at odds? You might not have an "enemy" in that traditional sense, but most of us have been in conflict with other humans.

Instead of calculating how to best them, or get them back,

cause them humiliation or even harm them;

Love them.

Recognize that they are living out of a mindset of confusion. The only true antidote to whatever is driving their conflict to you, is love.

The Buddha says in *The Dhammapada, Verse 5:*

> *"For hate is not conquered by hate:*
>
> *hate is conquered by love.*
>
> *This is the law eternal."*

Awakened beings understand this!

A Piano Player and the Klan

In a dark, smoky bar in 1983, a piano man was shredding through his songbook. He played blues, rock & roll, country, and R&B. His audience was captivated.

His name was Daryl Davis.

He was a black man, playing for a room full of white people, in a small town in Maryland. It wasn't white-only because it was the 80s, but that was the vibe.

After the show Davis was packing up his piano and a white man approached him, complimenting his playing. He thanked the man, who then said he had *"never heard a black man play as well as Jerry Lee Lewis"*. Davis replied that actually, *"Jerry Lee learned to play from black blues and boogie woogie piano players and he's a friend of mine."* [30]

The white patron seemed skeptical.

Despite this, they got a drink at the bar, and entered into a conversation. Over a drink, the man shared the fact that he was a member of the Ku Klux Klan, a white supremacist hate group, infamous for primarily targeting black Americans.

The two became friends and eventually, the man gave Davis

contact information on KKK leaders. Over time Daryl Davis has become friends with dozens of Klan members, including "Imperial Wizard" Roger Kelly, and Richard Preston. He gave away the bride at Preston's wedding. And over the years Davis has collected over forty robes from Klan members who have left the organization thanks to their friendship with him.[31]

Davis explains:

> *"I am a musician, not a psychologist or sociologist.*
>
> *If I can do that, anybody in here can do that.*
>
> *Take the time to sit down and talk with your adversaries. You will learn something and they will learn something from you.*
>
> *When two enemies are talking, they are not fighting. They are talking. It's when the talking ceases that the ground becomes fertile for violence.*
>
> *So keep the conversation going."*

Daryl Davis is a living example of praying for those who persecute us.

He had every right to hate these men. Merely being in the presence of the KKK, Davis was enduring hatred. But he recognized that through understanding, he could transform those men from enemies to friends. Throughout his life he has operated from a place of fearlessness—which is what love and transcendence ultimately generate.

"They Know Not What They Do"

The true teaching of Jesus is Love.

The mystic understanding of that wise man from Galilee is that he entered a space of Oneness with all. Transcending division. Transcending retribution.

I can't emphasize how powerful the concept of 'loving our enemies' truly is... hardly anyone is doing this two thousand years later! It's radical inclusivity and compassion. It's the highest perspective of humanity.

In his final moments on this planet, there are different gospel accounts of his trial, crucifixion and resurrection. Through textual analysis and historical understanding, we can recognize certain moments as being more or less likely.

In *Mark* & *Matthew*, as he is dying on the cross, he cries out:

> *"My God, my God, why have you forsaken me?"*
>
> *—Jesus, Gospel of Mark 15:34, Matthew 27:46*

If you think of this man achieving the heights of spiritual evolution, what a strange thing to say.

Now of course, death by crucifixion must be unimaginably painful. It was designed by the Roman military to be particularly humiliating. Spending your (body's) last hours like this could bring out this type of mentality of forsaken-ness and abandonment by God. But there are a few reasons why this attitude of desperation is less likely to have occurred with the historical Jesus.

For years this line made me question what I thought I understood about Jesus, until I learned that it is a direct quote from *Psalm* 22:1.

The *Book of Psalms* is in the Old Testament, an ancient book of Jewish spiritual songs. *Psalm* 22 is essentially 'the song of the persecuted holy man'... when a Jewish man was enduring suffering of some kind, typically at the hands of his enemies.

Psalm 22:1 is the exact saying, word for word, as *Mark* 15:34.

This psalm is from before the Babylonian exile of 567 BCE, hundreds of years before the time of Jesus of Nazareth.

Many Christians point to this identical line as being a legitimate and sacred 'fulfillment of prophecy'. Upon further research however, you can see that the entire sequence of the crucifixion in *Mark* is constructed from more themes in *Psalm* 22 (and 69)[32]:

> *Ps. 22:18: They divide my garments among them. They*

cast lots for my clothing.

Mark 15:24: Crucifying him, they parted his garments among them, casting lots on them, what each should take.

Ps. 69:21: They also gave me poison for my food. In my thirst, they gave me vinegar to drink.

Mark 15:23: They offered him wine mixed with myrrh to drink, but he didn't take it.

Ps. 22:16: For dogs have surrounded me. A company of evildoers have enclosed me.

Mark 15:27-28: With him they crucified two robbers; one on his right hand, and one on his left. The Scripture was fulfilled, which says, "He was counted with transgressors."

Ps. 22:15: My strength is dried up like a potsherd. My tongue sticks to the roof of my mouth.

Mark 15:36: One ran, and filling a sponge full of vinegar, put it on a reed, and gave it to him to drink, saying, "Let him be. Let's see whether Elijah comes to take him down."

Ps. 22:7-8: All those who see me mock me. They insult me with their lips. They shake their heads, saying, "He trusts in Yahweh. Let him deliver him. Let him rescue him, since he delights in him."

Mark 15:29-32: Those who passed by blasphemed him, wagging their heads, and saying, "Ha! You who destroy the temple, and build it in three days, save yourself, and come down from the cross!" Likewise, also the chief priests mocking among themselves with the scribes said, "He saved others. He can't save himself. Let the Christ, the King of Israel, now come down from the cross, that we may see and believe him." Those who were crucified with him also insulted him.

Mark 15:34: My God, my God, why have you forsaken me?

Ps 22:1: My God, my God, why have you forsaken me?

The Markan author even explicitly narrates the fulfillment of scripture occurring in 15:28!

Like I said, many Christians (ancient and contemporary) cherish these connections in the life of Jesus to ancient scripture, as though they were prophetic fulfillment—not seeing them as many scholars (and I see them)—as poetic license.

The gospel authors were no dummies.

Their arcs are complex. Their plots rich with heavy symbolism—like the fig tree representing the traditional institution. It is quite clear that they knew their Jewish audiences would have thought it would be prophetically powerful for the dying Jesus to utter these exact words with many psalmist themes, and took the liberty to add these components themselves.

So if he doesn't say *"My God, why have you forsaken me?"*, what are his other dying words on the cross?

If you're not familiar, a line from *Luke* is one of the most sublime, unitive teachings in all of human history:

> *"Father forgive them, for they know not what they do."*
>
> *—Jesus, Gospel of Luke 23:34 (NSRV)*

It's one thing to teach love to others; it's an almost unbelievable, inspirational thing to pray for the forgiveness of your killers as you're dying a brutal death at their hands.

This is the message of Jesus, of Christ Consciousness, of Abject Unity with All Creation.

Imagine being imprisoned for a crime you didn't do. Some made up charges that don't make any sense. You go through a trial, which despite any real evidence, proceeds into your very public, very humiliating execution. Soldiers walk you through the city as you haul a massive plank of wood on your beaten body. Your mother is there. You get mercilessly nailed to the wood and hoisted up. The priests who condemned you look on. Your closest friends are crying, watching you in the crowd, helpless to intervene on your behalf. You're experiencing pain as you realize this is the end of your mortal frame.

The mental, emotional, and spiritual space in which Jesus occupied was so benevolent, so full of unconditional love that he prayed for his killers' own well-being.

This verse cannot be understated.

It exemplifies the level of higher consciousness that carries him into significance today. It's this level of teaching, of practice, and of living example—this absolute height of human advancement and compassion is the reason we're still talking about this man, an uneducated working class, otherwise historically insignificant person, two millennia later.

Now I would not be an amateur Bible scholar if I didn't mention that this line is not in Papyrus Bodmer XIV–XV (P75), an early papyrus manuscript from Alexandria, Egypt.

I could spend a few dozen pages on why it is still legitimate despite this, but this book is not a Biblical studies textbook. It's an intro to spiritual philosophy and an undoing of fear-based institutional falsehoods.

While he doesn't make a conclusive statement, Bible scholar Nathan Eubank highlights the following reasons suggesting *Luke* 23:34's authenticity ("Forgive them Father")[33]:

- The verse is in other early manuscripts: the *Diatessaron*, the *Codex Sinaiticus*, *Codices A, C, N, L, 700, 1424*, Family 1, and Family 13—plus the Byzantine minuscules, which constitute a huge mass of the Greek manuscripts
- It is referenced in the correspondence of very early church fathers such as Irenaeus, Marcion, Hippolytus and Origen
- There is an ignorance-forgiveness motif in *Luke-Acts* (*Acts of the Apostles* operates as the "sequel" to the Gospel of Luke, and has parallel moments, particularly *Acts* 7:60)
- Early interpreters understood the line as a prayer for the Jews during an especially anti-Judaism period, and so early second century scribes could have actually removed the

prayer as a result of their unwillingness to forgive the Jews (explaining its absence from Papyrus Bodmer for example)

It's easy to get lost in the analytical side of this study. We have been arguing about these texts since they were written. But ultimately, it's important to understand that the Bible is a human document.

It's not the sole, living, perfect 'Word of God'.

And yet at the same time, it has incredibly beautiful, ethical teachings that can guide us into a greater harmony with ourselves and others.

Tío

My wife's Catholic uncle was an interrogator for U.S. Customs and Border Patrol for several decades. He was the guy who would get the call to come in at 2am because they just captured one of El Chapo's lieutenants and only our tio would be able to get reliable intel.

He's a big imposing badass—a bald Mexican-American man with a monster mustache, cool shades and a loud Harley. He looks like he could be an enforcer in one of the very cartels he has pledged to fight against.

I am the friendly loud white man drinking tequila at my in-laws' parties. They are my wonderful Latin familia and I'm the token white guy at every holiday. Perhaps due to his impressive presence Tío doesn't always have a ton of conversations at social gatherings so he's often stuck with me, as I enjoy getting the perspective of a kind man who lives a life many dimensions differently from my own.

One night I asked him, being a longtime veteran of the force, what is the biggest mistake young officers make in the interrogation room.

His reply was they're too tough.

Tío saying that someone being too tough is a mistake is like

Elon Musk saying not to multitask.

He explained that the reason he's good at what he does is because he meets them where they are. According to my uncle-in-law, you must see the human being underneath the outer image of themselves that they've constructed to survive and excel in that hellacious cartel culture. "Blessed are the meek", indeed. These young interrogators don't understand this, so they get angry. They try to be an action hero and all they do is increase the fear in the room, which helps no one.

It's perfectly likely for me, joyful Namaste Bob, to tell you that outward toughness is just a mirage, a paper mask worth nothing, but for Tío to get this across... it's worth contemplating.

Layers of the Teaching

Beyond even the perspective of 'it ain't perfect but it's good', I'll take a view of the New Testament one step further: there are layers of the teaching. Then we'll get to those profound and accessible Hindus.

Actually it was Swami Vivekananda, an enthusiastic admirer of Jesus, who put it as well as anyone on this topic:

> *"To the masses who could not conceive of anything higher than a Personal God, he said, 'Pray to your Father in heaven.'*
>
> *To others who could grasp a higher idea, he said: 'I am the vine, ye are the branches,'*
>
> *but to his disciples to whom he revealed himself more fully, he proclaimed the highest truth, 'I and my Father are one'."* [34]

This idea is hardly brought up in Western, Christian discussions of Jesus' teaching, but it's so simple. We can better understand what he was saying by recognizing his audience.

Despite usually lacking context for each audience in each scene in the gospel stories, thankfully there is a taste of this idea in both

Mark and *Matthew.*

> *"When he was alone, those who were around him along with the twelve asked him about the parables. And he said to them, "To you has been given the secret of the kingdom of God, but for those outside, everything comes in parables..."*
>
> *—Mark 4:10-11 (NSRV)*
>
> *"The disciples came, and said to him, "Why do you speak to them in parables"*
>
> *He answered them, "To you it is given to know the mysteries of the Kingdom of Heaven, but it is not given to them...."*
>
> *—Matthew 13:10-11*

You don't teach calculus to kindergartners. You teach calculus to high schoolers. And even they have trouble with it. I did.

Spiritual information isn't entirely different.

Direct, literal declarations like "blessed are the peacemakers" went to the largest groups of people. The Beatitudes, from the Sermon on the Mount, had one of his biggest audiences.

The parables, or short example story teachings, went to smaller groups—people who might have been more familiar with him, but were not quite the direct disciples. The Parable of the Good Samaritan was shared with those gathered around Jesus in the conversation with the expert in the law. This does not mean that they don't have value! On the contrary. The parables are provocative, anti-institutional and ripe with meaning, but they were designed for carrying the teaching beyond his intimate friends.[35]

It was the pronouncement of who he truly was, and the height of his attainment, that was saved for the close disciples, his direct students and friends. This is where you get the mystical, symbolic truths. This is where you get the revealing of the true identity.

> *In John, speaking to "those Jews who believed him", he*

said,

"...Before Abraham came into existence, I AM."

—Jesus, Gospel of John 8:58

This is the Christ Consciousness. This is not the identity of a mere mortal man named Jesus, but the height of human attainment entering into the Oneness of All.

Poet and author Ethan Walker highlights the timelessness aspect:

> *"In the state of being which is Christ's consciousness there is no past or future but only the eternally present shining singularity of existence..."* [36]

This pronouncement is not literal, because it isn't rationally logical—it is free of the time dimension. Being before the founder of your religion? It's an idea that doesn't make much sense unless you've been living closely with a master, submerging yourself into the teachings... not everyday folks sitting idly by listening to 'sermons' on 'mounts'.

Expanding on the revealing of True Identity, there's a "transfiguration" experience revealed to the direct disciples. It even takes place in all three Synoptic Gospels (*Mark-Matthew-Luke*) which makes it highly significant.

> *"After six days Jesus took with him Peter, James and John the brother of James, and led them up a high mountain by themselves. There he was transfigured before them. His face shone like the sun, and his clothes became as white as the light. Just then there appeared before them Moses and Elijah, talking with Jesus.*
>
> *Peter said to Jesus, 'Lord, it is good for us to be here. If you wish, I will put up three shelters—one for you, one for Moses and one for Elijah.'*
>
> *While he was still speaking, a bright cloud covered them, and a voice from the cloud said, 'This is my Son, whom I love; with him I am well pleased. Listen to him!'*

> *When the disciples heard this, they fell facedown to the ground, terrified. But Jesus came and touched them. 'Get up, and don't be afraid.'"*
>
> *—Matthew 17:1-8, parallel to Mark 9:2–8, and Luke 9:28–36*

He didn't reveal his Ultimate Pure Vision of Unity to the crowds. The crowds weren't ready, and they wouldn't have been able to interpret the message in the same way. During this moment even his closest disciples were afraid when it was a wholly loving vision. But it is the disciples who get the true message—the symbols to be interpreted by spiritual minds.

Another great example of this is when he's speaking to "the Twelve":

> *"Do not suppose that I have come to bring peace to the earth.*
>
> *I did not come to bring peace, but a sword."*
>
> *—Jesus, Gospel of Matthew 10:34*

When I was around eight years old, accompanying my Baptist friend to his Christian summer camp, I remember how surprised I was hearing that famous line.

My thought process was probably familiar to you: "Wait I was really liking this guy, the 'love your enemies' thing is right on, but now he's talking about bringing swords? He's either terribly inconsistent or they got some translations wrong."

I was completely unaware of the underlying figurative language behind this verse. And Vacation Bible School did a pretty miserable job of conveying the literal vs. the symbolic.

Literally, Jesus gave a sermon up on a mountain.

Symbolically, he brought a sword...

Many years later after my exposure to the great Paramahansa Yogananda and Kriya Yoga, I discovered a lesser-known Biblical commentary book by the late Hindu master, entitled *The Second Coming of Christ: The Resurrection of the Christ Within You*. Even the title contains a shining symbolic example! When I bought the book I immediately flipped to Yogananda's commentary on this line. It is as follows:

> *"Think not that I came to bring material peace for souls to be settled complacently in earthly life. I came not to offer short-lasting material happiness, but to give to the valiant spiritual soul a two-edged sword of wisdom and self-control, divine strength and determination by which he can sever the compulsions of material passions... that might obstruct his attainment of the everlasting happiness and freedom."*[37]

Joseph Campbell, one of the most impactful 20th century scholars on classical mythology, spent his life discussing the significance of world myths, and how humanity's ancient stories about the cosmos, cultures, and Creator, use narrative to point at what can't be conceived.

In the PBS special *The Power of Myth*, Bill Moyers asks Joseph Campbell about this same line from *Matthew*, and Campbell points to the Sanskrit term "*viveka*" meaning discrimination.[38] He mentions Manjushri, one of the most significant bodhisattvas (enlightened saints) in Mahayana Buddhism, who symbolizes transcendent wisdom and universal sight.

Manjushri is almost always pictured with a mighty flaming sword, cutting away the veil of illusions and temporality.

I come not to bring a sword to cut through an enemy, but rather let us cut through the idea of enemies, the idea that we are separate and embrace our inherent Unity!

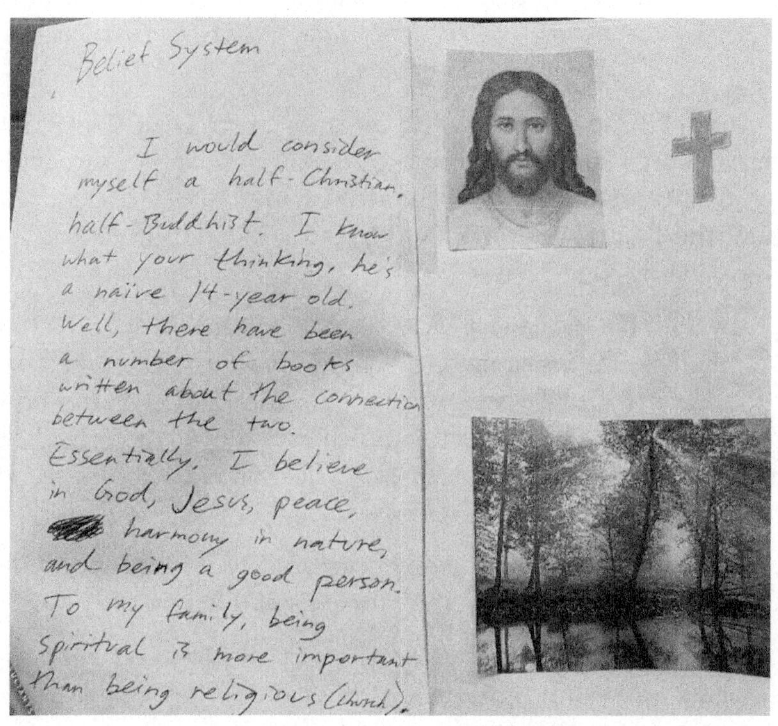

Photograph: An early journal entry. (2002)

Source: Author's personal collection.

CHAPTER 3

Who Is He? Who Am I?

From Christ to Kriya

My mom and I moved to Austin, Texas from Beaumont when I was ten to be closer to my spiritually open-minded dad. A few years later I read a book by the venerable Thích Nhất Hạnh, the late great Buddhist monk who was a friend of Martin Luther King Jr., called *Living Buddha, Living Christ*.

True spiritual exploration really began for me the moment I realized that the love spoken of by Jesus was the very essence of the compassion taught by the Buddha.

In high school I read Buddhist and Taoist texts, along with a few modern commentaries. I read *The Mystic Christ* by Ethan Walker III. *The Cloud of Unknowing*. I learned about Gnostic Christians, Hindu schools of thought, and the connective bridge between all religions: mysticism.

At the same time, I was also interested in film. I was never the little kid with the camera, but I did start filming things in high school. It was around that time that my dad (a former UT film major himself) helped me understand how cinema can deeply affect the way people think and feel. That stuck with me. Both of my parents told me that I had as much value as every other person out there, and I would be well-equipped with growing wisdom and eagerness to enter the competitive world of filmmaking. My gratitude for my parents' encouragement is not without the awareness that so many other artists come from significantly less supportive backgrounds.

I was in film school when zombie movies were happening. Hollywood dramedies about werewolves and vampires. And so that was a lot of the work my peers were emulating. There was some nice technical proficiency by my pals but a lot of the content itself was pretty uninteresting to me! At the same time I was taking every religion class I could get into: Shamanism, Buddhism, Sufism, and what became four classes on Jesus, two on Paul, two on "apocrypha" (non-canonical gospels) and my beloved Hindu philosophy.

Film was the vessel, while religion and philosophy became the substance. Towards the middle of my fourth year with an imminent bachelor's degree in film, an advisor told me that because I took so many elective classes in Religious Studies, if I stuck around for year five I could have enough credit for a second degree in Comparative Religion. I was probably stoned, hearing him justify another year in this amazing place, thinking, "COOL, man!" Another year it became.

During my last year of college, I also read Yogananda's timeless *Autobiography of a Yogi.*

There are very few writers that can compete with Paramahansa Yogananda. The man was very likely an awakened being, and his clarity of mind comes forth perfectly in his writing. I consider him a Buddha and a Shakespeare in one.

His early life in India is nothing short of miraculous. The boy Yogananda, Mukunda Lal Ghosh, met saints and masters of many different paths who passed along their teachings, ultimately meeting and studying under his own guru, Sri Yukteswar Giri, who eventually suggested he go to America.[39] Yogananda arrived in Boston in 1920. He lived the remainder of his life in California, becoming the first Hindu swami to live in the states for decades. All American spiritual seekers are forever indebted to him.

His seminal work about his life, *Autobiography of a Yogi*, was passed around by George Harrison in the 60s—who even placed Yogananda and the Kriya masters on the cover of *Sgt. Pepper*. It was the only e-book on Steve Jobs' iPad when he died.[40] And its nearly unparalleled influence is absolutely justified.

I was thrilled to read about how Yogananda and many other Hindu gurus have great admiration for Jesus. They get him. They all understand the wisdom in his teachings of love and unity and consider him an avatar, or an incarnation of the divine. Whether this state is born-as or achievable-in-man is another topic... but just know that that familiar (falsely-Europeanized) Galilean face adorns millions of Hindu altars, along with the idea that anyone can achieve the same state of Pure Love.

One of my favorite analogies of spirituality comes from a chapter in Yogananda's autobiography when Yogananda was studying in the ashram of his guru, Sri Yukteswar.[41] It was the early 20th century. The technology of radio was being discovered and implemented, expanding what humanity thought was possible. His parable goes like this:

Radio waves are all around us. They're very large. Their waves are as long as city blocks and they travel hundreds of thousands of miles.

But we can't hear them.

Our physical senses aren't aware of them.

Of course, scientifically we understand that they are moving through us. You just need a radio receiver tuned to the right frequency in order to hear the music.

Similarly, spiritual energy is constantly moving through us. The heart is our radio. Most of us have rusty wiring, faulty technology. But by living in a compassionate, mindful, forgiving, and loving way you will start to hit the right frequency and you'll begin to 'hear the music'. May we all begin to hear the song of our divine union.

The Sanskrit term for the Hindu religion is actually *"Sanatana Dharma"*, translated as "The Holy Science", which is quite purposefully the name of the only surviving book written by Sri Yukteswar. In his autobiography, Yogananda shares an important note on Christ's attainment from his own endlessly-perceptive guru:

> *"In this passage Jesus calls himself the Son of God. Though he was truly united with God, his reference here has a deep impersonal significance," my guru explained.*
>
> *"The Son of God is the Christ or Divine Consciousness in man.*
>
> *No mortal can glorify God. The only honor that man can pay his Creator is to seek Him; man cannot glorify an Abstraction that he does not know."*
>
> *–Swami Sri Yukteswar Giri, quoted by Yogananda*

The Kingdom Within, "Inside" not "Among"!

A spiritual mentor once told me that the Christian religion only missed the true teaching of Jesus by one letter. It wasn't Christianity, it's "Christ-I-AM-ity".

One of the most important lines in the Bible—to mystics, but truly to humanity itself—is *Luke* 17:20-21:

> *"When He was asked by the Pharisees when the kingdom of God would come, He answered them, "The kingdom of God does not come with observation.*
>
> *Nor will they say, 'Here it is!' or 'There it is!' For remember,*
>
> *the kingdom of God is within you."*

Powerful to Christians, but also to Hindu swamis and Buddhist monks. Anyone and everyone who has gotten a taste of the real beauty of an internal spiritual practice finds the value in this verse. Traversing our own depths to find the pearl... this line from Jesus is a vital affirmation. He found that non-physical 'kingdom' of presence, of realization, of unification with oneself and with all. And here it is, in the middle of the gospels of the New Testament.

While the King James Version of the Bible (a medieval

translation) has no shortage of translation issues, somewhat surprisingly, it has nailed this one for centuries. However when the New International Version was released by publishers in 1978, this line started to become 'updated' to reflect their own understanding of the original Greek: "the kingdom of God is in their midst", or in the New Revised Standard Version, which is highly influential, likewise translates: "For, in fact, the Kingdom of God is among you."

Clearly, this change carries a significant difference in meaning.

"In their midst" or "among" would be an implication that Jesus was being self-referential: that he was the exclusive holder of this divinity, and because he was speaking, being among them at that time, it could imply that therefore the kingdom was among them. With this translation, he could have been speaking in third person about his own uniquely divine self.

You'll find several proud Christian apologists online happily correcting us naïve Kumbaya-singing mystics about this supposed update.

Here's the problem.

They're wrong!

There has been considerable, recent scholarship done on ancient Syriac (a dialect of Aramaic, the language spoken by Jesus), and the conclusion is clear:

The word is ἐντός, which means "within", specifically "inside".

Professor Ilaria L. E. Ramelli's work on this translation explains that the best argument for ἐντός is "inside you". [42] There is only one other occurrence of ἐντός in the entire New Testament. It occurs in *Matthew* 23:26, where it undoubtedly bears the meaning, "inside":

> *"Blind Pharisee! First clean the inside of the cup and dish, and then the outside also will be clean."*

The line could not possibly be translated to 'clean the *among* of the cup', it means *internal part,* the *interior,* the *inside.*

There are other uses of the word "among" in the New Testament, but it's not ἐντός, it's ἐν μέσῳ + genitive, occurring in the New Testament 27 times: for example:

- *Luke* 2:46 "sitting *among* the teachers"
- *Luke* 8:7 "another fell *among* thorns"
- *Luke* 10:3 "like lambs *among* wolves"

There are more examples in the Old Testament of ἐντός being used to clearly connote 'within/inside':

- *Psalm* 108:22: "My heart was frightened *inside* me"
- *1 Maccabees* 4:48: "The *internal part* of the building"
- *Sirach/Ecclesiasticus* 19:26: "What is *inside* him is full of deception."

I can't emphasize this enough.

The kingdom of God, of Heaven, is inside you.

You.

Reading this.

Underneath our layers of fear, anxiety, self-doubt and all of these psychological traumas we've subjected ourselves to, is Perfect Peace.

And that is what the spiritual path helps us to access, and live from. Thank you, Jesus, for the reminder. And thank you Prof. Ramelli for straightening out this essential verse—validating the mystic's view with rigorous scholarship.

The Spiritual Gospel of John, Its Beauty and Its Issues

In the Synoptic Gospels (*Mark, Matthew,* and *Luke*), Jesus mostly talks about the "kingdom of God". In both the *Gospel of John* and the *Gospel of Thomas,* he makes statements about himself and his own divine nature—statements which are direct, mystical, spiritual statements of identity.[43]

Before we cover *Thomas,* it's important to mention the very significant differences between the "Synoptics" (meaning 'to be read together') of *Mark, Matthew,* and *Luke,* in contrast to the *Gospel of John.*[44]

There are two primary components about *John* to understand:

- *John* is clearly later historically than the other three canonical gospels (the Synoptics are understood to have been written from 70-100 CE, *John* was written from 100-125 CE)
- *John* is often called the "Spiritual Gospel" (initially by the highly respected Clement of Alexandria, because it's so different in terms of tone and theme)

These two facts do not invalidate the text entirely (it has its moments!), but they do mean one thing very strongly:

That it should not be taken literally.

It's in *John* where we get the authoritative, 'kingly' Jesus proclamations. It's also where we get "the only begotten Son" line, *John* 3:16—one of the most significant verses for modern day American Christianity:

> *"For God so loved the world that he gave his only begotten Son, so that everyone who believes in him may not perish but may have eternal life."*

You might remember *John* 3:16 on football player Tim Tebow's facepaint.[45] Stone Cold Steve Austin? I've even seen it on food menus in Laredo, Texas. This verse is almost always interpreted literally. With religious exclusivity—that Jesus, the man, the Son, is the sole holder of the keys to the kingdom.

As I mentioned, the statements of identity are almost always intended for the direct disciples. Very spiritual, mystical, to be interpreted deeply. *John* 14:17 has Jesus actually saying that point specifically:

> *"This is the Spirit of truth, whom <u>the world cannot</u>*

> *receive, because it neither sees him nor knows him. You know him, because he abides with you, and he will be among you."*

The disciples get the real identity, not the surface-level crowds… they aren't yet able to interpret these more in-depth spiritual teachings. *John* has:

> *"Before Abraham came into existence, I AM."*
>
> *—Jesus, Gospel of John 8:58*

How can a man in linear time come before the founder of his own religion? — a Jew speaking of predating Abraham, the father of the Jewish people. If Jesus is speaking about his identity in *John* literally, this doesn't make sense at all. This is because I AM is the eternal higher consciousness of Christ, of unity, of inclusive unconditional love. With this understanding, the famous line in *John* 14:6 takes on a whole new meaning:

> *"I am [I AM] the way, the truth, and the life. No one comes to the Father, except through me."*
>
> *—Jesus, Gospel of John 14:6*

No one comes to the Source of All Creation, except through the embodiment of unconditional love.

Making the distinction between the I AM and the man Jesus, there is a striking contrast of identity in *Mark,* when a man calls him the benign title of "Good Teacher". To which Jesus responds,

> *"Why do you call me good?*
>
> *No one is good except God alone."*
>
> *—Jesus, Gospel of Mark 10:17-18*

This is the true humility of an awakened human being.

In our purest form we are vessels of the light of our Creator, mirrors with all blemishes cleaned off to fully capture the image of the light's reflection. How can Jesus *not* be good, if he is the "one and only Son" of God?

Yogananda helps us interpret this one:

> *"The confusion between 'Son of man' and 'only begotten Son of God' has created much bigotry in the community of churchianity, which does not understand or acknowledge the human element in Jesus—that he was a man, born in a mortal body, who had evolved his consciousness to become one with God Himself. Not the body of Jesus but the consciousness within it was one with the only begotten Son, the Christ Consciousness, the only reflection of God the Father in creation.*
>
> *In urging people to believe in the only begotten Son, Jesus was referring to this Christ Consciousness, which was fully manifest within himself and all God-realized masters throughout the ages, and is latent within every soul. Jesus said that all souls who lift their physical consciousness... ...to the astral heaven and then become one with the only begotten Christ Intelligence in all creation, will know eternal life."* [46]

Yogananda is not alone here.

Prominent early Christian fathers Basilides, Theodotus, Valentinus, and Ptolemaeus all considered the "only begotten Son" to be the cosmic unifying aspect to all creation. The Greek word is "*Nous*", meaning "intelligence, mind, or thought", as opposed to the personhood of Jesus, the man from Nazareth. Clement of Alexandria quotes from Theodotus that "the 'only begotten Son' is *Nous*".[47]

John really comes alive when you read it allegorically, in the fuller spiritual meaning beyond the literal.

John has no nativity scene.

The birth of Jesus is only present in *Matthew* and *Luke*, and again there are a few differences between those accounts, but *John* starts off in a beautiful and fascinating way:

> *"In the beginning was the Word, and the Word was with God, and the Word was God.*
>
> *He was with God in the beginning.*

> *Through him all things were made; without him nothing was made that has been made.*
>
> *In him was life, and that life was the light of all mankind.*
>
> *The light shines in the darkness, and the darkness has not overcome it."*
>
> —*Gospel of John 1:1-5*

The "Word" is an English translation of the Greek λόγος, pronounced *"Logos"*, which originated from the Jewish wisdom tradition of Philo of Alexandria.[48] This term doesn't just mean a "word" but rather the Universal Law Governing All Things. There's a correlation to the *"Tao"* in Taoism, and *"Aum"* in Hindu philosophy. The term itself was first used by Heraclitus, an Ancient Greek philosopher (535-434 BCE), one of the most important pre-Socratic philosophers, writing:

> *"The Logos is as here explained; but men are always incapable of understanding it,*
>
> *both before they hear it, and when they have heard it for the first time."*

The author of *John* is tapping into a spiritual cosmology, about a Knowledge or an Awareness that is in tune with every fabric of existence. He specifically uses the *Logos* as a way of describing the level of attainment or divinity achieved by his main character.

The ancient Chinese sage Laozi writes in the opening lines of the *Tao Te Ching*:

> *"The Tao that can be stated, is not the eternal Tao;*
>
> *The name that can be named, is not the eternal name.*
>
> *The nameless is the origin of heaven and earth…"*

This "Word" is spoken and unspoken. It is intellectually unfamiliar and yet intimately knowable. It is intuitive, not analytical. Its truth transcends the world of form.

And lastly, the most striking comparison to *John* 1, comes from the *Rig Veda*:

> *"In the beginning was the Lord, and second to Him, was the Word.*
>
> *The word was truly the Supreme Brahman (God)."*

The *Vedas* are foundational texts for the Hindu religion. Not only are they the oldest texts of India, they are some of the oldest writings of human civilization. My head was spinning when I first read that line from another continent, in a previous era (~1900 BCE), as it is almost 'word' for 'word' in perfect alignment with *John* 1:1.

It's all connected...

There's another beautiful moment in *John* that fundamentalist Christians have been trying to explain for years but they just can't do it. I'm not persuaded about the exclusivity of Jesus Christ when this line roars out of the opening:

> *"He was in the world, and the world was made by him, and the world knew him not. He came unto his own, and his own received him not.*
>
> *But as many as received him, to them gave he power to become the sons of God, even to them that believe on his name: Which were born, not of blood, nor of the will of the flesh, nor of the will of man, but of God."*
>
> —*Gospel of John 1:10-13*

If Jesus is the one and only son of God, how is he able to give power to "those who received him" to "become the sons of God"?

It's a crucial, typically-overlooked moment that re-examines the divinity of Jesus. Is he "saving us" from original sin—that again, wasn't even a concept at the time of John's Gospel—or is his teaching offering us access into becoming what he became, another child of God? The manifestation of the *Logos* in man? And how can he be the literal only Son, if the beginning of the gospel has "sons" in plural? Bishop Athanasius of Alexandria, called the "Pillar of the Church", wrote:

> *"He was made human,*

> *so that he might make us gods."* [49]

Professor Howard Clark Kee contextualizes the power of the *Logos*:

> *"In 1:14 John states explicitly that the Logos is manifest in human form. The revelation of God that the Logos brings is accessible to all who are willing to receive it, not just to those who by ethnic descent or by pious mode of life consider themselves to have some special claim on God."* [50]

This is why I get excited about deeper reads with these texts.

This analytical process rigorously questions those old mainstream Christian tropes: that Jesus is the only way, the only divine being ever, and you don't have it in you. That you can't get to where he got because you're sinful.

Hopefully you're starting to see through those misplaced falsehoods as later constructions by lesser men—which are in direct contrast to the true message of Christ.

Gospel of Thomas: The Fifth Gospel, or The Book That Changes Everything

Before we move out of New Testament scholarship, we must cover one of the most important archaeological discoveries of the 20th century: the Coptic *Gospel of Thomas*.

While the New Testament only has four gospels about the life of Jesus, it is important to understand that there were hundreds of gospels written about his life and teachings. Many of these other gospels came centuries after these first four and are frankly, laughably ridiculous. Shoutout to the insane *Infancy Gospel of Thomas* where the adolescent Jesus is basically an evil warlock who kills other children.

The Nag Hammadi Library was found in 1945, and the Dead Sea Scrolls were found in 1947, both of which have completely transformed our understanding of Christianity. These finds are so significant because we already knew about these gospels, but we didn't have the texts themselves.

From a historical perspective, these later gospels can help us understand how later Christians were attempting to understand Jesus, but most are unreliable as historical accounts or evidence of his true teachings.

However, there is one gospel in particular that, according to most scholars, could have been written as early as the four gospels in the New Testament: *The Gospel of Thomas*.

In 1945, a Bedouin named Muhammad Ali was digging for fertilizer near his village of Nag Hammadi in Egypt. He and his brother discovered an earthen jar buried beside a boulder that contained 13 leather bound books.[51] Included in the jar were Coptic (ancient Egyptian language) versions of the *Gospel of Thomas*, the *Gospel of Philip*, the *Gospel of Truth*, the *Apocryphon of John*, the *Dialogue of the Saviour* and more.. totaling 49 separate documents. There was even a Coptic version of Plato's *Republic*. While we date these manuscripts back to the 3rd and 4th centuries CE, there is a healthy debate among scholars for the dating of the actual source texts that these manuscripts were based on—with *Thomas* being very likely the earliest for a variety of reasons.

We actually have correspondence of early church fathers arguing about which gospels should become official and which ones should be thrown out. Hippolytus of Rome (170–235 CE) quotes from the "Gospel inscribed according to Thomas", and then claims: "This, however, is not (the teaching) of Christ, but of Hippocrates, who uses these words…" [52]

With all these different gospels and accounts and documents floating around about Jesus in those early centuries, the church needed to make a list: a canon of scripture covering the authentic teachings of Jesus. Most notable was Bishop Irenaeus who wrote *Against Heresies* specifically calling out the issues with these extra gospels. He especially hated the Gnostics, condemning their teachings as being against God.

I mentioned Marcion earlier, the Gnostic teacher who saw the

Old Testament god as a false creator. The Gnostics were fascinating, and constantly coming into conflict with the mainstream or orthodox Christian leaders.

The term "Gnostic" comes from the Greek "*gnosis*" meaning "knowledge", but not analytical knowledge, more like intuitive spiritual knowledge: awakened information about existence, about liberation.[53] This *gnosis* was accessible by the teachings of the master. It was the kingdom, inside.

There were many Gnostic teachers: Marcion, Valentinus, and Basilides were an early big three, and they weren't all teaching exactly the same thing. But they all endorsed this idea of the human potential for divine self-realization through this spiritual process of escaping our mortal, human, separate selves.[54] Where the Gnostics lose me is their exhaustively complex cosmology of what they call 'the Archons', or dark spirits that helped to create this world and the planes of existence. But those works are typically later.

The *Gospel of Thomas* is generally considered Gnostic, although nowadays it's usually considered "proto-Gnostic" which means the text likely predates the later metaphysical Gnostic teachings. The prevailing opinion among scholars more recently is that *Thomas* is an example of earlier Wisdom literature derived from sources both Jewish and Hellenistic, that contains later Gnostic additions.[55]

It's a "sayings gospel", meaning there's no narrative plot. It's just "Jesus said" for 114 verses.

There's a strong case for it being earlier than *Mark* because it is a sayings gospel with no plot. The "logion" genre itself could have easily predated later accounts that included narrative elements.

Another huge clue: almost two-thirds of the *Thomas* sayings are in the canonical gospels. Scholars think the author might have had access to *Matthew* & *Luke* or the hypothetical Q source document itself, which places it anywhere from 60 CE—140 CE (60 CE making it in the timeline of the Pauline epistles and the *Gospel of Mark*, the earliest canonical). Highly respected scholar, Professor John Dominic Crossan considers *Thomas* "very, very early" thanks to its 'primitiveness', as well as the Gnostic-later-addition hypothesis, carrying a "very high degree of authenticity." [56]

From the canonicals, *Thomas* has:

- The *"Kingdom of God is like a mustard seed"* (*Thomas* Saying 20, *Matthew* 13:31-32, *Mark* 4:30-32, *Luke* 13:18-19)
- The *"first will become last"* (*Thomas* Saying 4, *Matthew* 20:16)
- The parable of the wedding banquet (*Thomas* Saying 64, *Matthew* 22:1–14, *Luke* 14:15–24)
- "Give Caesar what belongs to Caesar, give God what belongs to God" (*Thomas* Saying 100, *Matthew* 22:21)
- "*He who seeks will find*" (*Thomas* Saying 94, *Matthew* 7:8, *Luke* 11:10)
- "You see the speck in your brother's eye, but you do not see the plank in your own eye." (*Thomas* Saying 26, *Matthew* 7:3)
- *"Blessed are the poor"* (*Thomas* Saying 54, *Luke* 6:20)
- "Do not be concerned about what you will wear" (*Thomas* Saying 36, *Matthew* 6:25)
- The "*Kingdom is inside of you*" (*Thomas* Saying 3, *Luke* 17:21) The full saying in *Thomas* is stunning:

> *"Jesus said, "If those who lead you say, 'See, the Kingdom is in the sky,' then the birds of the sky will precede you. If they say to you, 'It is in the sea,' then the fish will precede you. Rather, the Kingdom is inside of you, and it is outside of you. When you come to know yourselves, then you will become known, and you will realize that it is you who are the sons of the living Father. But if you will not know yourselves, you dwell in poverty and it is you who are that poverty."*
>
> *—Gospel of Thomas, Saying 3*

So there are parallels to the earliest gospels, and there are even extensions as you see in Saying 3. But a major reason why both scholars and mystics are so excited about it, is because it has several sayings we've never seen anywhere else.

Even the first line of *Thomas* generates mystery and interest:

> *"These are the secret words which the living Jesus spoke and which Didymus Judas Thomas wrote down."*

Calling back to our discussion of layers to the teaching—it's been surmised that *Thomas* is purely the disciple-focused, secret teachings. They are loaded with symbolism. They are radically unique, and distinct from mainstream Judaism and later orthodox Christianity. According to the opening line, they were the collection of spiritual information hidden from the crowds, reserved for those only studying very closely with a true spiritual master.

The *Gospel of Thomas* is not the only ancient book where the apostle Thomas is considered a recipient of 'secret knowledge'. This is a literary component of both the *Book of Thomas*, a 'revelation dialogue' work, and the previously known *Acts of Thomas*, a work in the collection of apostle-biographies.[57] Not only are the disciples getting a deeper message, among a variety of ancient sources, Thomas is traversing the depths on the absolute floor of the ocean.

The sayings that are divergent from the canonical parallels, are nothing short of incredible:

> *"Jesus saw infants being suckled. He said to His disciples, "These infants being suckled are like those who enter the Kingdom." They said to Him, "Shall we then, as children, enter the Kingdom?" Jesus said to them,*
>
> *"When you make the two one, and when you make the inside like the outside and the outside like the inside, and the above like the below, and when you make the male and the female one and the same, so that the male not be male nor the female; and when you fashion eyes in the place of an eye, and a hand in place of a hand, and a foot in place of a foot, and a likeness in place of a likeness; then will you enter [the Kingdom].""*
>
> —*Gospel of Thomas, Saying 22*

Making the two, one.

The mystics see the One in All. The spiritual path is about

transcending separation and division. As we'll cover in later chapters, the process is about going from this dualistic plane of oppositional energies, to a non-dualistic state of Infinite Union. This is explicit in Saying 22.

> *"I took my place in the midst of the world, and I appeared to them in the flesh.*
>
> *I found all of them intoxicated; I found none of them thirsty.*
>
> *And My soul became afflicted for the sons of men, because they are blind in their hearts and do not have sight; for empty they came into the world, and empty too they seek to leave the world.*
>
> *But for the moment they are intoxicated. When they shake off their wine, then they will repent."*
>
> *—Jesus, Gospel of Thomas, Saying 28*

Attaining the heights of human understanding must be a lonely place! Awakened beings feel intimately connected with all creation, but that level of unity can be hard to relate to with other people. He only found a dozen or so people that could keep up with his level of understanding, and even they struggled to interpret his message.

In a way he's lamenting for the state of humanity, being caught in delusion. We're drunk with sensual indulgences and being distracted by our own egos. He understood that when we shake off our wine (delusion), we'll let go of our past and be able to find the peace he's found.

The brilliant Chinese sage Zhuangzi has a similar musing on the challenges brought about by a heightened state of awareness:

> *"Great truths do not take hold of the hearts of the masses. And now, as all the world is in error, how shall I, though I know the true path, how shall I guide? If I, while knowing I cannot succeed, still attempt to force success, this would be but another source of error. Better then, to desist and strive no more. Yet if I do not strive, who will?"*

58

The uniqueness of Christ's teachings in *Thomas* continues:

> *"The disciples said to Jesus, "Tell us how our end will be."*
>
> *Jesus said, "Have you discovered, then, the beginning, that you look for the end?*
>
> *For where the beginning is, there will the end be.*
>
> *Blessed is he who will take his place in the beginning; he will know the end and will not experience death."*
>
> *—Gospel of Thomas, Saying 18*

This is particularly mysterious to the non-adept. No wonder mainstream Christianity doesn't read this thing.

He's talking about the illusion of time. And how time is ultimately transcended with the inner realizations of presence, of detachment, of liberation.

It's also a brilliant and playful play on words. During that period, the Jews were concerned with the end of times (eschatology), and Jesus makes pronouncements about 'the end' and 'the coming' in the canonicals. But in this moment, he's playing with the relationship of the end to the beginning. Itß reads like a Zen koan.

> *"If you bring forth what is within you, what you bring forth will save you. '*
>
> *If you do not bring forth what is within you, what you do not bring forth will destroy you."*
>
> *—Jesus, Gospel of Thomas, Saying 70*

Beautiful verse emphasizing the inner work. It's not about external rules and doctrine. The practice is about traversing one's own heart, and one's own mind.

> *"He who will drink from my mouth will become like Me.*
>
> *I myself shall become he, and the things that are hidden will become revealed to him."*

—Jesus, Gospel of Thomas, Saying 108

There you have it friends, the explicit declaration that Christhood is attainable by all. It's a similar read to the *John* verse on 'becoming the sons of god' (*John* 1:12) but it is especially clear here. By 'drinking from my mouth'... by understanding my message that I'm preaching, you *"will become like me. I myself shall become he..."*

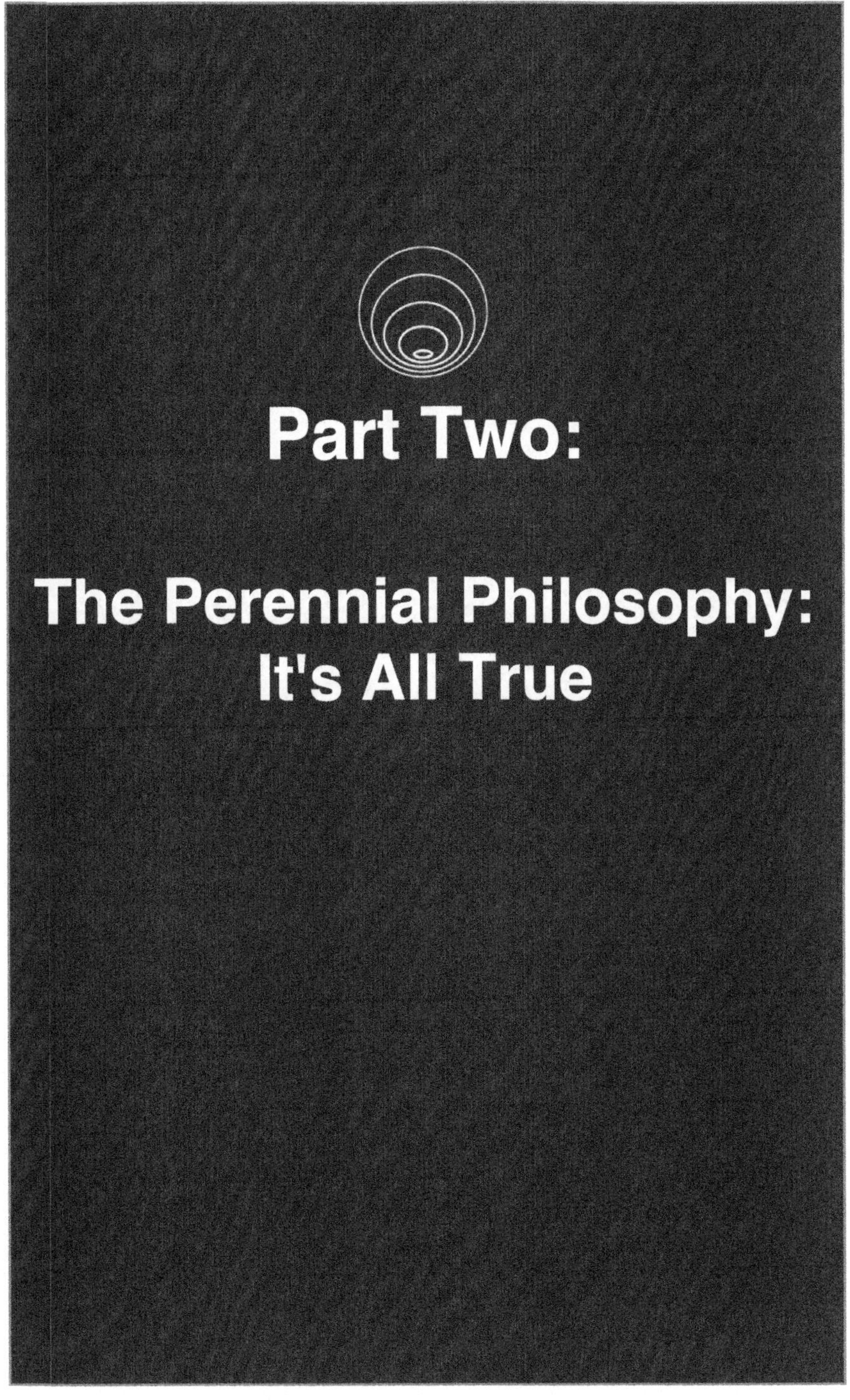

Part Two:

The Perennial Philosophy: It's All True

Original sin is a lie,

because every sage
who realized the truth,

says the same thing:

that our dark past is forgivable,

that our harmonious future is
inevitable,

and that our present is packed
full of the beauty of all existence.

CHAPTER 4

Many Paths Up the Mountain

The Apache Medicine Man

In the sixties, my grandfather Bob Peck played saxophone in nightclubs, and wrote copy for TV commercials.

In the nineties, my father Bob Peck wrote books, and handled home insurance claims for every state in the country.

In the past decade, I've made documentary films, and worked within digital marketing in Big Tech.

We're creative and also resourceful.

In the early nineties, my dad dated an amazing woman named Marcy who introduced him to "alternative" spiritual beliefs. She was a massage therapist, into essential oils, reiki healing, and using pendulums for decision-making. These are all more commonplace now, but in 1992 in Texas she was practically Madame Blavatsky.

Marcy influenced my dad's life in profound ways.

His incarnation's journey began as a Catholic, and then due to the overwhelming hypocrisy of the modern Catholic Church, he wound up a militant, confrontational atheist.

After many years and many arguments against believers, Marcy redirected him back into the reality of spiritual philosophy and ultimately spiritual living.

He had over a decade of spiritual synchronicities throughout his relationship with her. They were very in love and sadly, she became very ill. She passed away in 1997. He has recently finished a book about her life and experiences called *Tribute to an Angel.*[1]

Less than a year after Marcy's death, Dad was 'working a storm' unusually close to home.

Half an hour outside of Austin, he was visiting just another insurance claim that he was assigned to. He knocked on the door and a stoic Native American man answered.

Richard's house was hit by a hailstorm, and Bob was his insurance adjuster.

In decades of working storms, his tens of thousands of conversations had never reached the depths of spirituality at such lightning speed, as it did inside that hail-damaged house in Pflugerville, Texas.

While I do lean more spiritual than the average person, I still try to retain a healthy amount of rational skepticism. And truly I wouldn't be a believer in this man unless I saw his results. And I have. He's done a considerable amount of healing work on my father, and on my wife, and he's given me personal insight that has helped me to improve myself immensely.

Richard was born on a reservation in New Mexico in the 1950s. A proud Chiricahua Apache, he learned tribal customs and the ways of shamanic healing from his grandfather. He eventually enlisted in the military, and after his service he was a police officer in Dallas for several years. In his later years, he has been a probation officer for the state.

What better place for a holy man, than to work closely with an endless list of people suffering from damaged psychological states in need of care, understanding, and counsel?

He also communicates intuitively with ethereal entities. They've been called a variety of names: Guardian Angels, Spirit Guides, Ascended Masters. He refers to them as "The Old Ones" or "The Grandfathers"... again, I wouldn't believe this if their guidance through him hadn't come true so often, proving to be beneficial many times over the years. And his wisdom is usually enhanced with little synchronicities, or cosmic coincidences. He's a pretty unique guy.

We often say that we lost Marcy and got Richard.

I met Richard when I was a kid. My dad took me to meet him at a restaurant on the outskirts of north Austin, and at one point during dinner he asked me if I saw anything on a piece of brick that was the interior wall of the restaurant. I tried really hard to see something, I really wanted to. But I didn't. "A dolphin?" I asked. He smiled and said "A brave." The instant he said that, I could see the face of a Native American warrior in the brick, as lucid as a painting in a museum.

As a great healer, Richard has never once charged a penny. He has no website, no business card, no Instagram. He has also never taken credit for the results of his healing.

"I'm just a vessel," he says, shrugging off any admiration.

In 2012, my dad was diagnosed with cancer. We were shocked and saddened as he went in for surgery within days of the news. When they wheeled him out of the operating room, coming in and out of the anesthesia, the surgeon explained to us that there were additional tumors discovered, metastasizing: "He has about five years". My stepmom burst into tears. Resisting full-blown panic, we called 'the family doctor', our Apache shaman friend Richard, who came by to offer his support. When the room was considerably calmer with the warmth of genuine family love, Richard conducted a healing ceremony. We all circled my dad in his hospital bed, following Richard's instructions in asking for healing. Dad spoke later about the 'vision quest' aspect of his dreams that day. They were filled with striking spiritual imagery: two horses running up a hill, a pack of wolves surrounding aspen trees, and a series of red feathers which he eventually understood to be Richard's fellow Native brothers and sisters praying for my dad from a reservation.[2] A post-op visit a week later with an associate of the initial surgeon resulted in a drastically different analysis than the one immediately following the surgery. This follow-up concluded that something did something, because every single body part listed on their chart was read out loud to my dad and his wife: "Non-malignant". A decade later, he's been in complete remission.

Among the variety of metaphysical truths Richard has affirmed over the years, one of the most powerful is that there are many paths up the mountain. One time we asked him if he goes to church. "We're standing on it!" he said with a smile, implying of course that there is nowhere on this green earth without a sacred connection to the Divine. He has explicitly confirmed my intuitive understanding: there's only one summit—call it Liberation, the Kingdom of Heaven, Self-Realization, or Enlightenment—but you can get there, that one destination, in a multitude of ways. We all have our own psychological strengths and opportunities for growth. We have our unique past traumas. And so there is a wide variety of "ways back home" in order to match the needs of each type of human being.

The great saint Ramakrishna explained it simply:

> *"You must know that there are different tastes. There are also different powers of digestion. God has made different religions and creeds to suit different aspirants.*
>
> *...The mother brings home a fish for her children. She curries part of the fish, part she fries, and with another part she makes pilau. By no means all can digest the pilau. So she makes fish soup for those who have weak stomachs. Further, some want pickled or fried fish.*
>
> *There are different temperaments.*
>
> *There are differences in the capacity to comprehend."* [3]

Those differences are what make up this plane of seeming separateness, and I have deep gratitude for our shamanic mentor who has helped us to heal, to contemplate, and to start to make sense of it all.

Other Names for God

It's the 21st century. The word "God" could be the most loaded term in the English language. There is not a more diverse set of meanings for the same grouping of letters, which is why I personally try to avoid using that term as often as I can.

One of the extremes is an old bearded white man on a cloud passing judgments. Michelangelo, despite his nearly unparalleled talent, is substantially responsible for that image.[4]

The other extreme is a nebulous Cosmic Energy, Formless Love transcending this existence as we know it.

I side more with the latter—and even beyond that, the further I get into mysticism and nonduality via Advaita Vedanta and *A Course In Miracles,* the more I start to understand that God is actually the Only Reality… with everything else being a projection of our Mind, seemingly-endless layers of substance-less form, a dream brought about by the "tiny mad idea" of separateness[5]… okay we'll get there.

In a certain way, monotheism could be considered the beginning of the journey towards nondual mystical spirituality. Monotheism is dualism, really, because what it maintains is that God exists as a single entity, and the rest of us are here down on earth. While every religion's mystics blur these theological lines, the three Abrahamic religious institutions (Judaism, Christianity, Islam) are ultimately monotheistic.[6]

For example if you're a Christian: God sent his Only Son once, along with a few prophets, but otherwise God is pretty removed from the situation. At least in proximity. There's variance within that of course, but the point here is that within monotheism, God is distinctly separate from us.

Despite this separation, it would be unfair to not mention the extent of their adoration for Him. Islam in particular has "99 Attributes of Allah", from All-Compassionate, to The Giver of Peace, to the All-Seeing, to The Just, to Giver of Life and Bringer of Death.[7]

And I can't exclude the name He gave Himself, upon Moses' inquiry—in *Exodus*, a book holy to all three Abrahamic religions, Moses asks what he should say to his tribe, to Whom was he speaking? The reply received was, *"I AM THAT I AM."* Adding, *"Say this to the people of Israel, 'I Am has sent me to you.'"* (*Exodus* 3:14) In this moment with Moses, the god of the Bible self-defines as the Presence of Being.

Pantheism has an interesting take, expanding that framework a bit further. God exists, yes, but not in one concentrated place, rather within all things. Everything you see is God, or godlike, according to Hinduism, as well as a variety of indigenous, shamanistic beliefs. The Vedic religion of ancient India certainly has an indigenous aspect to it and pantheism is a doctrinal overlap with many of the non-Abrahamic religions.

> *"Where can we go to find God,*
>
> *if we cannot see Him in our own hearts,*
>
> *and in every living being?"*
>
> —*Swami Vivekananda*

Hinduism is considered pantheistic, but has more difficulty being considered polytheistic (many gods). While there are thousands, if not millions of separate gods in the Hindu pantheon, they all emanate from Brahman. This is extremely important. They are all masks of the One. The famous scholar Max Müller and others have referred to this ideology as "henotheism"—many iterations of the one God, or one single higher, more exalted deity within a larger framework.[8]

The term "panentheism" was coined by Karl Krause and later expanded upon by Charles Hartshorne, (a student of both Martin Heidegger and Alfred North Whitehead) which helps make the jump from standard pantheism "god is in all things", to a new definition that includes transcendence. The "en" after "pan" indicates that not only is God everywhere, but also beyond time and space as well as within it.[9] In my film, *The Kingdom Within*, Dr. Stephen Phillips makes the analogy for panentheism as follows: "

> *As human beings transcend our bodies by doing yoga and other spiritual practices, so does God transcend the universe."* [10]

Native American tribes have several names, many of which I find lovely: "Creator", "The Great Spirit", "The Great Mystery".

Aristotle wrote about a "Prime Mover" or "Unmoved Mover", the translation being "that which moves without being moved".

Zoroaster used the name Ahura Mazda meaning "Wise Lord".

Rumi and the Sufis spoke of God as "The Beloved", from the perspective of a lover.

Guru Nanak of Sikhism uses the symbol Ik Onkar meaning "One All Pervading Spirit".

Mahavatar Babaji, the timeless Hindu sage refers to "The Infinite Current".

Baha'is refer to God as many names but their most cherished name is "All-Glorious" or Bahá in Arabic.

In Subud, "The Great Holy Life Force".

Emerson and the Transcendentalists called God the "Over-Soul".

Carol Howe and the *A Course in Miracles* crowd often substitute the usage of the word "God" for simply "Love". So instead of Lesson 29: *"God is in everything I see"*, the phrase *"Love is in everything I see"* is a perfect substitution.

Madame Blavatsky had a variety: "Incomprehensible, Unknown and Unnamed", "The One and Secondless Principle in the Universe", the "Rootless Root of All".

Laozi called it the *Tao*, or "The Way", writing[11]:

> *"There is a thing inherent and natural, which existed before heaven and earth.*
>
> *Motionless and fathomless,*
>
> *It stands alone and never changes;*
>
> *It pervades everywhere and never becomes exhausted.*
>
> *It may be regarded as the Mother of the Universe.*
>
> *I do not know its name.*

If I am forced to give it a name, I call it Tao, and I name it as supreme."

Adi Shankaracharya, the Advaita master, refers to God as the "Supreme Self":

"Like bubbles in the water,

the worlds rise,

exist,

and dissolve in the Supreme Self,

which is the material cause and the prop of everything." [12]

There's also a movement within New Age circles to refer to God as a Her—an idea so ancient that it dates back to the earliest relics of civilization.[13] It certainly seems strange that we would consider the One That Birthed The Cosmos to be a male… as birthing anything is the defining characteristic of femininity. Archaeologists have found hundred-breasted idols dating back to before the modern patriarchal civilization as we know it, which begs the question: What could be more sacred than the life-giving aspect of the female?

Richard, the Apache shaman, prays to "Mother-Father-God", paying respects to both aspects of our parental Creator. As these common parallels are no longer surprising… this is the same translation of the name for God in the Tamil Nadu branch of Shaivism (Hindu).[14]

It's easy to get lost in the isms.

While it can be helpful to understand the sheer spectrum of the word "God", ultimately too much obsession over the word, or the form, fixates us on something finite.

Anything finite is destructible by definition and, according to the mystics, consequently unreal. The Source of All Creation is ultimately ineffable—it cannot be contained by words alone. The Jewish Kabbalists, Muslim Sufis, Advaita Vedantans and many others inquire: how can you label what simultaneously encompasses, and is also beyond, all known things?

Even William Winwood Reade in his humanist, rational-thinking "secular Bible" *The Martyrdom of Man*, writes[15]:

> *"The Supreme Power is not a Mind;*
>
> *not a Force;*
>
> *not a Being;*
>
> *but something higher than a Being;*
>
> *something for which we have no words, something for which we have no ideas."*

While there are five major religions in the world: Judaism, Christianity, Islam, Hinduism, and Buddhism, there are dozens if not hundreds of other faith traditions as well. And within the main five, there are hundreds if not thousands of sectarian divisions within each central faith.

So pick one, or many, or honor every variation, or reject them all.

Just know that the angry old Italian man on the ceiling of the Sistine Chapel doesn't quite cover it.

CHAPTER 5

Parallels Among the Central Religious Figures

The Avatars

Over the last few decades, our society has become more and more accustomed to religious coexistence. On college campuses and coffee shops in the 21st century, it's not unusual to hear the idea that "religions are mostly the same." As someone who embraces unitarian principles, it is a sweet melody to me, but looking back throughout history at how combative religions have been during certain periods, this fairly new, extremely valuable idea is worth understanding fully.

Thankfully we have the benefit of rigorous modern-day scholarship within comparative religion to help us see the luminous parallels. A hugely important aspect to the "sameness" of the world religions are their central figures: the *Avatars* and their teachings.

Hinduism is the oldest active faith in the world. The *Rig Veda* (~1900 BCE) is the oldest scripture still in use today.[16]

> *"Truth is one;*
>
> *Sages call it by many names."*
>
> —*Rig Veda*

I want to be absolutely clear here: many principles of ancient Hindu (*Vedic*) knowledge contribute to an incredibly helpful understanding of spirituality.

The *Vedas* carry the early creation stories, rituals, and songs, while the *Upanishads* came a few centuries later, giving us metaphysical commentaries that detail the nature of our existence.[17] They explain the fleeting impermanence of all creation, and these seers (*rishis*), sitting at the peaks of the Himalayas, mapped our human consciousness with such sophistication that we're still untangling them thousands of years later. Here are some core concepts offered by the Vedic and Upanishadic traditions:

- *dhyana* (meditation): the bedrock of spiritual practice
- *ahimsa* (non-violence): non-harm, compassion to all things
- *karma* (action): the cause-and-effect nature of vibratory phenomena
- *samsara* (reincarnation): the wheel of lifetimes; what Plato and the ancient Greeks called "*metempsychosis*", or the "transmigration of the soul"[18]
- and the *avatars* are those who guide us through darkness, connecting the world's religions through their mutual uplift of humanity

The avatar is a human manifestation of the Divine, born out of Absolute Compassion to serve and illuminate the rest of humanity.[19] They teach us to realize our True Nature. Almost every system of religious or spiritual belief contains divine, or awakened personas who guide the rest of us stuck in primal mud.

The term comes from Sri Krishna in the *Bhagavad Gita,* who comforts his cousin Arjuna with the following:

> *"Whenever righteousness wanes and unrighteousness increases I send myself forth.*
>
> *For the protection of the good and for the destruction of evil,*
>
> *and for the establishment of righteousness,*
>
> *I come into being age after age."*

—Krishna, Bhagavad Gita 4.7–8

Human civilizations rise and fall. Everything in the world of form happens in a cyclical framework.

During the peaks, humanity experiences harmony and brotherhood in the world. During the valleys, when evil takes over, a spark of divinity ignites within a human being who is intimately connected to our Creator, that ultimate Cosmic Energy from which all things spring.

This Manifestation of Light centers their entire human life around teaching how to liberate us from our earthly bondage.

The plot points of their lives are eerily similar: all avatars have wondrous births. Their coming is prophesied by sages. As youth, they radiate compassion and knowledge far beyond their years. They correct institutional hypocrisies and misdeeds. And they ultimately teach us how to walk the path of peace and love.

In introducing the primary three avatars who guide my heart, it's worth mentioning the two opposing points of inherent divinity vs. culminated realization. This debate is so conceptually unimportant to me but it's important to many religious people.

On one end, Buddha was very explicitly born a man who realized enlightenment sitting under the Bodhi tree, while Sri Krishna is considered realized even as a baby boy.[20] While Jesus is somewhere in the middle: devout Christians claim his complete, constant divinity, while the mystics point towards his trials in the desert as being pivotal for his spiritual evolution after which he began his public ministry.

Additionally I should say that Krishna's stories are by far the most ancient, so it makes sense that he would be the most heavily mythologized of these three, to be born a god. He is portrayed with blue skin after all.

To me, being 'born realized', or acquiring it later in life is not the point, that doesn't really matter. What matters is that the realization occurred—and what teachings spring from its well.

Unsurprisingly, Yogananda, who authored a two-volume

commentary on the New Testament, similarly wrote *God Talks With Arjuna: the Bhagavad Gita*, a two-volume interpretation of the *Gita*'s eighteen chapters. He explains the nature of our highest potential:

> *"All human beings are potential gods; the wise man and the ignorant one both are true image-incarnations of God. The Divine Omnipresence fills each soul-image even as the mighty ocean is present in each wave. However, unless a wave dissolves itself and becomes one with the ocean, it remains inordinately limited. Until a devotee is fully liberated, he cannot truly assert: 'I and my Father are one.'"* [21]

Krishna

One of the most famous holy texts of Hinduism is the *Bhagavad Gita*. It is an excerpt from the *Mahabharata*, an ancient Indian epic fifteen times longer than the Bible and eight times the length of Homer's *The Iliad* and *The Odyssey* combined.[22] The *Gita* is merely a scene within its expansive drama, but it contains vital ethical explanations for Hindus and humanity at large.

The timeline for the *Mahabharata* and Sri Krishna's life is as with all world mythologies, academically murky; despite this most scholars accept the historicity of Krishna, living on Indian soil by at least 1000 BCE, potentially as early as the 3200s BCE.[23] ("Sri" is a title of respect in India, it means "lord" for deities and holy people but can even mean "mister" in front of a respected man's name.)

During Sri Krishna's life, there was a massive war between clans. There were brothers against brothers and teachers against students. It was a horrible, bloody civil war and the protagonist, Arjuna, was hesitant. Arjuna was a great warrior. He was one of the finest archers in the world. And he was beyond fortunate to have his own cousin, Sri Krishna, as his charioteer.

Sri Krishna is considered to be a manifestation of *Vishnu*, one of the three Hindu gods of the *Trimurti*: *Brahma* (Creator), *Vishnu* (Preserver), and *Shiva* (Destroyer) comprise a Hindu "trinity" that doesn't exactly resemble the Trinity in Christianity (Father, Son, and Holy Spirit) but is an interesting similarity nonetheless.[24] Vishnu is "The Preserver" and occasionally takes on an earthly, human form in order to help humanity. In the *Gita*, Vishnu occupies an earthly body as Sri Krishna in order to guide Arjuna through his monumental existential crisis on the frontlines of war.

Yogananda elaborates:

> *"In the Bhagavad Gita our attention is focused on the role of Sri Krishna as the guru and counselor of Arjuna, and on the sublime yoga message he preached as preceptor to the world—the way righteous activity and meditation for divine communion and salvation—the wisdom of which has enthroned him in the hearts and minds of devotees throughout the ages.*
>
> *We hear of saintly ascetics, or prophets in the woods or secluded haunts, who were men of renunciation only; but Sri Krishna was one of the greatest exemplars of divinity, because he lived and manifested himself as a Christ and at the same time performed the duties of a noble king. His life demonstrates the ideal not of renunciation of action—which is a conflicting doctrine for man circumscribed by a world whose life breath is activity—but rather the renunciation of earth-binding desires for the fruits of action."* [25]

Eighteen brief chapters cover a wealth of religious, philosophical, and even psychological topics. The beauty of the *Gita* is its practicality. Krishna provides a contextual framework and then discusses how to apply these principles in our daily life—how to walk on the path to truth, accessing the integrity behind right action, understanding the immortality of spirit, how meditation disciplines the mind, and seeing the Divine in All.

Gautama Buddha

Siddhartha Gautama, also known as the *Buddha*, meaning "the

Awakened One" in Sanskrit, was another such avatar.

He was born a wealthy prince in India (~563 BCE) who was sheltered from the world. On the eve of his birth, his father the king consulted a priest who made a powerful prediction based on his birth. The king's son would either be a great warrior-king known for his conquests, or a famous saint known for his teachings. Due to the intense paranoia of losing his heir to a monastic life, his father tried to shelter the young boy from suffering.

In what became known as the "Four Sights", the famous religious scholar Huston Smith writes:

> *"No effort was spared to keep the prince attached to the world. Three palaces and 40,000 dancing girls were placed at his disposal; strict orders were given that no ugliness intrude upon the courtly pleasures. Specifically, the prince was to be shielded from contact with sickness, decrepitude, and death; even when he went riding, runners were to clear the roads of these sights. One day however, an old man was overlooked…"* [26]

And the seed was planted. Prince Siddhartha began to understand the inevitability of the decay of the material world. On his next ride he saw a sick man: illness. Then a dead man's corpse, showing him mortality and impermanence. And lastly, a monk, offering the potential of a way out of the other three—a spiritual practice in the attempt to end suffering by withdrawing from it all.

He couldn't endure the sensual charade any longer. In the middle of the night, Siddhartha left his royal upbringing and became an extreme ascetic, nearly dying from prolonged fasting. He eventually realized that sensual renunciation was not the ultimate answer, as that only ended up affirming the seeming reality of the body.

So that wasn't it either.

The path of the ascetic was no closer to ultimate peace than his sheltered princely life.

Sitting under the Bodhi tree, he reached enlightenment, or "awakening".

The Buddha intimately understood what later became known as "The Four Noble Truths":

- *Dukkha:* This world is suffering. (The translation is closer to the idea of 'un-satisfactory-ness'.[27])
- *Samudaya:* External desire (*tanha*) causes suffering.
- *Nirodha:* Ceasing desire, ceases suffering.
- *Magga:* The path of ethics, meditation and wisdom, more detailed as "The Eightfold Path", is the method for ceasing desire and consequently ceasing suffering.

In addition, he taught 'loving-kindness' to all beings. He disavowed superstition and empty ritual. His methods emphasized practicality. Because he preached moderation in a world of extremes, the Buddha's path is often called "The Middle Way".

Jesus of Nazareth

Considering how much time we spent in Part One, I'll be brief:

Jesus of Nazareth is quite possibly the most well-known person in human history. This becomes a fascinating fact considering how average his life was historically and economically. His family members were low-to-middle class laborers in antiquity! Millions of people lived and died in his time period without leaving a trace of their existence to us contemporary humans. So why are we still talking about him?

Considered the "Christ", which means "the Anointed One", or the "Messiah" ("Khristos" in Greek), the Messiah is a term for a Jewish savior. The original, Jewish definition is more simply: a leader, who unifies the Israelites as a prophesied warrior-king. Although Jesus eventually became to be considered the "Son of God" by Christians—unlike the Judaic concept of the Messiah. Despite this difference, Jesus is also an important figure in both Judaism and Islam, the three Abrahamic religions. (They are so-called because the followers of each faith consider themselves to be descendants of the ancient Israelite, Abraham.)

Jesus's origin story (born ~4-8 BCE) involves 'immaculate conception', that he was born of a virgin. To be fair to non-religious, skeptical readers, there are many other ancient figures born of a virgin mother, and Christian readers should know that only two of the four gospels include accounts of his birth. The earliest gospel, *Mark*, starts his narrative when Jesus is thirty, and the last, *John*, gives us that cosmological background devoid of the nativity.

In addition to, or aside from this divine persona, he was a teacher who preached radical love, humility, and forgiveness. He was also a miracle worker, not uncommon in first century Judaea, who met the end of his earthly persona after a few years of public ministry.

Arguably one of the most well-established facts in historical scholarship, Jesus was crucified by the Roman authorities in the first century—the Roman Empire being the hardened executioner of many anti-institutional voices.[28]

Despite his young death, his teachings live on.

What Did They Teach Us?

Quite simply (reductively), the primary mystical messages of each of these avatars are:

- The Path to Peace and its Internal Nature
- Compassion to All Beings
- Releasing Dependence on the External World

There are entire libraries dedicated to the teachings of these ancient masters so I'm only offering a meager flyover summary here, but a basic understanding of these teachers' parallels is important for the avenues and alleyways we'll be traveling in later pages. And of course, our lives at large.

<u>On the Internal Path:</u>

While the *Gita* is set on a battlefield of an epic war, for centuries yogic masters have interpreted this conflict as being two armies at war within one's mind: sensual egoic thinking vs. the illumined Self. The raging battle of Kurukshetra is merely the metaphor used for Krishna to guide his cousin Arjuna through a series of conceptual precepts and practical techniques leading to transcendence. Yogananda and others have even interpreted every major character in the *Mahabharata* as a symbolic representative of a unique aspect of self![29]

The method Krishna prescribes for avoiding temptation is self-control through meditation as well as the mental withdrawal from their importance.

> *"O Mighty-Armed Arjuna, undoubtedly the mind is fickle and unruly;*
>
> *But by yoga practice and by dispassion, the mind may nevertheless be controlled.*
>
> *This is My word: Yoga* is difficult of attainment by the ungoverned man;*
>
> *but he who is self-controlled will, by striving through proper methods,*
>
> *Be able to achieve it."*
>
> —*Krishna, Bhagavad Gita 6.35-36*

*Yoga as defined by Patanjali in the fourth century CE, is "the stilling of the mind fluctuations", the discipline to do so. Not quite modern 'American gym yoga' but its ancient antecedent.

This avoidance of external temptation is a key feature in the map of the hero's journey. It's an important plot point in their life story because it affirms their greatness. And the overcoming itself has a transformative power.

After his baptismal initiation by John the Baptist, Jesus walked off into the desert to be tested for forty days by Satan, who offers him different offerings of power and prestige, all of which he refused. In an especially striking parallel, the Buddha sat under the Bodhi tree for forty days, as Devaputra Mara ("chief of demons") offers him pleasure and power and other external trappings, all of which he refused.

"Ask, and it will be given you.

Seek, and you will find.

Knock, and the door will be opened to you."

—Jesus, Gospel of Matthew 7:7

"The kingdom of God does not come with observation.

Nor will they say, 'Here it is!' or 'There it is!' For remember,

the kingdom of God is within you."

—Jesus, Gospel of Luke 17:20-21

"Let those who are wise seek the Way.

Those who find it will not return."

—Krishna, Bhagavad Gita

"Those who seek to find the One without ceasing,

will find the Lord

dwelling in their own hearts."

—Krishna, Bhagavad Gita

"Seeking within, you will find stillness.

Here there is no more fear or

attachment—only joy."

—Buddha, Dhammapada

"Irrigators channel waters;

fletchers straighten arrows;

carpenters shape wood;

the wise master themselves."

—Buddha, Dhammapada

On Compassion:

"Bless those who curse you.

Pray for those who mistreat you."

—Jesus, Gospel of Luke 6:28

"A new commandment I give to you, that you love one another,

even as I have loved you, that you also love one another.

By this all men will know that you are My disciples,

if you have love for one another."

—Jesus, Gospel of John 13:34-35

"The best type of yogi is he who feels for others,

Whether in grief or pleasure, even as he feels for himself."

—Krishna, Bhagavad Gita 6.32

"Do everything you have to do,

but not with greed, not with ego, not with lust, not with envy

but with love, compassion, humility and devotion."

—Krishna, Bhagavad Gita 2.45

"Radiate boundless love towards the entire world

above, below, and across

unhindered, without ill will, without enmity."

—Buddha, Karaniya Metta Sutta

"We will develop and cultivate the liberation of mind by loving-kindness,

make it our vehicle,

make it our basis,

stabilize it,

exercise ourselves in it,

and fully perfect it."

—Buddha, Samyutta Nikaya

On Releasing External, Worldly Desire:

"It is easier for a camel to pass through the eye of a needle than for a rich man to enter the Kingdom of heaven."

—Jesus, Gospel of Matthew 19:24

"Therefore I tell you, do not worry about your life, what you will eat or what you will drink, or about your body, what you will wear. Is not life more than food, and the body more than clothing?

Look at the birds of the air; they neither sow nor reap nor gather into barns, and yet your heavenly Father feeds them.

Are you not of more value than they? Can any of you by worrying add a single hour to your span of life?

And why do you worry about clothing? Consider the lillies of the field, how they grow; they neither toil nor spin, yet I tell you, even Solomon in all his glory was not clothed like one of these."

—Jesus, Gospel of Matthew 6:25-29

"When one's mind dwells on the objects of Senses, fondness for them grows on him,

from fondness comes desire, from desire anger.

Anger leads to bewilderment, bewilderment to loss of memory of true Self,

and by that loss intelligence is destroyed, and with the destruction of intelligence he perishes."

—Krishna, Bhagavad Gita 2.62-63

"He who feels neither rejoicing nor loathing toward the glad nor the sad, who is free from grief and cravings, who has banished the relative consciousness of good and evil, and who is intently devout - he is dear to Me."

—Krishna, Bhagavad Gita 12.17

"A mind unruffled by the vagaries of fortune,

from sorrow freed,

from defilements cleansed,

from fear liberated—this is the greatest blessing."

—*Buddha, Mangala Sutta*

"I do not dispute with the world;

rather it is the world that disputes with me."

—*Buddha, Samyutta Nikaya*

They also discuss *karma*.

The concept of karma is pretty familiar to even non-spiritual Western readers, and I'm relieved to say that it's mostly well understood.

In Sanskrit, karma means "action", and so *karma yoga* is the yoga of action, or technically the 'unitive path of action'.

It's Newton's "Third Law of Motion" (every action creates an equal and opposite reaction), but it also incorporates our thoughts, emotions, and actions. Karma is a Hindu principle explained thoroughly by Krishna in the *Gita*. I cover Krishna's karma yoga in greater depth later, but in the meantime, here are two moments where Buddha and Christ agree on the reciprocal nature of the universe:

> *"Give, and it will be given to you. A good measure, pressed down, shaken together, running over, will be put into your lap; for the measure you give will be the measure you get back."*
>
> —*Jesus, Gospel of Luke 6:38*
>
> *"Everything is based on mind, is led by mind, is fashioned by mind.*
>
> *If you speak and act with a polluted mind, suffering will follow you, as the wheels of the oxcart follow the footsteps of the ox.*
>
> *If with a pure mind a person speaks or acts, happiness follows him like his never-departing shadow."*

—*Buddha, Dhammapada*

I recently finished *The Gospel of Buddha,* a short compilation book edited by Paul Carus, published in 1894 out of an attempt to assemble the narrative of Buddha's life in a similar fashion to the gospels of the New Testament. Carus did a fine job, and I found a few lines that made me stop, re-read, and immediately archive for future discussions. One of these moments was the fact that the Buddha offers the exact same line as Paul's from *Galatians* Chapter 6: *"What you reap is what you sow."* [30] Of course, this is exactly how a sage would explain the law of cause and effect to a farmer—remember "the mustard seed" as an image for the Kingdom of Heaven by that Jewish teacher from Galilee? Jesus also wandered the countryside, ambling through agricultural societies, teaching any and all who would *lend their ears to hear.*

This law of cause and effect is intertwined with right action. It's one thing to read these quotes and feel the transcendental warmth, but how do we live out these concepts in the world?

One major aspect of living out these truths is service to humankind, which is emphasized by all avatars. Despite Jesus' clear instruction, some modern Christians are content to sit comfortably on faith alone… which absolutely happens in Eastern spirituality too. We all know that image of the meditator sitting on a pillow lost in meditation, similarly unaware of his own dharmic responsibility to help others.

Whereas other Hindus like Mahatma Gandhi, Paramahansa Yogananda, and Amma Sri Karunamayi have worked tirelessly to feed, clothe, and lift up the lives of the underprivileged. As do the Christians down at my local soup kitchen who have been feeding our local homeless population every Saturday morning free of charge for over two decades. More evidence that all faiths have the full spectrum of devotees!

Jesus encourages us to serve others many times in the Gospels:

> *"'For I was hungry and you gave me something to eat,*
>
> *I was thirsty and you gave me something to drink,*
>
> *I was a stranger and you invited me in,*

I needed clothes and you clothed me,

I was sick and you looked after me,

I was in prison and you came to visit me.'

"Then the righteous will answer him,

'Lord, when did we see you hungry and feed you,

or thirsty and give you something to drink?

When did we see you a stranger and invite you in,

or needing clothes and clothe you?

When did we see you sick or in prison and go to visit you?'

"The King will reply,

'Truly I tell you, whatever you did for one of the least of these brothers and sisters of mine, you did for me.'"

—Jesus, Gospel of Matthew 25:35-40

Service is an essential component of not only the teachings of the Buddha, Christ, and Krishna, but authentic spirituality as a whole.

And lastly, the avatar helps correct the clunky, decaying institutions of their day.

The cosmic duty (*dharma*) of Krishna's manifestation is outlined in the *avatara* doctrine itself, *"Whenever righteousness wanes and unrighteousness increases, I send myself forth."* The Hindu religion in those times was heavily intertwined with the governing rulers, and their corruption brought adverse effects to the religion, and consequently to the people of that time. Krishna clarifying the misinterpretations of a devolving civilization was an essential aspect of his purpose in this world.

In later centuries, the Buddha was born a Hindu, and Jesus was born a Jew. The new religions that later came out of their teachings were a direct result of the extreme contrast between their reformative message and the stagnant state of their respective religious cultures.

The Buddha's own enlightenment disproved his fellow Hindu ascetics' misdirection. There were also others, worshipping fire and making animal sacrifices, all of which he discarded.

In a typical scene, he comes upon a religious festival where the priests prepare to sacrifice many animals. The Buddha makes the following rebuke:

> *"Ignorance only can make these men prepare festivals and hold vast meetings for sacrifices. Far better to revere the truth than try to appease the gods by shedding blood.*
>
> *What love can a man possess who believes that the destruction of life will atone for evil deeds? Can a new wrong expiate old wrongs? And can the slaughter of an innocent victim blot out the evil deeds of mankind? This is practicing religion by the neglect of moral conduct.*
>
> *Purify your hearts and cease to kill; that is true religion.*
>
> *Rituals have no efficacy, prayers are vain repetitions, and incantations have no saving power. But to abandon covetousness and lust, to become free from evil passions, and to give up all hatred and ill-will, that is the right sacrifice and the true worship."*

Jesus similarly condemns the religious orthodoxy of his day. As we covered, he calls attention to the hypocrisies of the Pharisees, a priestly class of other Jews who had considerable political power and who were more concerned with the appearance of piety than the truth underneath their actions.

In another instance Jesus calls out the dietary restrictions of his religion, joking lightly, "*It's not what goes into the mouth that defiles a person, but what comes out of the mouth*"—a clear illustration that words and actions determine a person's character and commitment to God, as opposed to the avoidance of certain foods or following ancient rules ultimately irrelevant to one's capacity to love.

I can't resist pointing out the Buddha's parallel:

> *"Anger, drunkenness, obstinacy, bigotry, deception, envy, self-praise, disparaging others, superciliousness*

> *and evil intentions constitute uncleanness, not verily the eating of flesh."*

Christ also famously picked heads of grain on the Sabbath, an unlawful act on the Lord's Day garnering accusations from the Pharisees. He responded, *"The Sabbath was made for man, not man for the Sabbath."* (*Mark* 2:27-28)

Vivekananda, the greatest disciple of Ramakrishna, elaborates on these parallels:

> *"Krishna preached on this idea of love [in the Gita]. There are [in] other great books, sermons on love — as with Buddha, as with Jesus. ...*
>
> *There is a great deal of similarity between the lives of Jesus and Krishna. A discussion is going on as to which borrowed of the other. There was the tyrannical king in both places. Both were born in a manger. The parents were bound in both cases. Both were saved by angels. In both cases all the boys born in that year were killed. The childhood is the same. ... Again, in the end, both were killed. Krishna was killed by accident; he took the man who killed him to heaven. Christ was killed, and blessed the robber and took him to heaven.*
>
> *There are a great many similarities in the New Testament and the Gita. The human thought goes the same way. ... I will find you the answer in the words of Krishna himself: "Whenever virtue subsides and irreligion prevails, I come down. Again and again I come. Therefore, whenever thou seest a great soul struggling to uplift mankind, know that I am come, and worship. ..."*
>
> *At the same time, if he comes as Jesus or as Buddha, why is there so much schism? The preachings must be followed! A Hindu devotee would say: It is God himself who became Christ and Krishna and Buddha and all these [great teachers]. A Hindu philosopher would say: These are the great souls; they are already free. And though free, they refuse to accept their liberation while the whole world*

is suffering. They come again and again, take a human embodiment and help mankind..." [31]

Other Masks of the One

While the altar of my mind contains the teachings of Krishna, Buddha, and Christ, I'm not an authority on whether Abraham, Moses, Muhammad, or other famous prophets throughout history were avatars as defined as the fullest aspect of the Creator in the flesh (despite the Buddha's agnosticism).

I know the above three and I have little need for more nourishment—they are each continental reservoirs overflowing the meager table pitcher of my heart.

That said, I fully endorse listing Abraham, Moses, Muhammad, Confucius, Zoroaster, Laozi, Socrates, Plato, Adi Shankara, Kabir, Mirabai, Bahá'u'lláh, Meister Eckhart, Guru Nanak, St. Francis of Assisi, The Great Peacemaker, Anandamayi Ma, Ramakrishna and countless others as avatars, as extremely important divine figures, prophets, sages, saints, or as the Ba'hai faith refers to many of these, "Manifestations of God".[32]

I've drawn out some of the parallels between the Masks of the One most cherished to me, but in my admittedly still feeble understanding of the Infinite Nature of our Creator, categorizing these illuminated beings doesn't seem to be very useful for conscious development.

What is useful however, is acknowledging the wisdom to be gained from each Holy Voice, and realizing that Spirit can come through in a variety of time periods and a variety of cultural backgrounds.

Ultimately the main reason I hold the avatars in such high regard is very simple: because I see the immense value in applying their teachings to practical living. There have been absolute giants of humanity who have found peace by connecting to an ever-present Divinity dwelling within themselves and the rest of creation. The fact that their teachings overlap so greatly is worth being aware of!

Photograph: "Filming swamis" (2011); (from L to R)
Swami Chidrupananda, Srinidhi Baba, Srinivasa Krishna Srinidhi, the author.
Source: Author's personal collection.

CHAPTER 6

The Inclusive East

The Kingdom Within, the Movie

In that fifth year to obtain the secondary Religious Studies degree, I read an article about an angry Christian pastor, Mark Driscoll, who publicly spoke out against yoga, considering it a "demonic" practice.[33]

And it wasn't just Driscoll. The president of the Southern Baptist Theological Seminary, Rev. Albert Mohler, considers yoga "against Christianity." In addition to these prominent pastors, there is no shortage of articles and YouTube videos warning Christians about the harms of practicing this millennia-old tradition.

To some—jaw-dropping; but to others more familiar with the intolerance of certain areas of Church-ianity, like homophobia and religious exclusivism—not that surprising.

This was perfect timing for me: a novice New Testament scholar finishing Yogananda's *Autobiography of a Yogi*. After *Autobiography* and joining Kriya Yoga, I read more books on the parallels between the East & West, especially: *The Sermon on the Mount According to Vedanta* by Swami Prabhavananda, and Yogananda's *The Second Coming of Christ: The Resurrection of the Christ Within You*. I was prepared to begin shooting interviews.

The first interviews were local Kriya yogis, two of my former UT professors, and Rev. Patrick Gahan, the man who baptized me. It was off to an incredible start. I knew I had something really special by the time I finished shooting Father Pat's interview. In my film, a Christian pastor in Texas tells the camera:

> *"I don't know many mature Christians that discount other traditions' holy messengers.*
>
> *To me that's rather arrogant.*
>
> *Who knows what God is up to?*
>
> *Who knows who He is speaking to at different times?"* [34]

The film ultimately took three years to make. To this day I am deeply grateful for every one of my eighteen interview subjects. They were all terrific. I shot about twenty hours of footage to make an eighty-three minute movie.

One of the conceptual issues I struggled with in directing the film was whether or not to include the theory that young Jesus went to India.

A film reconciling yoga and Christianity ought to consider mentioning the idea, but whatever aspect of scholarship in me was hesitant.

For background, the alleged trip would have taken place during the "Lost Years of Jesus", so-called because in the two gospels covering his birth, only *Luke* mentions his childhood up to twelve briefly. In all four gospels he's suddenly thirty getting baptized by John in the Jordan River as he starts his ministry. Eighteen years of his life are completely absent from the Bible. To quote Paul Davids, the director of the film *Jesus in India,* "In the world of film we call that sort of omission a 'jump cut.'" [35]

As we discussed, the Christian "apocrypha" (Christian literature excluded from the Bible) is as early as the first century and as late as the present. It is so diverse because of the sheer number of attempts to fill in missing information in regards to the life of Jesus. To be clear, contemporary mainstream scholarship rejects any narrative during the lost years that doesn't have Jesus working as a carpenter with Joseph in Nazareth, or according to scholarship from the past century, in the nearby town of Sepphoris, an emerging cosmopolitan center near Nazareth.[36]

That said, the India theory itself has a variety of sources, one of whom was a nineteenth century Russian explorer of Tibet, Nicolas Notovitch. In *The Unknown Life of Jesus,* Notovitch claimed to have visited with monks in the Hemis Monastery in Tibet where he was allegedly shown a scroll titled *The Life of St. Issa.*[37] Issa is one of a few Eastern names for Jesus, as well as his name in Arabic, in the Quran. Notovitch translated this document into his own publication, but to date, no one has seen the original. After Notovitch's controversial story came to light, the nineteenth century scholar Max Müller wrote to the monastery and was told that a Westerner had not visited in at least fifteen years. Dr. Bart Ehrman, a highly respected contemporary New Testament scholar, considers Notovitch a notorious hoaxer. Although there was a British explorer, Col. Younghusband, who did chronicle a brief meeting with Notovitch near Kashmir[38] but made no claims to the authenticity of Notovitch's writings.

Swami Abhedananda and Swami Trigunatitananda, disciples of Sri Ramakrishna, at separate times journeyed to the monastery in Ladakh and said to have verified the existence of ancient Buddhist texts recording the life of Jesus.[39] Swami Trigunatitananda was also shown two paintings of Jesus by the Buddhist monks, and had a copy of one made from his memory when he was living in America as a Vedanta missionary. Abbot George Burke (Swami Nirmalananda Giri) chronicles these Vedantans, and many other 20th century author-explorers who traveled to the Hemis monastery in the attempt to validate Notovitch's claim: Dr. Nicholas Roerich, Henrietta Merrick, Elizabeth Caspari, and Robert Ravicz were all reassured by monks that Jesus had indeed lived in many Indian monasteries during those 'lost years'.[40] Even Edgar Cayce, the famous American "sleeping prophet", stated that young Jesus studied in India.[41]

The most fascinating reference to me is an ancient Kashmiri text called the *Bhavishya Maha Purana,* a fifth century Sanskrit document, with an unavoidably interesting scene:

> *"...When the king of the Sakyas came to the Himalayas, he saw a dignified person of golden complexion wearing a long white robe. Astonished to see this foreigner, he asked, 'Who are you?' The dignified person replied in a pleasant*

> *manner: 'Know me as Son of God [Isha Putram], or Born of a Virgin [Kumarigarbhasangbhawam]. Being given to truth and penances, I preached the Dharma to the mlecchas [non-Indians]....O King, I hail from a land far away, where there is no truth, and evil knows no limits. I appeared in the country of the mlecchas as Isha Masiha [Jesus Messiah/Christ] and I suffered at their hands. For I said unto them, '"Remove all mental and bodily impurities. Remember the Name of our Lord God. Meditate upon Him Whose abode is in the center of the sun."' There in the land of mleccha darkness, I taught love, truth, and purity of heart. I asked human beings to serve the Lord. But I suffered at the hands of the wicked and the guilty. In truth, O King, all power rests with the Lord, Who is in the center of the sun. And the elements, and the cosmos, and the sun, and God Himself, are forever. Perfect, pure, and blissful, God is always in my heart. Thus my Name has been established as Isha Masiha.' After having heard the pious words from the lips of this distinguished person, the king felt peaceful, made obeisance to him, and returned..."* [42]

The main source of my scholarly dilemma to include this Indian journey hypothesis was that my spiritual beacon, Paramahansa Yogananda, was very clear in his writings that Jesus studied under yogic masters in India.

Yogananda's explanation was based on the narrative that the wisemen ("magi") were actually Indian rishis, holy princes who traveled "from the East" (*Matthew* 2:1) to pay their respects to the avatar who had just manifested in Bethlehem. According to Yogananda and other sages, many years later the young Jesus took a caravan to India in order to return the honor of their blessing and long journey, by studying Eastern ways of living—most specifically God-realization.

About a year into filming, my wife Melissa and I were at Richard's house, our Apache shaman friend. When we visit him, we'll typically get a bite to eat out somewhere, and then head back to his place for a brief ceremony and some spiritual discussion. He could tell that something was gnawing on me and asked what the matter was. I said, "Well I'm not sure if you have the answer for me, but I can't decide whether or not to include the idea that Jesus went to India. I'm open to the idea of it, but Bible scholars don't think he did, and I really respect that." He sat still for a moment and said the name of an obscure spiritual book, *Lords of the Seven Rays*, and pointed to it. "There, pick it up, and read it aloud. They're saying to start at Part II, page 10." I grinned and grabbed the book, eager to discover what the Grandfathers wanted me to understand.

This is the excerpt I read:

> *"Many of you understand the journey of Jesus our Lord to the Far East, and you understand the purpose of his journey taken when a teenager, as many of you who are here today are. It was in pursuit of the teachings of the Far East and a teaching itself. It was preparatory to his final years in Palestine.*
>
> *And so he did meet the great lights of India, and he did take the teachings of Hinduism and Buddhism and make them come alive. And he did challenge, therefore, the priesthood, the classes who denied to the poor the full flowering of that Spirit. And he preached to the poor and he gave them back the dignity of life. And for this, they who held the reins of power in religion sought to take his life as they did later in Palestine.*
>
> *Beloved ones, I point out to you one of the most pernicious errors of orthodoxy this day, and it is the lie that Jesus is the only Son of God, and furthermore that Jesus came into embodiment in the full mastery of Christhood and did not himself have to follow the Path and realize his own inner God-potential before beginning his mission.*
>
> *These things are plain in scripture, but the scriptures have been read and reread so many times that the true intent is no longer heard by the soul. The layers of misinterpretation and then the removal of the very keys themselves have given to Christianity today a watered-down religion that does not have the fervor or the fire to*

meet the challengers of civilization..." [43]

I finished the page and started laughing out loud. Richard smiled. Melissa said something witty to the effect of, "So did you get your answer, Bob?"

The very next morning I had a volunteer shift. When I joined the Austin Kriya Yoga group, alongside learning the meditation technique, I was assigned to a community service group. It's called E.A.T. Outreach (Everybody Ate Today). The simple task is to bag a few grocery carts of day-old bread from a local grocer and take them to a distribution point for several food banks. I was paired up that morning with Valerie, a compassionate meditator devoid of religious allegiances. She asked me about what I was working on, and I mentioned the film and its subject-matter. She lit up and said, "Have you ever heard of the prospect of Jesus going to India?" Concealing my delight from the previous night's experience, I nodded and replied, "Sure, yes. Yogananda wrote about it a good deal." She excitedly declared, "You have to meet Ed and interview him for your film!"

It turned out that Valerie was well-acquainted with Edward T. Martin, a lovely, intelligent man who is the author of the book *King of Travelers: Jesus' Lost Years in India,* and star of Paul Davids' film *Jesus In India*. He was living about an hour away from Austin, and he became my tenth interview in shooting *The Kingdom Within*.

Hinduism as a Spiritual Foundation

Hinduism is a beautiful, ancient amalgamation of beliefs and practices. The name "Hindu" is what the colonizing British called people east of the Indus River. What the Hindus themselves call Hinduism, is *Sanatana Dharma*. It means "the Holy Science" or "eternal Law".[44]

Scholars maintain that Hinduism as a religion is so diverse that there is actually no such thing as "Hinduism proper", its developments over the past four millennia are so vast that admittedly I will be unable to properly contextualize its breadth in my few humble pages.

That said, the essence of its greatest beauty to me is ironically one of its most commercialized and appropriated phrases:

Namaste.

The word on bumper stickers and tote bags and the window of every yoga studio sums it all up pretty well.

Namaste is a Sanskrit word that translates to the equivalent of "the Divine within me, salutes and bows to the Divine in you."

We are all connected to our Cosmic Source, a celestial Higher Intelligence that exists in a plane beyond ours, and that Source is also present here, intimately, within every living being... of which Hindus acknowledge in both greeting and parting.

Mohandas K. Gandhi, the famous spiritually-inspired political activist of Indian independence defined namaste as follows:

> *"I honor the place in you where the entire Universe resides. A place of light, of love, of truth, of peace, of wisdom. I honor the place in you where when you are in that place, and I am in that place, there is only One of us."*

The Hindu religion is a vast spectrum of beliefs, deities, and practices. There are so many misconceptions about it, and it is my joy to debunk them.

The most common misconception is there are "a million gods!", which is not quite it. While there is a spectrum of worshipping multiple divine incarnations—some worship Vishnu, some worship Shiva, or Brahma, Shakti, Krishna, Kali, Durga, and so on—the One (or Brahman) is manifesting as the All. Every divine being, and every divine entity has the same underlying Oneness with all, and with Itself.

This is important:

The Divine is Within You.

The All.

The Everything.

You are a part of it and you are also a fragmentary representation of it. We are all—every being—a Mask of the One.

So by loving ourselves, we love all. By loving all, we love ourselves.

Again there's a wide variety of systems, but it begins here. Ancient-ly!

Within Indian philosophy, there are nine schools of thought. Six of these "orthodox" points of view accept the Vedas: Samkhya, Yoga, Nyaya, Vaisheshika, Purva-Mimamsa, and Vedanta. The other three—Carvaka (no longer existent), Buddhism (with its wide spectrum of sects), and Jainism do not accept the authority of the Vedas and are considered unorthodox.

Within Hindu scripture, there are two main categories: *shruti* and *smriti*. Shruti means divinely-inspired, ultimate authority. Smriti are also very influential as well, but the translation means "remembered", whereas shruti means "heard" [from a Divine Source]. The *Vedas* are the primary shruti within the orthodox schools, while smriti tends to be consistent philosophically with Vedic thought: the great epics (the *Ramayana*, and the *Mahabharata* containing the essential *Bhagavad Gita*), the *Puranas*, and the *Dharma Shastras*.[45]

All of which recognize the intuitive alignment with our own godliness as a source of philosophical truth.

The Hindus call this component of our godliness, the *Atman*. The atman is essentially the Sanskrit word for "soul" in Judeo-Christian spirituality, and Brahman is the name for the Formless Infinity, the One Manifesting as the Many. To be fair, there are variations on this relationship between the Atman and Brahman. Within some sects they are perfectly equal, to others the atman is a part of Brahman, and to others the atman is like the body of God while Brahman is like the Soul of God.

The "Four Principles" (*Mahavakyas*)[46] within Upanishadic thought are as follows:

> *- Prajñānam Brahma - "Consciousness is Brahman." ('Consciousness is Ultimate Reality')*

—Aitareya Upanishad 3.3

- Aham Brahmāsmi - "I am Brahman."

—Brihadaranyaka Upanishad 1.4.10

- Tat Tvam Asi - That thou art." ("You are Brahman; You are the Ultimate Reality.")

—Chandogya Upanishad 6.8.7

Ayam Atmā Brahma - "This Self is Brahman."

—Mandukya Upanishad 2

Sri Krishna highlights the untouchability of the atman in the material world to Arjuna:

> *"Weapons cannot shred the soul [atman], nor can fire burn it. Water cannot wet it, nor can the wind dry it.*
>
> *The soul is unbreakable and incombustible; it can neither be dampened nor dried. It is everlasting, in all places, unalterable, immutable, and primordial.*
>
> *The soul is spoken of as invisible, inconceivable, and unchangeable. Knowing this, you should not grieve for the body."*
>
> *—Krishna, Bhagavad Gita 2.23-25*

The atman is our true identity, underneath the body, and the atman is that which remains beyond lifetimes. Our earthly body is like a set of clothes that the atman wears for a time and then (at death) removes. This is what is often called reincarnation, which the Hindu scriptures refer to as *samsara*, or the "wheel" of existence.

We continually 'cycle through' a series of incarnations until we realize we are the Eternal Self, at One With the One. And by defeating or transcending this ignorance, we regain infinity.

> *"As the one fire, after it has entered the world, though one, takes different forms according to whatever it burns, so does the internal Ātman of all living beings, though one, takes a form according to whatever He enters and is outside all forms."*

— *Katha Upanishad 2.2.9*

This separate form of the individual self, despite being one, has many distinct layers.

A 20th century Hindu guru and yogi master, Swami Satyananda Saraswati, explains:

> *"Modern psychologists refer to the three dimensions of mind as the conscious, subconscious, and unconscious. In the philosophies of Vedanta and Yoga they are known as the gross, subtle, and causal dimensions of the human personality. These three dimensions are again subdivided into the five koshas or bodies which constitute the total expression of the human personality from the grossest to the most subtle dimensions of existence."* [47]

Body, mind, and spirit are interconnected, interpenetrating, with these layers populating each aspect. Many yogic commentators draw the comparison of these subtle layers of our body, mind, and soul, to electromagnetic fields, or radioactive fields. The physical body just doesn't have the solidity we think it does. In many ways, modern physics, neuroscience, and psychology are starting to catch up to the sophistication of these ancient Himalayan seers!

Adi Shankaracharya was a famous Hindu teacher born in 700 CE, who acts as a bridge between the ancient Hindu philosophers and the modern day. He wrote volumes of both original works and commentaries on the ancient scriptures. His school within Vedanta, is called *Advaita.*

Scholar George Cronk writes in the Wadsworth Philosopher's Series *On Shankara*:

> *"In Shankara's view... the individual soul or self (jiva) is essentially one with the Universal Self (Atman), which itself is identical with Absolute Reality (Brahman). The idea that there are many individual and separate selves (polypsychism) is a delusion caused by spiritual ignorance (avidya). There is only one True Self (Atman) (monopsychism). Since Brahman alone is absolutely and*

> *independently real, the entire world of ordinary experience has no independent existence. Rather, the world is a mere appearance of Brahman."* [48]

Within Indian philosophy, *maya* is the physical world as we know it, but like our own physical bodies, it has a dreamlike element to it. Of all the Hindu sects, Advaita is the most extreme in terms of its undoing of the seeming reality of the physical plane.

> *"You never identify yourself with the shadow cast by your body, or with its reflection, or with the body you see in a dream or in your imagination. Therefore you should not identify yourself with this living body, either."*
>
> —*Adi Shankara*

This view of the world has also been called nonduality, meaning "not two": that everything we see, hear, smell, taste, and touch is merely another appearance of the One.

This world is finite, and since only the Divine is Infinite, it is therefore the Only True Reality.

Modern science tells us that we can only see a few hundred nanometers on the electromagnetic spectrum. We can't hear ultra-low-frequency sounds. Machines are confirming hard evidence of what the wisdom traditions have been getting across for millennia: that this plane of existence is not quite what it seems.

This is why Hindu philosophy makes an incredible foundation for spirituality. Its starting point is our inherent divinity, the recognition that our soul is comprised of both our individual uniqueness and our collective Oneness.

Everything else: meditation & yoga, scriptural study, religious ritual, service to others & oneself begins there. Or shall I say, here.

Right here.

With our essence.

And our potential.

What's so powerful about Indian philosophy is this aspect of limitlessness. We are not weak beings.

We are conscious, compassionate, with the potential to know our true self, and according to those prior humans who have gotten there: we can and will experience the Fullest Unending Love greater than any earthly comparison.

This Love comes to us from Source, overflowing in attributes. Another name for God in Hinduism is *Satchitananda*, or Sat - Chit - Ananda, which means:

- *Sat*: truth, absolute being or existence--that which is enduring and unchanging
- *Chit*: consciousness, understanding and comprehension
- *Ananda*: bliss, a state of pure happiness, joy and sensual pleasure

A friend recently asked me: isn't the One lonely? And perhaps so from an Abrahamic image of that old white man on the austere mountaintop. Perhaps from the anthropomorphic Greek pantheon of flawed human divinities. But if Satchitananda accurately describes The Source, then this image contains Infinite Bliss (Ananda) as an essential component, grouped with Eternal Truth (Sat) and Consciousness (Chit).

20th century Indian philosopher and activist Sri Aurobindo considers Satchitananda to be the eternal, unified concept of the soul which is beyond matter, space and time:

> *"These three, Sat, Chit and Ananda are one Trinity, Satchitananda. They are not three different factors making a single sum, neither are any two of them merely attributes, even inseparable & invariable attributes, of the third. No doubt, they are always coexistent. Where there is no delight, latent or developed, there can be no existence; where there is no awareness self-absorbed or manifest, there can be no existence. Follow existence into utter & blind inertia, consciousness sits secret in that night; follow consciousness into the abyss of desolation, joy sits self-stunned in the mask of that misery. But their coexistence is only an exterior sign of their essential unity. They do not exist separately, because they are not*

> *different from each other—all three are one thing-in-itself seen diversely; seen sensationally, touching the fibres of conscious life in us it is delight; seen mentally, touching the fibres of living consciousness, it is comprehension; seen spiritually, touching the very core of this living & conscious I, it is being. But the thing-in-itself is one; it is Brahman."* [49]

Satchitananda is both the definition of Brahman (God), and also the highest ideal, the potential for our own attainment!

We are not a mistake.

We are not evil.

We are only momentarily blinded by ignorance of our true nature. We've only forgotten who we are, taken a detour, thanks to the endless distractions of all these material stimuli.

And the spiritual path, whichever way home that best suits our enjoyment and understanding, is the way we can be reminded.

> *"Once we become conscious, even dimly, of the Atman, the Reality within us, the world takes on a very different aspect.*
>
> *It is no longer a court of justice but a kind of gymnasium.*
>
> *Good and evil, pain and pleasure, still exist, but they seem more like the ropes and vaulting-horses and parallel bars which can be used to make our bodies strong.*
>
> *Maya is no longer an endlessly revolving wheel of pain and pleasure but a ladder which can be climbed to consciousness of the Reality."*
>
> —*Adi Shankara*

Yogas: Bhakti & Jnana, the Heart & the Mind

> *"However one approaches me, I approach them in the same way, for everyone follows My path in all respects."*

—Krishna, Bhagavad Gita 4:11

The Hindus have a lovely way of explaining different styles of spiritual students. They categorize different aspects of a spiritual practitioner based on distinct paths to the Divine.

These paths are types of *yoga,* (Sanskrit: "union") equating to the different personalities within the world of form.

And in explaining these "yogas", it's important to understand that contemporary physical yoga is only one method of a larger system of spiritual practice within Hinduism. When you go to a gym in America, you're moving through a series of postures called "*asanas*" that were developed mostly in the past two centuries. They do have Indian roots (a la Krishnamacharya, Iyengar, and others) but they don't go back as far as Vedic philosophy or meditation.[50] Patanjali's *Yoga Sutras* is an ancient commentary that discusses "eight limbs" (*ashtanga*) of yoga, where the physical asanas (mainly, sitting comfortably) are merely one of eight limbs of yogic union.

For the purposes of this section, I'm referring to *jnana yoga,* absolute discipline of the intellect; and *bhakti yoga,* boundless devotion of the heart.

A *jnani* is an intellectual philosopher. This is someone who understands the conceptual theology and the power of the Mind. They use rigorous mental analysis and discipline to deduce their identity down to their True Self… which merges back into the One. *Neti neti* for example is a jnana technique, meaning "not this, not this"—a mental practice of negation to help understand the true nature of the atman. I am nothing out here, or out there, I am rooted in the Self.

One of the highest teachers of Advaita, a path infused with jnana yoga, was Sri Nisargadatta, explaining this state of realization:

> *"When the mind is kept away from its preoccupations, it becomes quiet. If you do not disturb this quiet and stay in it, you find that it is permeated with a light and a love you have never known; yet you recognize it at once as your*

> *own nature. Once you have passed through this experience, you will never be the same man again; the unruly mind may break its peace and obliterate its vision; but it is bound to return, provided the effort is sustained; until the day when all bonds are broken, delusions and attachments end and life becomes supremely concentrated in the present."* [51]

Unlike the jnani, a *bhakta* is a devotional lover. This is someone whose emotions are their connection to Spirit. The bhakta is shedding ecstatic tears in a place of religious worship. They sing songs and write poems to God. They are the lover and God is the Beloved. For example, seeing every person as another face of their chosen deity is a bhakti practice. When I see my son smile at me, or a friend, or a cashier... and my eyes lock into theirs, I feel the Beloved underneath their smile.

Arguably the most famous bhakti saint in the history of the Hindu religion is Mirabai, a 16th-century Hindu mystic poet and devotee of Krishna with more than 1300 poetic songs (*bhajans*) attributed to her. You can feel the intensity of her devotion in *"Unbreakable"*:

> *"Unbreakable, O Lord,*
>
> *Is the love*
>
> *That binds me to You:*
>
> *Like a diamond,*
>
> *It breaks the hammer that strikes it.*
>
> *My heart goes into You*
>
> *As the polish goes into the gold.*
>
> *As the lotus lives in its water,*
>
> *I live in You.*
>
> *Like the bird*
>
> *That gazes all night*
>
> *At the passing moon,*

> *I have lost myself dwelling in You.*
>
> *O my Beloved - Return."*

The third path is called *karma yoga,* a spiritual path that is tread through action, which I'll discuss later on. But *karma yoga* seems like another level to me, as either a *jnani* or a *bhakta* can do service. (Especially bhaktas typically do.)

The fourth yoga is called *raja yoga,* meaning "royal". Considered the accumulation of all paths, *raja* has a strong emphasis on *pranayama,* or yogic breathing. Vivekananda associated *raja yoga* with Patanjali's ancient *Yoga Sutras,* while Yogananda considered his lineage of *kriya yoga* to be *raja yoga,* for example. Regardless, these varying yogas are essential in understanding and appreciating different spiritual points of view.

> *"Either melt by devotion (bhakti) the sense of separateness, or burn it by knowledge (jnana)—for what is it that melts or burns?*
>
> *Only that which by its nature can be melted or burnt, namely the idea that something other than your Self exists. What will happen then? You come to know your Self."*[52]
>
> —*Anandamayi Ma*

The distinctions between jnanis and bhaktas are clear.

I know many jnanis who aren't swayed by the beauty of a hymnal, but the right line of thought strikes them to the core.

Bhaktas lose interest in a heavy theological discussion, while a verse of poetry flutters and awakens their heart.

Rumi was a bhakta. Anandamayi Ma was a bhakta. Krishna Das is a bhakta.

Buddha was a jnani. Ramana Maharshi was a jnani. Eckhart Tolle is a jnani.

We've all seen spiritual people make judgments about others on the path who might be going about all of this with a different method.

Bhaktas might think jnanis seem cold and unemotional. While jnanis can have a tough time trying to analyze the seeming irrationality of bhaktas.

But we must remember (and appreciate) that these separate paths are all absolutely true. They are merely unique styles of the spiritual experience—all of which lead to Oneness.

Ramakrishna Validates Them All

> *"God is one, but His aspects are many…*
>
> *As the master of a house is father to one, brother to another, and husband to a third, and is called by different names by different people, so the one God is described in various ways according to the particular aspects in which He appears to particular worshippers."*[53]
>
> —*Ramakrishna*

Ramakrishna, the ecstatic mystic in near-constant superconscious communion with the Divine, was born Gadadhar Chattopadhaya in a tiny village in India in 1836. Although he had the humblest of beginnings, a mere decade after his death, his simple teachings had spread across India and even to Europe & America.

As Swami Abhedananda admires in *The Gospel of Ramakrishna* (1907):

> *"His life was so extraordinary and unparalleled that within ten years after His departure from earth it aroused the admiration, wonder and reverence not only of all classes of people in His own country, but of many distinguished English and German scholars of the nineteenth century. ...Professor Max Muller was deeply impressed by the originality of this great Saint and real Mahatman, who was not brought up within the precincts of any university and who drew the water of His wisdom neither from any book, nor Scripture nor from any ancient prophet but directly from the eternal Fountainhead of all*

Knowledge and Wisdom." [54]

Ramakrishna's parents were fervent devotees of the Hindu God Rama, both of whom had supernatural experiences during his mother's pregnancy… including Chandra, his mother, having a vision of light entering her womb.

While he was known for both his exceptional genuine sweetness and authentically sincere teachings, Ramakrishna was also known for his mystically ecstatic trances. These experiences were extremely powerful for him and for those around him as they took place. He would become so overwhelmed by a cosmic sense of bliss that he would (mentally, spiritually) leave his body. In the early years, his nephew Hriday would follow him around, helping Ramakrishna to stand upright so that the ecstatic saint wouldn't injure himself when he would inevitably lose bodily control entering these states.

His experiences began at an early age. He later recalled a moment as a boy walking in a field alone, looking up at a sky full of dark clouds. A flock of white cranes flew overhead, producing an indescribable joy, causing him to lose external consciousness.[55]

As a young man he wandered into becoming a priest in a temple of Kali outside of Kolkata. Ramakrishna's young adult life consisted of performing the daily ritualistic duties prescribed by the ancient Hindu texts. Singing hymns, guiding parishioners through the temple and the courtyard. His devotion intensified, growing into desperation for a vision of Kali, the goddess of the Dakshineswar Temple, which dramatically culminated in an attempt to end his life. He ran for a sword in the corner of a temple room, but before reaching it, he observed:

> *"Houses, doors, temples, and everything else vanished altogether; as if there was nothing anywhere!*
>
> *And what I saw was an infinite shoreless sea of light; a sea that was consciousness.*
>
> *However far and in whatever direction I looked, I saw shining waves, one after another, coming towards me." [56]*

The extent of Ramakrishna's visions, and his simple yet lucid teachings, generated followers young and old. The young generation became students, and after his death they created the Ramakrishna Mission, to spread his story and message. His direct followers as well as practitioners across varying Hindu sects consider Ramakrishna to be a modern-day avatar. In his masterpiece *Ramakrishna and His Disciples,* 20th century British novelist & Hindu convert Christopher Isherwood describes the great saint as a "phenomenon", due to the difficulty (and excitement) in defining such a being.

In some ways Ramakrishna is like a figure from thousand-year-old myths, being lost in supernatural sights and unspeakable devotion. His 19th century biography sometimes reads like an ancient scripture.

And in other ways he was centuries ahead of his time.

In the middle decades of the 1800s, India experienced tense internal conflict, both within its religious systems, and its politics. It was ruled by the British, creating a new generation of Hindu philosophers, re-examining the ancient ways.

Ramakrishna's simple, yet effective analogies of universalism and tolerance helped guide the occasionally fierce intellectual disputes among group leaders. The Brahmo Samaj were one such group, intent on creating a new era of Hindu belief focused on the Formless God. Their writings appealed to even the American Transcendentalists. The Samaj had no need for 'cartoonish' devotional ritual. Until of course their famous leader Keshab Sen met Ramakrishna, a holy man in his right, and came to see the wisdom and beauty in Ramakrishna's devotion.

One afternoon Keshab's followers were arguing about the 'power of God.' To which Ramakrishna questioned:

> *"Why are you always talking so much about the various powers of God? Does a child who's sitting beside his father keep thinking how many horses, cows, houses and estates his father has? Isn't he simply happy to feel how much he loves his father and how much his father loves him?*

> *...Instead of dwelling on that, a real devotee makes God his very own, through love...*
>
> *If you dwell so much on God's powers, you can't think of Him as your nearest and dearest. Thinking about His greatness makes Him seem distant from His devotee. Think of Him as your very own. That's the only way to realize Him."* [57]

While on the path of devotional Kali worship as a bhakta, Ramakrishna began to see that after the continual authentic experience of our True Nature, any barriers into other spiritual paths start to crumble.

You see God is Infinite; therefore, there are infinite paths to Him/Her/the All That Is.

As the young mystic's development increased, he met a nun called the Brahmani who taught him tantra. Then he met a swami called Tota Puri who taught him Advaita. He even practiced Christianity, and then Islam for a time.

Chronicled richly in the *Gospel of Ramakrishna* by Swami Nikhilanda, a later disciple, his life was a sequential validation of each path. He validated their capacity to reach God through his own experiential successes:

> *"Before accepting any statement, He must realize it in His own life and then He would speak of His personal experience to others in order that they might gain benefit from it. For nearly twelve years before He appeared in public or made any disciples, Sri Ramakrishna, like a scientific investigator, inquired into the beliefs of the various sects of every religion, followed their methods and performed their rituals and ceremonies with perfect faith and earnest devotion that He might realize the goal which could be reached by each of them. To His great surprise, however, He discovered that He arrived at God-consciousness through each sectarian method. Whenever, furthermore, He desired to follow any particular path, there came to Him a perfected soul of each sect who had*

> *realized the Ideal, to direct Him in that path. Every one of these great saints recognized in Sri Ramakrishna the manifestation of Divine powers, when in a short time He attained to that which they had not been able to acquire during years of austerity, worship and extreme devotion."* [58]

Each religion only gets at a singular aspect of the Divine, so by approaching the multiplicity with this understanding, the Totality becomes clearer. In explaining the truth of religious pluralism, Ramakrishna was fond of the ancient parable of the blind men and the elephant:

A group of blind men heard that a strange animal, called an elephant, had been brought to the town, but none of them were aware of its shape and form. The first man, whose hand landed on the trunk, said, "This being is like a thick snake". For another one whose hand reached its ear, it seemed like a large fan. Another blind man whose hand was upon its leg, said this is like a tree-trunk. The blind man who placed his hand upon its side said this animal is a like a wall. Another who felt its tail, described it as a rope. The last felt its tusk and said this is creature like a spear.

Of course, the blind men begin to argue, for its snake-ness, or its wall-ness, or its fan-ness. Then a man with sight walks by, observing the blind men bickering, and interjects, "This being is not like a thick snake, *its trunk* is like a thick snake. This being is not like a spear, *its tusk* is like a spear."

To the man with sight, the elephant contains all aspects; much like exclusivist religious bickering, only a person with spiritual sight can see that the Divine contains aspects of each faith tradition—and that every religious path is a unique, and equally valid, gateway into Truth.

But even in universalist, open-minded Hinduism, there were often disputes among sects. The starkest contrast was, and still is, if God is either with form as a deity, or without / beyond form / Formless? A devotee asked Ramakrishna this very question.[59] He answered:

"No one can say with finality that God is only 'this' and nothing else. He is formless, and again He has forms. For the bhakta (devotee) He assumes forms.

But He is formless for the jnani, that is, for him who looks on the world as a mere dream.

The bhakta feels that he is one entity and the world another. Therefore God reveals Himself to him as a Person.

But the jnani—the Vedantist, for instance—always reasons, applying the process of 'Not this, not this'. Through this discrimination he realizes, by his inner perception, that the ego and the universe are both illusory, like a dream. Then the jnani realizes Brahman in his own consciousness. He cannot describe what Brahman is.

Do you know what I mean?

Think of Brahman, Existence-Knowledge-Bliss Absolute, as a shoreless ocean.

Through the cooling influence, as it were, of the bhakta's love, the water has frozen at places into blocks of ice.

In other words, God now and then assumes various forms for His lovers and reveals Himself to them as a Person. But with the rising of the sun of Knowledge, the blocks of ice melt. Then one doesn't feel any more that God is a Person, nor does one see God's forms. What He is cannot be described. Who will describe Him? He who would do so disappears. He cannot find his 'I' anymore."

Cosmic Connections

While filming several yogis & scholars for *The Kingdom Within,* I realized I needed more Christian voices.

I found Rev. Dr. Jayme Mathias by searching online for a local Catholic priest interested in interfaith ideologies. He had taken a youth group to a Shambhala interfaith field trip which made the publication of a local website. I had a personal connection to most of my subjects but the wonderful Rev. Jayme came into the film from a cold email I sent to him about doing an interview. I was thrilled to see Asian artifacts from his many travels decorating his home. Generally speaking, well-traveled people tend to have a more tolerant view of other cultures and other faith traditions, and while I did interview fundamentalist Christians, I was always glad to add another open-minded priest to the film.

After we wrapped up his lovely, articulate interview, I was packing up my gear and he mentioned that a man had recently come up to him, after mass, inquiring about the ethical implications of doing yoga as a Catholic.

Rev. Jayme and I had already been emailing during that time and in the hectic bustle of a church immediately post-mass, the reverend was only able to say that to his knowledge it was not problematic to be Catholic and practice yoga. And beyond that, that this man should reach out to me, Bob Peck, a local filmmaker working on a film about that very topic. He didn't get the man's information nor share mine with him, but Rev. Jayme was compelled to tell me of the incident, affirming that this was a topic worth covering.

Several months later I was setting up another interview with a close friend's mother, Genevieve Yellin. Genevieve was a biochemistry researcher in her younger years and has since become a well-respected yoga teacher focusing on integrative yoga therapy for various types of emotional distress including PTSD, anxiety, and clinical depression. In our introductory emails, Genevieve agreed to explain the scientific benefits of yoga for the documentary, alongside vaguely mentioning a student of hers whom I should consider filming as well—as he has an unbelievable story and would love to be a part of the film. I was getting very close to finishing, having shot over twelve hours at that point, so I essentially said, "yeah sure", but I was mainly interested in getting her brilliant scientific angle on camera.

On my way to her interview, I called her about ten minutes away from her studio and she immediately apologized. "Bob I have come down with a horrible illness in the last hour, I'm not really even sure what it is, but I can't do the interview today." I told her I hoped she felt better soon and not to worry about the interview that day. She continued, "My husband's coming to pick me up, but the student I mentioned to you, Richie Flores, is here and you're welcome to interview him if you'd like to do it." I had all my gear with me and I had the hours booked anyway. Sure, why not?

I got to Genevieve's studio, she quickly said hello, introduced Richie and I, apologized profusely and zipped away to the doctor. I expected to only get ten or fifteen minutes worth of this new alternative interview.

Richie's story was so incredible, and he was so articulate and enthusiastic, that we filmed for nearly ninety minutes until my camera batteries died.

Richie has an extensive criminal background. He grew up in gangs, sold drugs, committed robberies, got DWIs. He was incarcerated for the majority of his twenties. The fourth time he was in prison, he was watching the communal TV and anticipated a fight breaking out due to half of the room wanting to watch *The Young and the Restless* instead of *Maury*. People don't know this, but these big guys in prison are obsessed with their soap operas. They'll beat up a new guy for unwittingly changing the channel during a heavily-anticipated emotional scene. The loudspeaker announced a "yoga class" starting soon and Richie decided to go to that instead, solely in order to miss out on the impending conflict over the remote.

Despite his initial hesitation, Richie's life became completely transformed by yoga.[60]

He learned yoga sequences, he learned meditation, he learned mindfulness. He began taking responsibility for his past actions. He started to forgive himself. He reconnected with God.

There was a time when Richie was in solitary confinement, with only one hour of sunlight a day, and he would be locked in a pose in perfect peace. In perfect stillness.

Richie had an amazing teacher, Geoff O'Meara, a dreadlocked

sage with a gentle smile and a rippling build emblematic of his dedicated asana practice. Geoff was a central figure of Community Yoga Austin, an organization dedicated to bringing contemplative practices to marginalized and incarcerated communities. Their friendship blossomed into a soulful brotherhood: Richie fully credits Geoff for his transformation and Geoff fully credits Richie.

In recounting those days, Richie said that at first other inmates would make fun of him in the yard. They would throw things at him holding a pose and laugh. But prisoners tend to have an appreciation for athletic physiques, and over time they became truly impressed by his ability to achieve certain physical feats with the more advanced yogic asanas. They had bigger muscles, some of them, but he explained to them that his strength didn't come from his arms, it came from his mind. It came from his spirit.

It was a stunning interview. It was so good that his story of transformation ended up taking up almost a third of the film I'd already been shooting for nearly three years. We wrapped the interview and I was ecstatic. I was so grateful for him opening his heart up to a complete stranger. He even mentioned that a Catholic priest told him to get in touch with me… Rev. Jayme.

Richie was the anonymous man inquiring after Jayme's mass.

Packing up my gear with a smile, he started to ask me about my life. What got me started making a film like this? What are my experiences of spirituality? He asked me specifically, "What do you know about spiritual energy?" I smiled and said, "Man, I'm just a student on the path, but I do know a teacher who knows a lot more about it than I do." "That's pretty cool. Who is he?" I responded, "Well he's an Apache shaman. He's been a close friend of my family for a long time."

He said, "Is his name Richard?"

I couldn't contain myself. I burst out laughing. I asked incredulously, "How do YOU know Richard?" He replied with a grin:

"He was my PO."

Of the thousands of yogis in Austin, and the dozens if not

hundreds of probation officers assigned to ex-cons, my new friend and most significant contributor to my debut feature film happened to be mentored by the very same, essentially anonymous teacher whose counsel I had taken to heart for over a decade.

Nothing has really been the same since.

Still Image: Richie Flores demonstrating yogic asanas (2013)
Source: *The Kingdom Within* (2015) dir. Bob Peck (the author)

CHAPTER 7

Ancient Religions and New Sciences

No Human System is Flawless

> *"Institutions are not pretty. Show me a pretty government. Healing is wonderful, but the American Medical Association? Learning is wonderful, but universities? The same is true for religion... religion is institutionalized spirituality."*
>
> *—Huston Smith*

While I have been captivated by Hindu philosophy in the previous years, and in the previous pages, it's important to get across that no human system is without flaws.

When I began practicing Kriya Yoga in Austin, Texas, over ten years ago, I was obsessed with the Hindus. I was reading everything Yogananda wrote, Ramakrishna and Vivekananda, the bhaktas, the jnanis, Advaita; each layer became more fascinating, feeling its truth intuitively in my heart.

I thought, 'finally, a path I can really get behind... it must be the truth-iest truth of them all!'

In those days I was living in south Austin, and most Sunday mornings I would drive to the outskirts of town where our Austin Kriya Yoga center was, in Dripping Springs.

I couldn't help but take it as a cosmic sign that on the way to my Hindu (Kriya) meditation practice, on a Texas country road, I would pass an entirely separate Hindu (Vaishnava) temple! My humble part of the country and the world is not overflowing with Eastern places of religious worship, so I would smile driving past the geometric beauty of Barsana Dham on my way to Kriya. Stopping in there once, I admired the beautiful peacocks walking the grounds, but ultimately (and disappointingly), felt no special connection to the place.

A few years later I read that the reigning guru of Barsana Dham was accused and convicted of sexual abuse of several young women including a girl as young as 12![61] Exhibiting a level of cowardice diametrically opposed to the "fearlessness" expounded in the *Vedas*, Prakashanand Saraswati disappeared, fleeing to India before he was arrested. The temple had been defrocked by the child abuse scandal and was renamed to Radha Madhav Dham, dissociating from the former guru entirely.

It reads much like the recent scandals of the Catholic churches, sickening to the heart. This episode helped to debunk my naïveté, and confirm my deeper intuitive feeling: that Hinduism, as a religion, is not inherently better than Christianity.

There are awakened Christian teachers who have accessed the heights of humanity, and there are terrible, barbaric, lost-soul Christians preying on the vulnerable.

There are awakened Hindu teachers who have accessed the heights of humanity, alongside terrible, barbaric, lost-soul Hindus preying on the vulnerable.

We can admire each path for its own unique offerings and spiritual flavors, but it is crucial to not get caught up in egotistic superiority that has plagued all religions and truly all of humanity.

It's the most unfortunate side effect of personal growth—that egotism tends to become associated with our own sincere developments towards mental/emotional/spiritual well-being.

Ram Dass called these people "phony holies".

Chogyam Trungpa Rinpoche called it "spiritual materialism".

Jesus of Nazareth used the term "wolves in sheep's clothing."

I keep getting sent a link to a new psychological study about egotism and narcissism developing within spiritual practitioners.[62] I don't know if it means they want me to be aware of this stuff as a commentator on spirituality or if their long-held suspicions about my egotism are finally verified by scientific research!

The name of this first study of its kind is: "An Exploration of Spiritual Superiority: The Paradox of Self-Enhancement" published in the *European Journal of Social Psychology*. The abstract states:

> *"Spiritual training is assumed to reduce self-enhancement, but may have the paradoxical effect of boosting superiority feelings. It can, thus, operate like other self-enhancement tools and contribute to a contingent self-worth that depends on one's spiritual accomplishments.*
>
> *Spiritual Superiority scores were consistently higher among energetically trained participants than mindfulness trainees and were associated with supernatural overconfidence and self-ascribed spiritual guidance. Our results illustrate that the self-enhancement motive is powerful and deeply ingrained so that it can hijack methods intended to transcend the ego and, instead, adopt them to its own service."*

Spiritual work is not just flowers in the meadow. It is a cliff-jump into the fullest exploration of our own humanity—the good, the bad, the ugly, and the beautiful. While ultimately this work can lead to a greater sense of Self and (as I understand it) liberation, exploring these peaks and valleys so thoroughly makes us especially susceptible to our ego, an extremely worthy adversary.

Transcending Ego

The human being is multi-layered.

Yes, the Kingdom Is Within Us, that's who We Truly Are, but most of the time for most of us, we are covering up our inherent

Infinite Awareness by listening to another voice: the voice of the ego.

The ego represents the separate self.

It's who we think we are, without investigating who we truly are.

The ego has needs, because it operates from a place of lack. There is never enough for the ego. No sense of validation or appreciation or even love can satisfy it. It's the deranged tyrant of our mind. The great Sufi poet Hafez was intimately familiar:

> *"There is a madman inside of you, who is always running for office."*

At the end of the 19th century, while Ramakrishna was illuminating listeners with his simple divine truths, Sigmund Freud was studying the mind.

To be fair, we have writings discussing 'mental disorders' in ancient India, ancient Greece, and ancient Egypt.[63] There were essentially mental hospitals even then, all the way up through the Middle Ages and the Enlightenment. But it was the Austrian neurologist and founder of psychoanalysis, Dr. Sigmund Freud, who pioneered the idea of the ego, within what he considered to be a three-layered model of the mind: ego, super-ego, and the Id.[64]

During the much more primitive phases of modern medicine, there was a lot of dissecting. Freud began as a young lab researcher, comparing the physical brains of humans to other animals. He cut open hundreds of eels. He analyzed neural tissue. And he worked in psychiatric clinics.

Freud also attended lectures on esoteric topics like hypnosis. He famously attended a three-month fellowship on hypnosis of a renowned neurologist named Jean-Martin Charcot. Charcot would demonstrate accessing trance-state conversations with audience members of his lectures. One particular work with a patient named Anna O. is credited with launching Freud's theories into what would become psychotherapy. A colleague of Freud, Josef Breuer, describes Anna:

> *"[She had] two completely separate states of consciousness which alternated very frequently and without warning, and which became more and more differentiated in the course of the illness. In one of these states she recognized her surroundings; she was melancholy and anxious, but relatively normal.*
>
> *In the other state she hallucinated and "misbehaved", that is, she swore, threw pillows at people... tore buttons off her bedclothes and linen with those of her fingers which she could move, and so on. At this stage of her illness if something had been moved in the room or someone had entered or left it [during her other state of consciousness] she would complain of having 'lost' some time and remark upon the gap in her train of conscious thoughts."* [65]

The difference in mental and emotional states between both of Anna's personas, was too much for Freud to grapple with. It became quite clear to him that there is much more to our mental health than what meets the eye—much more to our (unconscious) thought processes underneath the surface, like an iceberg.

Freud's terms are the id, the ego, and the superego, and they're all vying for power within our everyday thinking.

In Freud's model the id is the embodiment of our primordial needs under the surface. The id is instinctive and impulsive, seeking unchecked carnal pleasure (which he called "the pleasure principle") to push away the darkness of life. Then you have the ego; the barrier between the id and the external world—according to Freud the ego helps mitigate the id's illogical needs within the expectations of the external world. While the third section, the superego, persuades the ego to become moralistic, rewarding good thoughts and shaming the bad.

I don't subscribe to this breakdown exactly and neither does much of modern psychology but you have to give it to him. It is a wildly fascinating image of the internal politics governing patterns of everyday thought. Freud's concepts have been heavily debated, and refined in the now-century since his first publications, but the idea of subconscious motivations certainly holds up today.

Carl Gustav Jung, one of Freud's younger colleagues, took the baton in pioneering an even further understanding of the workings of consciousness. Freud saw Jung as a literal successor within psychoanalysis but Jung's philosophical differences ultimately created a painful schism between the two men.

Like Freud, Jung also wrote about dream interpretation, but expanded into pioneering terms like "synchronicity", archetypal phenomena, the collective unconscious, the psychological complex, and extraversion & introversion. Jung became a massive influence on not just psychology but other fields of academia: comparative religion, mythological history, literature, science, art, medicine, spirituality, and philosophy.[66]

Jung's concept of "the Shadow", or "Shadow work" is a highly relevant term for the spiritual path in that it is an excavation of that subconscious aspect of ourselves (Freudian) that we choose to repress. Our attempts at adapting to a societal construct defined by mainstream culture create this quality of both intentional and unintentional 'mask-wearing'. We hide away certain aspects of ourselves and emphasize others. This is the ego's specialty. Jung saw through humanity's various attempts at inauthenticity for self-gain, writing:

> *"People will do anything, no matter how absurd, in order to avoid facing their own souls…"* [67]

And that this avoidance only delays the self-reflection vital for understanding and growth:

> *"One does not become enlightened by imagining figures of light, but by making the darkness conscious."* [68]

These pioneering psychologists understood that there are many facets to our thinking; and as Jung proposed in a manner similar to ancient Eastern philosophers, that this level of inner exploration can lead to self-actualization.

Scientists are the Modern Shamans

Dr. Jill Bolte Taylor is a neuroscientist researcher who began studying the brain because she had an older brother who would be diagnosed with schizophrenia. From a very early age, her eighteen-months-older brother exhibited very different ways of thinking and behavior than she did. Because he was so different from her in the way he experienced reality, she studied to become a respected researcher and teacher at Harvard Medical School.

One December morning in 1996, Dr. Taylor woke up to a pounding headache behind her left eye.

She was a healthy person. Thinking that some light cardio would help alleviate the pain and get the blood flowing a bit, she hopped onto her exercise machine. Noticing the now very unfamiliar appearance of her hands, she had thought, these look *"like claws..."* ...as a powerful shift in perception began to take over. [69]

Dr. Taylor was now witnessing herself, exercising, from a distance, as a bizarre creature.

She noticed something was very wrong when she turned on the shower when the heavily amplified sound of the shower head startled her. She lost the capacity to understand where she ended and where the shower wall began. Her perception of her molecules were blending in and out of her environment, sinking her conscious mind into an expansive bliss, unifying her with a boundless all. In those moments she experienced her body to be composed of 'trillions of organisms' all working together to make her a functional human. She was aware, sadly that we so often forget the profundity of this unimaginably complex system that works so hard for us to exist.

As Dr. Taylor delved deeper into this understanding, it led to an unspeakable peace... a peace harshly interrupted by the thought *"We gotta get help!!"*, which she recognized as coming from her left hemisphere—the side of the brain that processes rational, analytical thought and language. Then she would melt back into the blissful euphoria of her right brain, the side of the brain containing our creativity, big picture perception, and imagination... later writing:

"To the right mind, no time exists other than the present

> *moment, and each moment is vibrant with sensation. Life or death occurs in the present moment. The experience of joy happens in the present moment. Our perception and experience of connection with something that is greater than ourselves occurs in the present moment. To our right mind, the moment of now is timeless and abundant."* [70]

She lost her personhood identity, losing *"thirty seven years of emotional baggage"* ... how liberating!

When Dr. Taylor's right arm went completely paralyzed she realized, *"Oh my gosh, I'm having a stroke... how cool! How many brain scientists get to study their brain from the inside out!"* Her gratitude and the accompanying peace of her right brain euphoria overwhelmed her, until the next left-minded-thought rattled in, which was: *"but I'm a very busy person! I don't have time for a stroke!"*

Dr. Taylor realized she needed to call someone but numbers on the phone pad at her desk looked like unintelligible pixels. Her office phone number on a nearby card looked like a series of squiggles, which she would then match to the corresponding squiggle on her phone. As she pressed each button, she sank back into the feeling of an inexhaustible peace, whereby she *"soared like a great whale through a sea of silent euphoria"*. Later she described that experience as feeling like an ocean of love and unity. In this unfolding paradigm of left-brain-disintegration, it took her what felt like eons to match the numbers. When her colleague answered on the other side, she said he sounded like a golden retriever. And then she heard her own voice, yet another golden retriever.

In the ambulance, Dr. Taylor, living in a state of expansive connectivity with all creation, surrendered to the universe. Surprised, she woke up in a hospital bed, able to remember her overpowering experience of what the mystics call an "ego death". Writing in her bestselling book *My Stroke of Insight*, she beautifully explains that everyone has this capacity to 'step to the right of our left hemispheres', to connect with the infinite potential of ourselves and of all things. In the years that followed she has become a tireless advocate for brain research, mental health, and wellbeing.

Richard, the Apache medicine man, told me once that society

will start to have more scientists having more spiritual experiences. He specifically referenced Dr. Jill Bolte Taylor and her stroke, calling it a "shamanic death". From a cosmic perspective, the purpose here is because in this day and age, scientists hold the power of knowledge—they are the new priests—and so they are the ones that will lead our current civilization into the next paradigm.

> *"Try and penetrate with our limited means the secrets of nature and you will find that, behind all the discernible concatenations, there remains something subtle, intangible and inexplicable.*
>
> *Veneration for this force beyond anything that we can comprehend is my religion.*
>
> *To that extent I am, in point of fact, religious."* [71]
>
> —*Albert Einstein*

My Jewish cousin, who calls herself "Jew-ish", had a conversation with me recently about science and religion.

She said, "I'm 100% science. It has to be proven or I have trouble with it."

And as a mystic, I understand this and can relate. Mystically-minded spirituality as a practice is based almost entirely on evidential experience—what has happened directly in our own lives—as opposed to the impersonal, inaccessible doctrines of institution.

I'm not a scientist, but I do appreciate the scientific method, and I greatly respect the commitment of genuine scientists to furthering this human civilization in a positive, harmonious way.

I am typing this book on a MacBook. I'm researching sources on the internet. And my wife has given our house over to Alexa's control.

I would be a massive hypocrite if I did not acknowledge and appreciate science and its incalculably valuable progeny: technology. That said, there are a few points I need to get across before continuing on this philosophical voyage through broader spirituality, its concepts and methodologies.

1) We don't know it all.

The current understanding of science is not the totality of absolute knowledge: it's just that, the current understanding. Imagine a medieval scientist peering into an electron microscope. Even two centuries ago, a person watching a space shuttle take off would be considered witchcraft. Where we are right now is in no way absolute.

To be fair, civilization's advances, particularly the last century, shouldn't be understated. We've come so far to get to this point, and again, we have accumulated a considerable amount of useful knowledge about this plane of existence. But it's that progression of knowledge that's the basis for the point I'm making here: thinking that what we understand in this moment in time is the ultimate understanding of reality, is completely ridiculous.

One of the best examples of the challenges of our current state is, what cognitive scientist and professor David Chalmers called, the "hard problem of consciousness".[72] Within neuroscience and neuropsychology, we understand *how*, the brain works. We know which sections light up with electrical charges and ions when certain emotions are felt and when various thought processes are taking place. ("Easy problems".) But there's not a single scientist on this planet that can tell you with any more assurance than anyone else, *where* our consciousness comes from. And why does this awareness exist at all?

Another component of our scientific uncertainty lies in the academic world itself.

Many pioneering scientists were initially ridiculed by the larger academic community, to then be redeemed when the current understanding catches up decades later. Physicist and philosopher Thomas Kuhn famously articulated this highly human tendency in his landmark study, *The Structure of Scientific Revolutions*, although it was put more bluntly by Schopenhauer:

> *"Every problem passes through three stages on the way to acceptance: First, it appears laughable; second, it is fought*

against; third, it is considered self-evident." [73]

A great example of this stubbornness of mainstream science concerns the Clovis period and the early discoveries of Canadian archaeologist Jacques Cinq-Mars.

While excavating at Bluefish Caves in the northern Yukon in the 1970s and 1980s, Cinq-Mars found traces of human hunters dating back to approximately 24,000 years ago. This was preposterous in the 80s, because the scientific community was still fiercely protecting the "Clovis first" model, the idea that the first modern humans arrived in North America 13,000 years ago. Since then, several other important archaeological discoveries across the continent have convincingly disproved "Clovis first". And now after so many decades of being called a crazy fool, Cinq-Mars is now rightly-considered a redeemed pioneer.[74]

2) Science is starting to point to the potential of spiritual principles.

"Those who are not shocked when they first come across quantum theory cannot possibly have understood it."

—Niels Bohr, Danish physicist and pioneer in quantum theory, Nobel Prize in Physics (1922)

As a spiritual commentator, a historian of religion, and a human being without any academic background in a scientific discipline, I am extremely hesitant to point out the parallels between quantum physics and spirituality.

Yes, I watched *What the bleep do we know?* and I've heard spiritual teachers and authors talk about this marriage for decades.

But after speaking with a variety of scientists about this overlap, many contemporary spiritual teachers attempt to connect spirituality and quantum physics without actually grasping the intricacies of what that elusive, zenith level of physics truly entails. From Deepak Chopra to Gary Zukav (both of whom I respect and admire), there are dozens of books in the pop spirituality section that veer into misappropriating the life's work of quantum physicists in order to make a shoddy point about reality from a spiritual perspective. It's unfair to the scientists themselves, and ultimately it's unnecessary. It's all in the heart and mind anyway.

So I'll keep it short. (Short compared to how much longer I would spend sledge-hammering these points in a late-night porch discussion-turned-soliloquy.)

Where I am comfortable connecting science and spirituality is the following:

- In the 20th century we shifted from an absolute model of reality (Newtonian) to a relative model of reality (Einsteinian). This is important in helping us realize the subjective nature of existence. Our own mind, our conscious awareness is not a stabilized control but rather just another variable in the experiment! Einstein himself was practically a pantheist who explicitly declared: *"I believe in Spinoza's God, who reveals himself in the harmony of all that exists, not in a God who concerns himself with the fate and the doings of mankind."* [75]

- We're starting to understand that the senses are pretty inadequate at detecting reality. Echoing the main point from my first chapter, mysticism is ultimately about releasing dependence on the external world. Thankfully science and technology are demonstrating just how unreliable our human senses really are! The human eye paired with our visual cortex can see a mere fragment of the ultraviolet spectrum. From the micro to the macro, we're missing out on the vast majority of matter itself. And if we can't detect other basic makeups of physical matter, how could we be so arrogant to think that our inability to detect divinity with the eyes, ears, and touch must make it absent? One of Ramakrishna's zingers uses the futility of the senses to make a theistic point: *"You see many stars in the sky at night, but not when the sun rises. Can you therefore say that there are no stars in the heavens during the day? Because you cannot find God in the days of your ignorance, say not that there is no God."* [76]

- There is a considerable amount of peer-reviewed research coming out explaining the practical benefits of meditation.

The trendy-ness of mindfulness meditation in secular circles, riding the coattails of American gym yoga, is gaining ground in academia. And despite plenty of early, hyperbolic misses that overstated the benefits, ultimately the results are in: regular meditation greatly reduces stress. It helps to focus our attention. It creates a fuller sense of well-being and self-compassion.[77] These are verifiable research papers, published in the last decade... proving what Himalayan yogis have been discussing for millennia. We're just beginning to see how impactful a sincere practice can be on the mind which is translating to other areas—mental, emotional, and even physiological. What other ancient methods and patterns of thought will we be able to prove in future double-blind studies?

3) **Science and mysticism are actually cousins due to their mutual emphasis on experiential learning.**

As I'll discuss in the next section, the spiritual mystics throughout history similarly left the 'blind faith' doctrine of religious institutions. George Harrison, "the Quiet Beatle" whose interest in Hindu philosophy introduced generations to Eastern mysticism, shared this need for tangibility:

> *"Ravi Shankar and the sitar was kind of like an excuse, trying to find this connection. I read stuff by various holy men and swamis and went around and looked for them. Ravi and his brother gave me a lot of books by some wise men, and one of the books was by Swami Vivekananda who said, 'If there's a God you must see Him. And if there's a soul we must perceive it, otherwise it's better not to believe—it's better to be an outspoken atheist than a hypocrite.' And after all my life I had been brought up... well they tried to bring me up Catholic. They told you to just believe what they're telling you, and not to have the direct experience. And this for me, going to India, and hearing someone saying 'No you can't believe anything until you have direct perception of it...' I thought 'Wow, fantastic, at last I've found somebody who makes some sense!"* [78]

—*George Harrison*

Echoing George and his love of the Hindu mystics, Yogananda says time and again that 'your life is the experiment'. The "scientific method" is centered on a hypothesis being testable and falsifiable, and the experiments and observations being repeatable. So, try these practices out. Have love in your heart, watch it grow, and see the results play out for yourself.

For a seeker on the spiritual path, ultimately the framework of how we look at the world has to open up a bit.

It doesn't have to change altogether immediately, as spiritual introspection isn't a cult requiring a full-fledged initiation. It's not a rapid conversion into some orthodox viewpoint, it's a gradual undoing. You might say the constraints start to melt away.

The migration goes from a purely scientific materialist worldview that humans are merely the latest development of that initial primordial amino acid pool, towards the idea that this world is a curriculum. An unfolding of experience. A reuniting of the Many into the One.

I should say, I don't dispute with evolution.

It's a perfectly rational way to understand the development of organisms, and how we pass along our genetic makeup down the generations. Science is excellent at doing what it was designed to do, but the issue is that it has expanded its province into encompassing all of reality as we know it. The scientific method has its limitations, because not everything is observable and repeatable. Yes, it's an undeniably useful and integral tool for civilization. But it struggles with value judgments, ethics, human connection, and the greater mysteries of existence.

I have had conversations with passionately science-minded friends where they are just as rigid and fanatical as the orthodox religious.

There is not one direct statement to prove God, or even to give some transcendental hope to another person. But there are pieces of evidence peppered throughout the sciences, the arts, and the human experience, that indicate that there is something more to all of this. And as so many great men and women throughout history have shared, we do have the capacity to reach a more advanced understanding about life and reality by breaking the chains on limited, conformist ways of viewing ourselves and the world.

The absolute beauty of science is that it keeps revealing new discoveries, new ways of framing our existence. Please, don't shackle science in the same way we have limited religion, as science is one of the most innovative tools for our collective self-discovery!

This book isn't about proving spirituality through science. But if you're interested, I highly recommend the work of:

- Rupert Sheldrake, Ph.D., a biologist, researcher, and Fellow of Clare College at Cambridge University who has authored more than 85 scientific papers and 9 books, including *The Science Delusion*.
- Bruce Lipton, Ph.D., an early stem cell researcher whose discoveries are related to our modern understanding of "epigenetics": that you can alter your genetics by modifying your behavior.
- Dean Radin, Ph.D., a psychologist, physicist, and the Chief Scientist at the Institute of Noetic Science (IONS). He has written more than 100 scientific papers and 5 books, including *Real Magic: Ancient Wisdom, Modern Science, and a Guide to the Secret Power of the Universe.*
- Brian D. Josephson, Ph.D., a physicist, researcher, director of the Mind-Matter Unification Project of the Theory of Condensed Matter Group at the Cavendish Laboratory, at Cambridge University. He won the Nobel Prize in Physics in 1973.
- John Hagelin, Ph.D., a quantum physicist, science and public policy expert, educator, peace activist, and author who is the current leader of the Transcendental Meditation (TM) movement. He has directed several research projects aimed at demonstrating what TM practitioners call "the Maharishi effect", the purported ability of a large group of meditators to affect the behavior of populations of

people.[79]

Hilariously, the Wikipedia pages of each of these distinguished scientists are written in dismissive tones, even considering Josephson afflicted by "Nobel disease": a "hypothesized affliction resulting in Nobel prize winners embracing strange or scientifically unsound ideas, usually later in life."[80]

Thank you scientific materialist Wiki editors for proving my earlier point: that pioneers are ridiculed before the rest of us come around.

One of the earliest proponents of heliocentrism (that we revolve around the Sun, not the Sun around us) was the Renaissance thinker Giordano Bruno. The initial idea of the altered rotation came from Nicolaus Copernicus, however it was Bruno who expanded the universe not as a finite, fixed set of spheres, but "instead it was an infinite, homogeneous expanse populated by an infinite number of solar systems like our own."[81] He was burned at the stake.

Ultimately, my inner work does not depend on the latest discovery in the newest scientific journal. If a discovery is beneficial in explaining this shift in awareness, wonderful—us mystical proselytizers can use all the help we can get.

But my path does not rely on them. My progress, the evolution of my consciousness, is measured by experiential learning and a rising sense of peace and joy.

Everything else is getting more and more trivial.

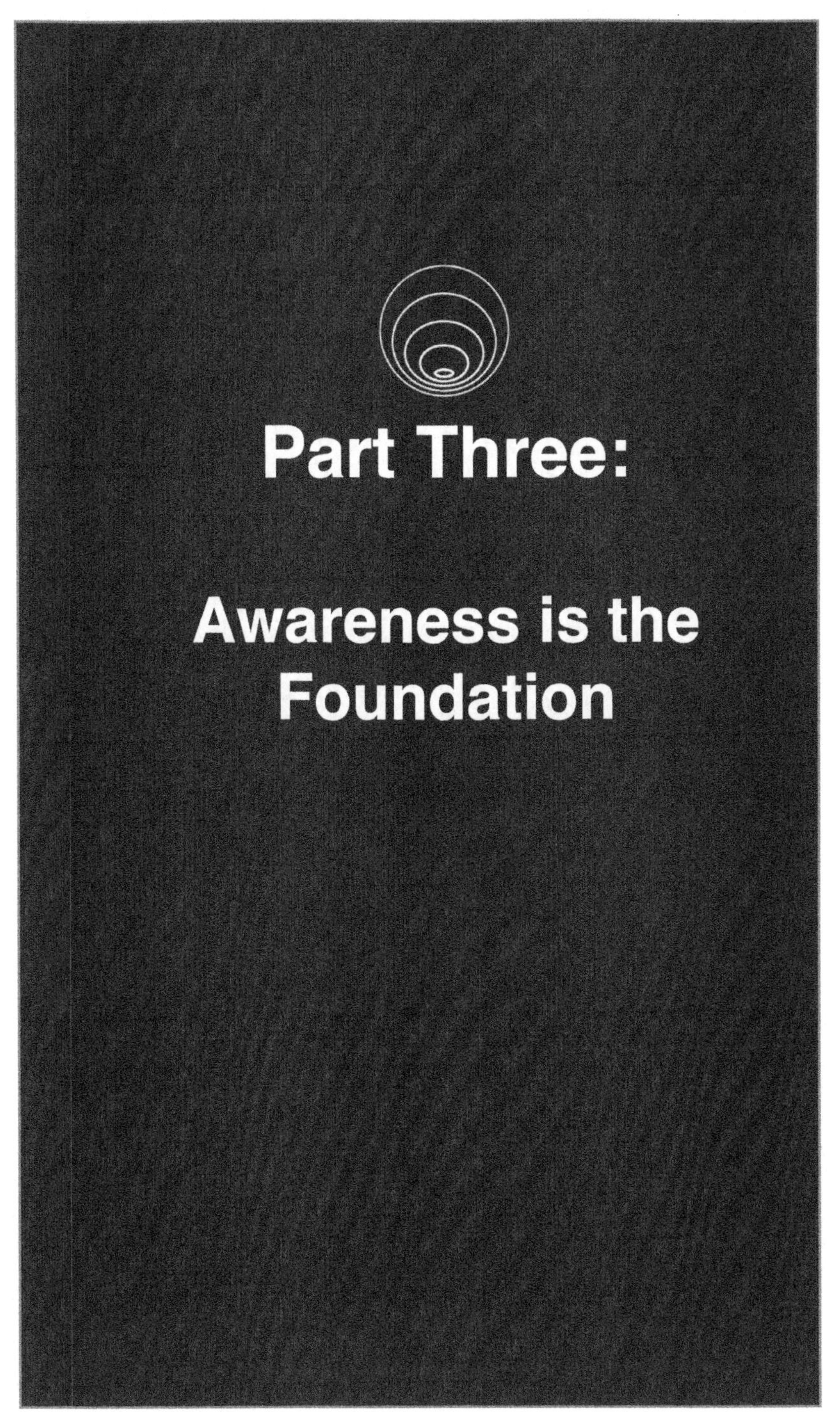

Part Three:

Awareness is the Foundation

Original sin is a lie,

because every human being has an automatic, unconscious thought system of self-interest;

but when we get still in our mind,

our heart opens—like a flower in bloom.

CHAPTER 8

Demystifying Mysticism

From the Outer to the Inner

"If you realize that all things change,

there is nothing you will try to hold on to."

—*Laozi*

This world is constantly attempting to provoke a response to its seemingly endless stimuli.

React to this!

Judge that!

Enjoy this!

Hate that!

And as soon as you finish engaging with one phenomena, a new one comes into view.

It's exhausting, isn't it?

All of the manifestations of mysticism that I've come across are based on the idea that the external world does not bring lasting peace—and that a redirection towards the internal brings about an unspeakably powerful, inner transformation of self.[1]

We may find external peace for a day, or a month or even a few years but some aspect on which that happiness is dependent will inevitably come crashing down. When we put our sense of well-being on the external world, we are Sisyphus, struggling to push that ancient boulder up the hill. Life will come rolling back down as we sigh in exasperation, throwing our hands up defeated again and again.

> *"He who looks outside dreams, he who looks inside awakens."*
>
> *—Carl Jung*

Classic Americana has two achingly accurate representations of the transitory joys of the external: Elvis Presley and Marilyn Monroe. Elvis had gargantuan fame and riches and yet he died depressed and unhealthy, overtaken by the ravages of drug abuse. Marilyn was, and is still (more than half a century after her death), the icon of female beauty. She was also riddled by anxiety, depression and excessive prescription drug use that ended her young life, shortly after her third divorce.[2]

There's really no shortage of famous, unfulfilled deaths in our society.

They couldn't find happiness despite having absolutely everything the world has to offer. According to our society which is fixated on material acquisition, sexuality, and social status, they should've had happiness. Why didn't they?

Then you have George Harrison. One of The Beatles, George was open about never feeling fully satisfied by everything they had acquired.

Imagine being a Beatle in the 1960s. The global popularity of unparalleled pop stardom alongside the admiration of their authentically evolving creativity. They had money, women, and their influence on music is staggering and nearly immeasurable. But as George articulates, none of those things made them truly happy. So if not there, then where?

He eventually found his peace after meeting Ravi Shankar, an Indian sitar player and philosopher in his own right. The Beatles met every famous person on this planet and George said no one ever truly impressed him, until he met Ravi. Sure movie stars and successful people were impressive in a way, but they were all trying to be someone else in front of the Beatles. Whereas Ravi's calm, loving authenticity touched Harrison deeply as someone who had a fuller grasp of the peace of the inner world.[3] Harrison's songs like "The Inner Light", "All Things Must Pass", and "While My Guitar Gently Weeps" show us how he was able to see through all of the traps awaiting us 'out there', living a long peaceful life thanks to this understanding.

Universally the mystics claim, by way of their own experiential learning that there is a unifying connectivity between all beings.[4] There is a Transcendent Oneness that radiates between every living thing and our ability to connect with that Unity is the only way out, or rather way in.

You aren't going to find lasting happiness here.

'Here' meaning the world, the external world of form.

But according to the mystics, you will find it Here, internally, within your heart in your connection to your Truest Self, beyond the influences of time and space.

> *"You will undertake a journey, because you are not at home in this world.*
>
> *And you will search for your home, whether you know where it is or not.*
>
> *If you believe it is outside yourself, the search will be futile, for you will be seeking where it is not."*
>
> —*A Course in Miracles, T-12.IV.5:1–3*

The word "mystic" derives from the Greek root *mu*, meaning "silent" or "mute"... indicative of an understanding so profound that only silence can provide its due respect.[5]

There is a mystical "version" of every world religion, while the orthodox institutions are typically on the opposite end of that spectrum. The Christians had the Gnostics, the Muslims have the Sufis, the Jews have Kabbalah, the Buddhists Zen, and Hinduism has the Vedanta. There are thousands of degrees in both directions for every system, but even most religious scholars will draw these parallels.

> *"Theologians may quarrel, but the mystics of the world speak the same language."*
>
> —*Meister Eckhart*

Mysticism, the non-institutional internal path, is the string connecting the pearls of each major faith.

A respected religious studies scholar, Dr. Stephen Prothero, wrote a book with a spicy title, *God Is Not One,* which covers the doctrinal distinctions between the world religions. The book's thesis is that it's intellectually lazy to say "oh well they're all the same", and that is an important point to make. On the institutional, exoteric side of each faith, they are very different—grossly oversimplifying for the sake of brevity: Judaism is based on following rules or commandments, Christianity is focused on the sacrifice of Christ, Islam means submission to God, Buddhism is concerned with ceasing desire and consequently ceasing suffering, and Hinduism is mainly a devotional attempt to break the cycle of birth and death.

But on the mystical, esoteric side of each faith, the distinctly institutional lines of division start to blur.

It's also important to emphasize that the mystic values the experiential understanding of Spirit. They are sometimes called "the ecstatics," based on the state of spiritual ecstasy generated by their realizations.[6] While institutional practitioners rely on the testimony of clergy, the sanctity of scripture, and the psychology of ritual, the mystic only needs their own intimately personal experience of Divinity / Awareness / Unity / Presence.

> *"Where the philosopher guesses and argues, the mystic lives and looks; and speaks, consequently, the disconcerting language of first-hand experience, not the neat dialectic of the schools.*
>
> *...Hence whilst the Absolute of the metaphysicians remains a diagram—impersonal and unattainable — the Absolute of the mystics is lovable, attainable, alive."*
>
> —*Evelyn Underhill*

The mystical experience is a defining component of this internal exploration, and its importance stems from its function. While there can be similar ecstatic emotions to drug-induced states of consciousness (which is a whole 'nother chapter), the distinction is that the mystical experience has a considerably higher purpose, which is that it acts as the connection between two seemingly-oppositional conceptions of divinity: the Transcendent and the Immanent.

The divine is both beyond this plane of existence, and simultaneously all-pervasive throughout. The Absolute is the unending substratum beneath all things, as well as the Experiencer of the world of form—and the mystical experience is the bridge between these two (ultimately unified) conceptions of the Infinite.

Swami Abhayananda covers this dynamic thoroughly in the *History of Mysticism*, writing:

> *"Yet while we do not possess the written testimonies of the mystic sages of the dim past... when we examine the mythologies of these earliest civilizations, especially those myths which describe the origin of the cosmos, we find a curious similarity in the religious symbols used by widely separated cultures. In almost every instance, we may discover the legend of an original Father-God, whose first Thought or Word, symbolized in the form of a Mother-Goddess, is said to have given birth to all creation."*

Despite their theological sophistication and spiritual practicality, the mystical sects were formerly less out in the open than they are today. There was less literacy and more danger from the orthodoxy. Today, there's no shortage of extensive, academic explanations of each of them. There are bookshelves full of their ideologies, entire university careers devoted to their study. But a brief summary of the main mystical sects will suffice here.

Gnosticism

In the time between Jesus's death and the formation of what

came to be modern day Christianity, there were several competing sects of Judaism: some of which were beginning to reflect the profound and newly radical teachings of Jesus, while other Jewish communities were holding fast to the ancient traditions of the Torah and the Jewish people. While early Christianity was primarily focused on the one major difference between traditional Judaism—that Jesus Christ was "the Messiah"—Gnosticism took their beliefs a step further.

As we touched on earlier, the name "gnostic" comes from the Greek word *gnosis*, meaning "knowledge", although the translation is closer to an intuitive understanding than to knowledge of the analytical mind. While the sect that would become Christianity was focused on scripture and faith, the Gnostics were bent on revelatory experiences, experiencing an intimately personal connection with the divine.

Like Christ, the Gnostics were reforming the way that the Jewish people came to understand God.

In some Gnostic sects, this world was considered illusory, and this personal connection was the answer for how to break through the veil between this world and heaven. The idea of the false creator god of the Old Testament was not exclusive to Marcion, and "Yaldaboath" or "the Demiurge" is only one player in a larger cosmic drama that is representative of the soul's journey into this plane of existence. *Sophia*, Greek for "wisdom", is a feminine figure who represents the human soul, but also the Divine Feminine who is in a variety of ways responsible for the creation of the sickly Demiurge, the creator of this world. There is a fall of Sophia due to her miscreation, but she guides humanity through the Holy Spirit, and works with the True Father, the Creator of All, to send forth the Christ—who reminds the lost earthly souls of their inherent divinity in order to "escape the bonds of the world ruler and return to their heavenly home and the blessed rule of the true Father."[7]

The Gnostics were by no means perfect. Some sects held spiritually-superior beliefs about themselves, like many other religious sects throughout history. While there were smaller groups of Gnostics who had the beautiful practice of drawing lots to see who would lead the day's service—because every human is capable of being a divine instrument—other Gnostic groups would look down upon the more traditionally religious because they were not in the process of spiritual awakening & material transcendence. (Sound familiar?)

Ultimately the Gnostics were considered heretics by orthodox bishops, Irenaeus being an exceptionally notorious persecutor. And while Marcion gave us the earliest "canon" in the second century, it wasn't until 367 CE that Bishop Athanasius of Alexandria was the first to name the exact twenty-seven books of the New Testament in today's version.[8] When Christianity became the state religion of the Roman Empire, many prominent Gnostic leaders and writers were executed as heretics.

And again, fortunately for our contemporary civilization, two of the most significant archaeological discoveries of the 20th century were those rural Egyptian shepherds stumbling across ancient leather-bound scrolls near the Dead Sea—in 1945 at Nag Hammadi and in 1946 at Qumran.[9] Many of the texts belonged to the Gnostics as they were mentioned by name in correspondence between early church fathers. Several of these Gospels we did not have complete copies of before the 20th century, including my beloved *Gospel of Thomas*. Accordingly, they have come to greatly influence how we understand the formation of Christianity as well as these alternative spiritual systems by early followers of Jesus.

"Split a piece of wood,

and I am there.

Lift up the stone,

and you will find me there."

—Jesus, Saying 77, Gospel of Thomas

Sufism

Sufism (*tasawwuf*) is even more diverse than the Gnostic tradition as it is not necessarily its own sect, but rather the mystical, internalized nature of each branch of Islam, with a deep focus on universal courtesy, awareness, and inner awakening.[10] There are Sufis in both the primary Sunni and Shia schools, as well as Sufi Orders that were disconnected from any element of traditional orthodoxy.

Rumi and Hafez being two of the most prominent Sufis throughout the centuries, Sufism tends to be comprised of the poets, musicians, singers, and dancers of Islam. The "Whirling Dervishes" are one such Sufi order that spins around and around in artful dances, mimicking the intoxication of the spiritual experience.

The word "Sufi" comes from the Arabic word *tasawwuf* meaning to "dress in wool" referring to the woolen garments of early Islamic ascetics. But the definition of their belief is the path of the heart. It is admonishing one's own worldly desires in place of Love for the Beloved. To the Sufi, God, or *Allah* in Arabic is considered in a sense to be an intimate partner, the One and Only recipient of one's devotion. By purifying the heart of greed, lust, and wrath we become unhindered to access the truth in our inner self, which translates to an outpouring of love to the Creator and all of creation.

> *"Love is*
>
> *The funeral pyre*
>
> *Where I have laid my living body.*
>
> *All the false notions of myself*
>
> *That once caused fear, pain,*
>
> *Have turned to ash*
>
> *As I neared God.*
>
> *What has risen*
>
> *From the tangled web of thought and sinew*
>
> *Now shines with jubilation*
>
> *Through the eyes of angels*

And screams from the guts of Infinite existence

Itself.

Love is the funeral pyre

Where the heart must lay

Its body."

—Hafez

In Sufism, the detachment from the world is so powerful that there comes a moment of annihilation (*fana*) in the love of the Divine. This is similarly referred to by Carl Jung as the "ego death" in modern psychology, and in many ways parallel Bhakti yoga of Hinduism.

The Sufis would give exceptionally more alms, they would fast for nine months instead of one, they would pray more than five times a day—they weren't pious for society's sake, they were pious out of the purest love for God.

When you love someone you want to make them happy, and these expanded practices were the surest way to do so.

"We did not take Sufism from talk and words,

but from hunger and renunciation of the world and cutting off the things to which we were accustomed and which we found agreeable."

—Junayd

One subtle yet very important theological distinction within mysticism that I would like to point out in regards to Sufism, is the difference between "annihilation" in the Divine, *fana*, and the "descent" of the Divine into a human body, *hulul*. There have been many Muslim dynasties with shifting sectarian divisions, decrees and renunciants, too many to contextualize here, but there was a very famous Sufi who was hanged for this very debate.

Mansur al-Hallaj was a Socrates-like figure in the 8th century CE who got in a lot of trouble for saying "*Anal al haq*", meaning "I am the Truth."

He was sent to the gallows for hulul, as his proclamation was considered blasphemous. The ruling imams' logic was that our bodies are bound by time and space—Almighty God cannot possibly descend into mortality in the way that we frail humans do. Whereas Hallaj's followers considered his declaration fana, emptying the soul in order to take on divine attributes. Hallaj was not making a "crude claim to divinity, but rather expressing the negation of his own separate existence."[11]

> *"I have seen my Lord with the eye of my heart, and I said:*
>
> *'Who are You?'*
>
> *He said:*
>
> *'You.'"*
>
> —*Mansur al-Hallaj*

Al-Hallaj famously sang and danced to the gallows in chains. He was so intoxicated by spirit that he was beyond any fear of death. He sang, "Kill me, my faithful friends, for in my being killed is my life."[12] His legacy endures to this day as one of hundreds of famous Muslim Sufi mystics who found peace and joy despite the external happenings of the body.

Kabbalah

Completing the Judeo-Abrahamic representation of mysticism is the *Kabbalah* of Judaism. Like Hinduism, Judaism is ancient. For nearly three millennia (~2,000 BCE to ~1280 BCE), the term "Kabbalah" in Hebrew simply meant "to receive" or "that which has been received through tradition."

It wasn't until the 13th century CE that Jewish esoteric mystics in Spain and Italy claimed to understand "hidden" or "secret teachings" of the ancient scriptures that represented a more psychodynamic view of the human mind, of metaphysical layers to this world, and of the cosmogony—the birth of the universe. These interpretations, the mystics claim, had been passed down from the earliest prophets (Moses, Elijah, Isaiah, King Solomon) of the

Jewish faith, secretly transmitted for generations from teacher to student.[13]

> *"In love is found the secret of Divine Unity.*
>
> *It is love that unites the higher and the lower stages of existence, that raises the lower to the level of the higher—where all become fused into one."*
>
> —*The Zohar*

The foundational text of Kabbalah is *The Zohar*, (meaning the Book of Radiance) which is a narrative of mystics traveling the Galilee that plays as a metaphysical commentary of the Torah—the five Books of Moses, the central documents of the Jewish faith. There are other Kabbalistic texts, but *The Zohar* is the masterpiece. A voluminous work spanning many concepts but most relevant for this humble summary is the definition of God as, ultimately, undefinable. The Divine Essence is beyond human comprehension, beyond space & time, for which the Kabbalists use the term *"Ein Sof"*, meaning "Nameless Unending Infinity". While the Ein Sof is unknowable by human beings, there are ten stages (*"sefirot"*) that act as vessels of Divine Energy through which we can come to know God. Each stage has its own characteristics that progress as the human being nears closer to the Knowable God in proximity.[14] They are highly symbolic, acting as a blueprint of the metaphysical experience within this realm. The famous 20th century Jewish scholar Gershom Scholem writes that the Kabbalistic symbolism is:

> *"...An expressible representation of something which lies beyond the sphere of expression and communication, something which comes from a sphere whose face is, as it were, turned inward and away from us. A hidden and inexpressible reality finds its expression in the symbol."* [15]

The Zohar categorizes the levels of textual interpretation as follows: direct interpretations (in Hebrew, *Peshat*), allegoric (*Remez*), imaginative or Rabbinic meanings (*Derash*), and the inner, metaphysical meanings of Kabbalah (*Sod*). As discussed in the *Thomas* section, a common theme among mystics across cultures is that there is oftentimes 'hidden wisdom' or 'secret teachings' withheld from the masses. Now my initial reaction to hiding anything is hesitation because that implies some kind of hierarchy between human beings, as ultimately I hold the firm understanding that We Are All One. Ironically, hierarchical elitism is something that made me (and so many others) thoroughly question organized religion and start to look elsewhere. However the more I work with these kinds of transcendental ideas I can see that they are indeed not for everyone, and that someone not living within these perspectives could easily misinterpret them. (I might be guilty of doing that myself!) So in that sense I understand some of the intention behind concealment.

The Zohar was allegedly written (or transcribed) by Shimon bar Yochai in hiding during the Roman-ruled 2nd century CE, later revealed to the public at large in the 13th century CE Spain by a Jewish writer named Moses de León. There is still a lively debate among Jewish rabbis and scholars over the original author being de León or Shimon bar Yochai. Regardless of its author, *The Zohar*'s commentary and insights have been appreciated by wider Jewish audiences for centuries, and in recent decades the Kabbalah has become more closely associated with New Age movements and a variety of universalist aspirants.

Taoism

Taoism is one of China's most cherished cultural legacies. It goes back to at least the 4th century BCE. You can feel its influence in a multitude of places, from Eastern Zen Buddhism to Western literature, cinema and culture. Chances are some of your favorite science fiction or fantasy stories have Taoist themes in them. In Brazil there are Taoist temples full of followers. Korea, Japan, Vietnam and Singapore also have long histories with Taoism. Even famous childrens' book authors in Europe have tried to channel Taoist philosophy in their stories.

The *Tao Te Ching* is the foundational text for Taoism. Its credited author is the mythic sage Laozi. Some scholars believe it was written by a collection of authors over time.

The Tao (translated as *"the Way"*) is an idea as large as God. It is the source and substance of everything, including us. Yet the tradition of Taoism says that the Tao is too deeply rooted in reality to even describe with words. This means the Tao we talk about is not the real Tao. Taoists understand that language can't express all of existence. Instead, they believe other forms of expression like music, dance, art and even non-action can better capture the true state of existence, or the true Tao.

> *"Existence is beyond the power of words to define."*
>
> *—Laozi, Tao Te Ching*

When you first read Taoist ideas and quotes, you might notice that they seem confusing or contradictory. They intentionally try to turn common knowledge on its head. They often compare opposing concepts like life and death, stillness and movement, emptiness and fullness. Instead of seeing these as opposites, a Taoist would see them as interconnected.

> *"Stop leaving and you will arrive.*
>
> *Stop searching and you will see.*
>
> *Stop running away and you will be found."*
>
> *—Laozi, Tao Te Ching*

Do you feel the confusion yet? Laozi pushes against your understanding of basic logic. Taoists say not to rush through this mental exploration. Sit on these thoughts patiently and the confusion will give way to a deeper wisdom.

Zen

I almost left this paragraph blank.

But that's too pretentious because the point is to give some necessary background, not be showy flashy guy. Or maybe I was worried about people thinking about formatting errors. I'll just start.

Buddhism is already a fascinating system. Even in its most general sense, the Buddha's search for truth is so penetrating and so profound that you might think there wouldn't be a reformation required. But ultimately Buddhism is still a religion, too. One that has been institutionalized over the centuries like all the others, and because of this we have the emergence of Zen, a lotus sprouting up from the mud.

> *"Zen does not confuse spirituality with thinking about God while one is peeling potatoes.*
>
> *Zen spirituality is just to peel the potatoes."*
>
> —*Alan Watts*

Admittedly Zen does not meet every definition of "mysticism", the mismatch being that mystic philosophy tends to rest on a theistic belief in an internal divinity—whereas Buddhism is generally categorized as an agnostic spiritual system—however, an integral component of Zen is experiential spiritual practice, which is why many academics have thought of it as a 'mystical branch' or 'esoteric Buddhism'.

A sub-school of the Mahayana branch of Buddhism, the Zen origin story actually dates all the way back to the "Flower Sermon", the subtlest of subtle moments in the Buddha's teaching career. While seated in front of his monks, he simply held up a white flower. No one seemed to make sense of it, except one monk, Mahākāśyapa, smiled quietly. His smile was clear to the Buddha as the true understanding of the teaching—causing Buddha to designate Mahākāśyapa as his primary successor.[16]

Centuries later, Buddhism made its way to China in the 5th century CE, brought by Bodhidharma, a semi-legendary Western Buddhist monk, credited for Zen's pioneering transmission. Zen developed further thanks to a flavoring from Taoism, the ancient Chinese religion of Laozi and the later writings of Zhuangzi. Bodhidharma is as good as it gets:

> *"People of this world are deluded.*
>
> *They're always longing for something-always, in a word, seeking.*

But the wise wake up.

They choose reason over custom.

They fix their minds on the sublime and let their bodies change with the seasons.

All phenomena are empty.

They contain nothing worth desiring."

—*Bodhidharma*

Zen koans are an example of how useless form is to Zen Buddhists. Koans are riddles designed to help us break out of our conceptual thinking, like "What is the sound of one hand clapping?" The answer is... up to the perceiver... which is why the late great religious philosopher Huston Smith calls Zen "a step through Alice's looking glass"[17] where confusing contradictions and playful paradoxes work to describe the nature of the mind.

But the real beauty of Zen Buddhism is its absolutist focus on presence and awareness. Dogen was a Buddhist priest who branched off from the Tendai School, founding the Soto school of Zen—further illustrating the tendency of religious systems to decay and need rejuvenation—and Dogen greatly emphasized the practice of *zazen*.

As a certified mindfulness meditation teacher, I've heard many new to meditation hesitate. They'll say something to the effect of 'I can't stop my thoughts'... to which I reply, that's okay! That certainly doesn't invalidate you as a candidate to enjoy and reap the benefits of meditation. There are many non-Buddhist modern styles of meditation—guided meditation, noticing thoughts, affirmations & mantras—all of which have value, and can be much more accessible to new practitioners. But the zazen of Zen Buddhism *is* that very thought-stopping type of meditation that causes so much secular resistance. It's so unique that some Buddhists consider zazen to be categorized differently than meditation altogether—when the head moves into the heart, or into a more holistic body-mind framework.[18]

In the Zen view, because enlightenment is already present,

non-striving is the key.

Everything else is in the way.

> *"The main practice of Zen is zazen, meaning sitting meditation,*
>
> *where the goal is essentially to concentrate on the breath and suspend all thought.*
>
> *If you are unable to find the truth right where you are,*
>
> *where else do you expect to find it?"*
>
> *—Dogen*

I am not compelled to speak at length about Zen because there's something funny and contradictory in speaking about Zen, whereas Zen is feeling the rhythm that my fingers find the keys as I type out these words filling these pages. Being right here and nowhere else.

There have been great many Zen masters from Bodhidharma to Dogen to contemporary teachers like D.T. Suzuki, Alan Watts, Shunryu Suzuki, and my beloved Thích Nhất Hạnh, all of which have helped many minds find the "no mind".

Advaita Vedanta

I've covered Hinduism at a decent length already but it's important to include Advaita in a summary of the world mystics.

As discussed, Hinduism as a whole tends to exemplify spiritually "mystical" traits across a much wider breadth than the religions of the West. Considering mysticism as a direct, personal connection to the Divine within one's own heart, this description holds true for all Hindus: from the Vaishnavas (worship of Krishna) to the Shaivites (worship of Shiva).

However, Advaita in particular, is where mystic philosophy really crashes through the surface and breaks into the atmosphere. After over ten years of study, I still find myself picking up my jaw:

"I am dead already. Physical death will make no difference in my case.

I am timeless being.

I am free of desire or fear, because I do not remember the past or imagine the future.

Where there are no names and shapes, how can there be desire and fear? With desirelessness comes timelessness.

I am safe, because what is not, cannot touch what is. You feel unsafe, because you imagine danger.

Of course, your body as such is complex and vulnerable and needs protection.

But not you.

Once you realize your own unassailable being, you will be at peace." [19]

—Nisargadatta Maharaj

Without sounding too redundant here, Advaita is the earliest system of "non-dual" thought. Non-duality, meaning "not two", is the idea that the atman (individual soul) and Brahman (formless Divinity) are one and the same. According to Advaitists, they are separate terms in concept only, ultimately there is no distinction. Whereas there is a distinction between your body-mind and Your Timeless Being, Your Spark of Infinity. The body comes and goes, "but not you", says Nisargadatta, one of the most profound Advaita teachers.

Advaita was mostly developed by Adi Shankara in the 8th century. He is rightfully considered one of the most sophisticated teachers in this system, and within world mysticism. In addition to the medieval founder, we've had several Advaita masters in the 20th century, namely Sri Ramana Maharshi and Sri Nisargadatta Maharaj, who have utterly destroyed the veil of the temporal self—and who are worth deep contemplation, as we'll cover soon.

New Age

After the breakthrough scientific discoveries of the Age of Enlightenment, religion was reeling from a global shift towards rationalism and a more sophisticated, scientific worldview. While many religious sects regressed into overly orthodox interpretations, from the Amish to the Wahhabis, many of the mystical sects and related schools were similarly rejuvenated. With major developments in chemistry, physics, astronomy, mathematics, and biology, the religious humans basically went either hardcore fundamentalist or heart-core spiritual.

There are many antecedents for the modern "New Age movement"[20] all contributing to a growing patchwork of spiritual beliefs from as early as the 1830s to the late 20th century:

- American Transcendentalist authors who rose to prominence in the 1830s (Ralph Waldo Emerson, Henry David Thoreau, Louisa May Alcott, and the great poet Walt Whitman, among others), themselves influenced by Kant and the German idealists, emphasized the inherent purity of the individual, personal freedom, and the guidance of intuitive direction
- Helena (Madame) Blavatsky co-founded the Theosophical Society in 1875 (with Henry Olcott), which originated out of contact and study under an alleged secret brotherhood of Eastern mystics and their scriptures; her followers included Annie Besant, Charles W. Leadbeater and Jiddu Krishnamurti, who ultimately left the organization and rejected the Theosophists' messianic expectation around his youth, famously defending his departure by maintaining that *"Truth is a Pathless Land"* [21]
- Phineas Quimby's "New Thought" and Mary Baker Eddy's "Christian Science" both focused on the power of the mind and its role in spiritual healing; alongside the writings of Joseph Murphy, Neville Goddard, Ernest Holmes, William Walker Atkinson and Napoleon Hill

- The work of Carl Gustav Jung, a psychoanalyst and colleague of Sigmund Freud, who founded analytical psychology and made contributions to many fields of knowledge, including mysticism and comparative mythology
- Edgar Cayce, a Christian mystic who gave over 14,000 channeled readings in a trance state in the early 1900s—his psychic readings provided answers on healing, reincarnation, and a multitude of predictions, helping to make terms like "auras", "soul mates" and "holistic healing" household terms[22]; as well as a new genre of channeled texts from a variety of sources over the next century, with some of the most popular works being *A Course in Miracles* by Helen Schucman and the Abraham material by Jerry & Esther Hicks
- 20th century physicists, notably Einstein, Planck, and Heisenberg, many of whom were interested in questioning scientific materialism, with Einstein's relativity theory and the larger field of quantum physics pointing to the potential of consciousness as fundamental to the universe, as opposed to matter
- Unitarianism, an emerging Christian denomination in the early 19th century considering Jesus a human being, and rejecting the doctrines of original sin and Biblical infallibility
- Early religious academics helping to document and in some ways legitimize the esoteric: from Max Muller translating Eastern sources, to Rudolf Otto's syncretistic commentaries, to William James pioneering a psychology-based understanding of mystic states, and Evelyn Underhill's theological exploration of mysticism
- George Gurdjieff, an Armenian and Greek mystic philosopher who emphasized the unification of mind-emotion-body in a series of teachings he called "The Work"[23]

- The arrival of Hindu swamis and Buddhist teachers to America—Swami Vivekananda, Paramahansa Yogananda (the founder of Self-Realization Fellowship), Maharishi Mahesh Yogi (the founder of Transcendental Meditation), Osho, and Swami Prabhavananda to name a few; while Shunryu Suzuki set up the San Francisco Zen Center and began to lecture Westerners in the 1950s on Buddhist teachings and practices[24]
- The Beat authors (Jack Kerouac, William S. Burroughs, Allen Ginsberg, and others), a collective of writers embracing non-conformity and spontaneous creativity, and the later 1960s "Counterculture Movement" of American hippies embracing the use of psychedelics (due to the work of Dr. Timothy Leary, Ram Dass, Aldous Huxley, and others), as well as sexual liberation, and questioning the societal norms of previous generations

Beyond these overlapping oceans of the last two centuries, "New Age spirituality" also tends to have an appreciation for 'archaic' beliefs such as shamanism, Vedic tantra, various forms of astrology, channeled literature and other pagan practices. From the ancient Greek Stoics (highly secular) to the medieval Celtic Druids (highly metaphysical), the West has truly begun to embrace more earth-centric, non-Abrahamic spirituality. New Age generally refers to an amalgamation of most interfaith understandings of spirit in what might be previously dissimilar capacities.

In conclusion, mysticism is simply a focus on connecting to the internal when everyone and everything else is focusing on the external.

Every religion has a spectrum with exoteric orthodoxy on one end and esoteric mysticism on the other. Throughout history, those who have controlled the power behind religious institutions have persecuted these mystics, either by excommunication or death.

Fortunately we live in the 21st century. Not only has this condemnation lessened significantly, but the public at large has gained access to formerly withheld esoteric scripture, ritual, and practice, along with a larger cultural movement embracing alternative perspectives on traditional religion and spirituality.

This is all to say that, it is a hell of a thin read to associate all spiritual thinking as being ancient, irrelevant "fairy tale" mythologies.

That dismissive attitude neglects so many multitudes of sincere seekers. They diverged from institutional norms. They transcended the everyday drudgery of this world by way of authentic mystical experiences that reflect the beauty and peace within us all.

CHAPTER 9

The Present Has Everything

The Present Never Runs Out

> *When the Buddha was asked, "Sir, what do you and your monks practice?" he replied, "We sit, we walk, and we eat."*
>
> *The questioner continued, "But sir, everyone sits, walks, and eats."*
>
> *And the Buddha told him, "When we sit, we know we are sitting. When we walk, we know we are walking. When we eat, we know we are eating."*
>
> *—Thích Nhất Hạnh*

All this speculating and categorizing and book-reading and thinking and doing!

You ever just, be?

The mystics saw through the stimuli of the world. And as much as I know this, I still get trapped by it.

It's a very captivating phenomenon. And it's why being firmly rooted in the present is such an artform.

There's a lovely spiritual cliché from Vonnegut: we are human beings, not human doings. But there's just so much to do! In my life, in the world. There are so many great books to read. My movie and TV show watchlist keeps getting larger, not smaller. There are so many places to see, foods to try, people to meet.

And yet, here we are.

I am sitting.

In a chair.

Breathing.

Noticing the thoughts come up.

That's the primary technique for being rooted in the present, in meditation.

Echoing the explanation on zazen: most people think that meditating is stopping your thoughts. That's a misunderstanding. Even experienced meditators don't stop the thoughts completely. That's Dogen's zazen, or Ramakrishna's samadhi… where you're merely an empty vessel for the sunyata or the Divine. That might be the eventual goal, but that's not *my* morning meditation.

All I'm doing is being aware of being aware.

> *"Flow with whatever is happening and let your mind be free. Stay centered by accepting whatever you are doing."*
>
> *—Zhuangzi*

The present actually has everything. All of it. It's the restlessness and resistance to this fact that brings us anxiety or regret. Anxiety of course is concern for the future, regret is concern for the past. When we're here, fully, those feelings lessen. Because you're in the truth! The truth of this unceasing present moment.

I am not always mentally in the present. But when I am, what peace comes to me! Ram Dass talked about how he was getting to a point where, while yes he still loved connecting with people, he could sit in an empty white room for hours and be happy. He was rooted in the power of the present moment.

Alan Watts the great British Buddhist had a wonderful image. He said we think the present is a little tick mark on your wrist. We've been deceived that the present is a *snap* and not the *ringing of a long sustained bell*. We've been lied to!

It's here.

And here.

And here.

And it never runs out.

And we are starting to grasp how important staying rooted within it can be.

> *"If, then, I were asked for the most important advice I could give, that which I considered to be the most useful to the men of our century, I should simply say: in the name of God, stop a moment, cease your work, and look around you."*
>
> —*Leo Tolstoy*

Krishna and the Hindu masters have preached about meditation for millennia. The Buddha attained enlightenment meditating under that tree. Even Jesus would go off into nature "to pray".

But we didn't know what it actually does to our bodies and brains until very recently. In the 1970s when Americans like Ram Dass, and then Daniel Goleman and Jon Kabat-Zinn went to India, meditation was still very esoteric. It was not studied scientifically until Dan Goleman and Richard Davidson started looking into actually scanning the brains of meditators. There were only a handful of studies published by the end of the 20th century. Then a shift happened. Every year since 2010, scientific studies on mindfulness & meditation have increased exponentially. There are tens of thousands of research studies evaluating every dimension of what it does for us.[25]

The results are undeniable.

Meditation, or being rooted in the present, benefits our respiratory system, our cardiovascular system, our neurological system, our ability to regulate emotions, and our ability to reduce stress. These benefits are published in the most established medical journals in the world.

An especially exciting new realization from this research on the brain is called "neuroplasticity".[26] It means that our neural pathways can be changed. In much of 20th century psychology our brain chemistry was thought to be fixed. Now we understand that many of the ideas proposed by Eastern and contemplative philosophy are being validated.

In Buddhism they say we are "always arriving". In meditation, we are practicing coming back to the present moment. And according to modern neuroscientific research, we are actually getting better at doing that. We can build the mind muscle to come back to the present, even better than we could prior to meditating. This is a very useful image because it shows that we have the power to improve our own lives. Our own sense of peace and happiness is attainable by coming back into the present, coming back into love. It's this slow, gradual but deliberate, incremental increase that I rely on to work towards a fuller sense of self and a greater connection with others.

Bobby the Zen Master: Emptiness & Presence

We're so bound by conceptual thinking.

For me it's either task-related or concept-related. Sometimes I'm cooking and thinking deep things like how Adi Shankara borrowed some of Buddhism to help refine medieval Hinduism. That the idea of "wholeness" or "fullness" could act as a parallel to "emptiness", because the opposite ends of a spectrum start to bleed into each other, like a circle. And then I flip the tortillas.

But probably more often, I'm thinking about all the things I need to do throughout my day.

I'm a father, I'm a husband, a son, a brother, and a friend; my loved ones have certain needs that I help them fulfill in a variety of ways. I'm a co-worker and marketer; my teams and clients have certain expectations of work I do on their behalf. And I'm a writer, filmmaker, and content creator; my humble audience, my collaborators, and my own need to be creative bring forth my expressive qualities as actions to be done.

Well not my boy, Bobby.

He's a year-old next month. And there are very few, if any, concepts going on in there. Certainly zero task-related to-dos. And how liberating that must be!

His primary state is so firmly rooted in the present... he's a gargantuan boulder immovably grounded at the bottom of the valley of time.

> *"The baby looks at things all day without winking; that is because his eyes are not focused on any particular object. He goes without knowing where he is going, and stops without knowing what he is doing. He merges himself within the surroundings and moves along with it. These are the principles of mental hygiene."*
>
> *—Zhuangzi*

Mystics throughout history have admired the care-free-ness of children and babies. The world of industry, of economy, of responsibility, chides children for their naïveté. But the mystics recognize their effortless capacity for being in the here and now.

Yes, there are illogical tantrums. But that's hardly a scratch against the joys.

Most of my friends don't have kids yet, and a few of my guys have expressed their reasons for hesitating: 'I don't know if I can mentally deal with kid stuff, watching the cartoons, hearing the kid songs on endless repeat', etc.

I can't express how insignificant those things are compared to hanging out with a being who is rooted in presence and joy.

He's tumbling around the house, in the moment, in the moment, in the moment. Traveling through time and space as this sphere of Zen: no past, no future. Fully here now, unintentionally yanking his mother and I into what he's focused on. It's very powerful.

> *"Most certainly I tell you, unless you turn and become as little children, you will in no way enter into the Kingdom of Heaven.*
>
> *Whoever therefore humbles himself as this little child is*

the greatest in the Kingdom of Heaven."

—Jesus, Gospel of Matthew 18:3-4

I'll often walk over to where he is, coming from my office with work thoughts of today's happenings and tomorrow's to-dos, and all that energy is a puny candle extinguished by a tornado. Suddenly I am wrangled into this moment, free of obligations, free of ideology.

Despite all the tears, dishwashing, diapers, food costs, and sleeplessness throughout a global pandemic, seeing a miniature human crack a grin is ineffable bliss. His laugh disintegrates the Monkey Mind, dissolving my analytical thoughts and constant concerns of day-to-day living. It's his unaware offering of awareness… of purity… and of presence.

There's nothing going on and there's everything going on, you know?

As adults, we're seemingly distant from this innate capacity to be grounded in the here and now. I'm teaching him many concepts, but he's teaching me concept-less-ness.

The Unpleasantness as an Anchor

When I started meditating, I would feel so good. Actually that's not true, when I very first started meditating I couldn't do it and nothing happened. But after a while of trying to do it anyway, I started to notice that I would feel calmer, more at peace. All those things you read about. And then I would lose it throughout the day, but I would come back into it on the cushion.

You really don't become a regular meditator until you see the benefits kick in.

I was five to seven years on and off until I realized 'wow, this is increasing my clarity and peace' and it became a feeling of really *needing* to sit. It wasn't an obligation anymore, it's 'I want to keep the magic going!'

That's the phase where we can actually begin to grasp the

moment too tightly. Buddhism talks about clinging to external objects, well you can even cling too hard to this present moment. Not wanting it to change or end. And so noticing that, and releasing, is a key practice along the way.

The positive healthy side of this is called savoring.

The negative trap side of this is called grasping or clinging.

When you're clear and detached you'll know which aspect you're bringing to each moment.

How can I be detached and present? That is the balance!

We're here but we're letting things go. The image from Buddhism and Taoism is that we're sitting on the bank of a stream watching the water roll on past us. Joyful, present, calm. It's coming and going, endlessly like our thoughts, but we're just here.

A few Saturdays ago I was about to watch a favorite show, sitting with my tiny guy smiling up at me at lunchtime. Press play on the new episode. My hunger is about to be subdued, and here's a cherub. It was several very good things all colliding into one beautiful moment. If you've gone to Tulum you know this feeling: overwhelming positive sensual phenomena!

And so a real clinging, covetous thought came up.

Like 'I don't want this to end, this is just too amazing'. And almost immediately after that thought, Bobby started crying for no reason. Annoyed baby is not a good sound. It launched me out of the pleasure overload and into a more balanced acceptance of the moment. It's good and bad. Pleasure and pain. Loss and gain.

The world of form's unpleasantness can be used to reduce our grasping tendencies. As we become more aware, we can see through the situation more deeply. We can learn. And be gentle with ourselves.

Unraveling "PRAY. REPENT. OBEY."

I was driving down the highway working with a new mantra:

"I am at peace with the way things are."

I like it because not only could I feel presence but even my heart was starting to flutter a bit... the HeartMath Institute[27] studies this kind of thing... and the whole vibe of the family car was excellent. When I was fully in the space of "I am at peace with the way things are", really believing it, there was harmony with my wife Mel, baby Bobby and even our dog Toto. The cars around me too. I was vibrating high.

So I'm in that state and see a billboard for Christianity. Not sure of the church, but it was that Iron Age type of mantra. All caps:

"PRAY. REPENT. OBEY."

Here's the typical read: medieval subservience to white-bearded patriarch. It's the same energy that's responsible for the sinking ship of modern institutional Christianity. Decades into the twenty-first century, most of us are no longer praying, repenting, or obeying.

But I was in the place of real presence. And what I realized was that when you look at this phrase from a lack of ego-resistance, it takes on a whole new meaning. That phrase could have started from a place of deep spirituality, but it has been so downgraded by semantics, bad translations, and misinterpretation. Ego got it.

I broke it down by each word:

Pray: well that basically means meditate, right? Sit in stillness.

Repent: Repent means examine your past behaviors. Contemplate them and move forward from them. Let go of the past.

Obey: Obey means you're not in charge. You don't decide. There's a higher decision above your conscious one and you have trust in the universe. So you surrender to it all.

Well, "Meditate, Let Go of the Past, and Surrender", is Ram Dass 101. That's New Age Instagram. Those three aspects of the spiritual path are constantly being emphasized in my universalist mystic circles.

It's possible that whoever paid for that billboard could have held conflict in their hearts. Were they trying to spread Jesus' message of radical love? Or were they trying to spread fear and indoctrination?

Ultimately, this exercise proved the inadequacy of form and how diabolical the ego is at twisting the meaning towards conflict. The way out of our confusion is being in presence, and coming at life from a place of peaceful acceptance. By avoiding initial resistance to "Pray-Repent-Obey", I was able to unravel it a bit and get a glimpse of a new holistic perspective.

CHAPTER 10

Noticing Is The First Step

Sri Ramana, Self-Inquiry, and the Bull in the Stable

"There is no greater mystery than this:

being Reality ourselves,

we seek to gain Reality."

—*Ramana Maharshi*

In 1896, a boy was sitting in his uncle's house, alone. His father had just passed away, and he was thinking about death.

He had just seen his father's lifeless body earlier that day. This thought of the physical body dying consumed him. The fact that all humans, all beings, appear to meet an end within the body. An immense fear took over him, and he was struck by "a flash of excitement" or "heat", a "current" or "force" that seemed to possess him, while his body became rigid.[28]

The boy experienced the feeling of death... but it was more like the feeling of death *occurred,* absent of a subjective experiencer. As the limbs, organs and everything started to shut down, he was taken through a process of self-inquiry: he began to ask himself *what it is that dies.*

He concluded that the body dies, but that this "current" or "force" remains alive, and recognized this "current" or "force" as his Self.

In one of his rare written comments on this process he later wrote,

> *"Inquiring within 'Who is the seer?'*
>
> *I saw the seer disappear, leaving That Alone which stands forever.*
>
> *No thought arose to say 'I saw.'*
>
> *How then could the thought arise to say, 'I did not see?'"* [29]

This boy was Bhagavan Sri Ramana Maharshi (1879-1950), a liberated being (*jivanmukta*) who experienced sudden liberation (*akrama mukti*) at the age of sixteen, a liberation that remained consistently throughout his entire life.

While most of us have to slog through our incremental evolution of consciousness for years, decades, lifetimes... there is the occasional luminary of humanity who breaks through the veil instantaneously.

After this experience, he felt a completely pervasive sense of bliss. He was so immersed into that Eternal Union with All, that as a teenager he had trouble with school and living a normal life for a time. The young Ramana (born Venkataraman Iyer) ultimately left his childhood home for the holy hill of Arunachala, a couple hundred kilometers away. Arriving as a young renunciant, Sri Ramana spent the rest of his life on top of that hill. He sat for years in a state of such powerful peace that eventually followers began to come to him.[30]

Sri Ramana's primary teaching was silence.

If you didn't understand that primary teaching—silence—then he would speak about self-inquiry (*atma vichara*).

Asking the question "Who am I, truly?" It's a deeply powerful question to sit with, and it can transform everything as you start to find out the truth. In the West we say, "Hi I'm Bob, I'm a filmmaker." "Hi I'm Morgan, I'm an account manager." "Hi I'm Whitney, I'm a realtor." We reduce ourselves down to what we do to make money. What a frustratingly thin layer of who we actually are!

We are all of our roles simultaneously, but even still, we are Fullness, Wholeness underneath them all. This is what sitting in prolonged silence can reveal to us. This is what Sri Ramana asked us to find out about ourselves.

> *"Your duty is to be and not to be this or that. 'I am that I am' sums up the whole truth. The method is summed up in the words 'Be still'.*
>
> *What does stillness mean?*
>
> *It means destroy yourself.*
>
> *Because any form or shape is the cause for trouble. Give up the notion that 'I am so and so'. All that is required to realize the Self is to be still.*
>
> *What can be easier than that?"*
>
> —*Ramana Maharshi*

Like Jesus with his agriculture parables, Hindu gurus put these concepts in simple terms for our unawakened minds. Sri Ramana explained the process of self-inquiry with the metaphor of a bull in a stable.[31]

He said imagine that you have a bull, and you keep it in a stable.

If you leave the gate open, the bull will wander outside of the gate and go graze on other cultivated fields of grass. The owners of these fields will beat it with sticks and throw stones at it to chase it away, but it will come back again and again because the bull doesn't understand field boundaries—it's just following its instinct to eat grass when it's hungry.

The bull is the mind, and the stable is the heart (or The Self).

The other fields are like the pleasures of the senses, outside of the stable of the heart, they tempt us to roam around aimlessly, following our carnal instincts. Other ascetic spiritual techniques are like tying up the bull, which can work temporarily but as soon as those renunciant-restraints are loosened, the bull is outside in the other fields again.

Sri Ramana said that the practice of self-inquiry is like putting a handful of fresh grass under the bull's nose, and gently walking it back to the stable.

Eventually the bull will learn that the abundance of fresh grass is in the stable. There is no need to go out into the countryside, looking anywhere else but inside. Wandering outside the heart will eventually bring us self-created punishment, but if the mind remains in the heart, we will understand that it has everything we could ever need.

This is what self-inquiry can help us accomplish through its repeated practice.

Another interesting fact about Sri Ramana is that he never once encouraged a devotee to go off and become a renunciant like he was. In many ways he was a "stereotypical guru", sitting on top of a hill, where devotees would come to him for an experience of awakening. Despite this, he encouraged those who came to him to do their duty in the world—to not detach from the world, but to detach from their way of thinking about the world.

If this existence is a dream, then what does it matter where you are? And what you do? It only matters how you perceive.

> *"Happiness is your nature.*
>
> *It is not wrong to desire it.*
>
> *What is wrong is seeking it outside when it is inside."*
>
> *—Ramana Maharshi*

Going to 'the thing'

I skipped class and went to the Austin City Limits Music Festival in 2004. We drove to Bonnaroo in 2006, 2007, and 2008. I have been to hundreds of bars in Austin, and I've met musician heroes of mine backstage at festivals that no longer exist. I got thrown out of Barbarella's, although it was mostly their fault. Okay don't order six drinks (for a group!) at last call.

So yeah, I'm good!

Now I like sitting down, listening, and talking.

I don't need to go to 'the thing' anymore.

I'm losing interest because the hype around a seemingly important cultural social event is usually plastic. Our celebrity heroes are actually just normal people, holding surface-level conversations, dealing with their own human-life-obstacles and blockages. That kind of hype is empty.

Ultimately, we have two choices: We're either sharing with other people in an authentic way that reminds them of their own inner light, or to quote Terence McKenna, we're "dithering while Rome burns".

We're all going to die.

Initiate a genuine connection with as many people as you can while breath is going through the lungs.

Byron Katie and the Work

In 1986, a deeply depressed 43-year old woman was trying to get some sleep. She had lived a normal life—a successful career, two marriages, and three children—but for the previous ten years she had gone through life in a state of unbearable rage, paranoia, and sadness. She spent weeks in bed, finally checking into a center for women with eating disorders, the only facility covered by her insurance. She was lying on the floor. She had such a burning sense of self-hatred that she felt like she didn't even deserve to sleep in a bed. As she lay there on the ground, overcome with anguish, a cockroach ran over her foot. But it wasn't *her* foot.

She woke up "without any concepts of who or what she was."[32] It generated an experience of becoming the Observer of All. She understood that she had been attached to her personal "story", and that by stepping outside of this narrow lens, she could see the fullness of existence.

Unburdened by her previous stories, Byron Katie emerged.

"Katie" spent a few years having difficulty explaining this new way of seeing the world. Her family was happy that she was no longer depressed but they were also concerned because she was so radically different than who she appeared to be before.

> *"I discovered that when I believed my thoughts, I suffered.*
>
> *But that when I didn't believe them, I didn't suffer, and that this is true for every human being."*
>
> *—Byron Katie*

This process of seeing the world, she began to call "The Work": a series of four questions that take us through the process of self-inquiry. Her sequence of questions allows us to see through the flimsiness of our personal stories, and that they hide the truth of who we are and the truth of what is.

Upon writing down a judgment (a thought), about yourself or others, the process is to go through four questions. It is strongly encouraged to be in a meditative, contemplative state of mind as you go through the questions. And it can take time—Katie worked on her thoughts about her own mother for three years.[33] The more tightly-held the belief, the more time it can take to sit with each question when examining the thought.

Her four main questions are:

> *-Is it true?*
>
> *-Can you absolutely know that it's true?*
>
> *-Does this thought bring peace or stress into your life?*
>
> *-Who would you be without that thought?*

Afterwards there's a "turnaround", where you write out the exact opposite of your initial thought, and then list out examples of why the turnaround is true.

Byron Katie has been going through this process with people 1-on-1 for decades now. There are hundreds of recordings of her doing this on YouTube. It's unbelievable. There's also a free app,

"The Work" by Byron Katie, that helps you go through the process. It includes a few extra questions to get you in this state of self-awareness.

I'll be vulnerable here and share one I've done. It is my book after all!

When I started publishing my writing about mystic philosophy, I was extremely self-conscious. Many of my acquaintances, and even friends really, are pretty secular. I know that this material is not for everyone and I carried plenty of self-doubt in writing about it publicly… things like the chakras, reincarnation and so on… I work at a tech company! So I did the Work on it:

> *My friends and acquaintances perceive me as a crazy mystic.*

Is it true?

> *Yes.*

Can you absolutely know that it's true?

> *No.*

How do you react when you believe that thought?

> *I feel judged.*
>
> *Or I feel like others think that I'm corny, or that my material or interests are 'cringe'.*

Does that thought bring peace or stress into your life?

> *That.*
>
> *Brings.*
>
> *Stress.*

What images do you see, past and future, when you think that thought?

> *Mostly being excluded from things, events. I see people whom I admire, talking about me to others as being crazy.*

What emotions arise when you believe that thought: *"My*

friends and acquaintances perceive me as a crazy mystic"?

> *My heart drops down into my stomach. I feel anxious and lack self-confidence.*

Who would you be **without** the thought?

> *I would be able to be fully present.*
>
> *To write and discuss and communicate in a much more whole, integrated way.*
>
> *Assured!*

Turnaround:

> *My friends and acquaintances do not perceive me as a crazy mystic.*

What are some examples that make that thought as true or truer?

> *-People tell me I'm thoughtful and compassionate.*
>
> *-My beliefs are backed by self-inquiry, academic study, and even some new science.*
>
> *-I have a successful career at a legitimate organization.*
>
> *-A beautiful woman has been with me for over a decade.*

(And then as Katie typically says, there's another turnaround in this one…)

> *I perceive myself as a crazy mystic.*

What are some examples that make that thought as true or truer?

> *-In some ways, I like the identity of being a crazy mystic… it's mostly good company.*
>
> *-Who wants to be normal? Isn't it more fun to be a little crazy? A little bit mystical and open to the mysteries of the universe?*

By the end of the process, the initial fear-based thought disintegrates into a thousand particles. Most of Katie's couch companions start their conversation in tears, and end in bursts of laughter, acceptance, and love.

It's a beautiful, transformative process of self-inquiry, and I am extremely grateful to Byron Katie for sharing her deep practical approach that has truly helped millions of people investigate their thoughts, and love themselves a bit more than they did before. In many ways, she's similar to Zen monks, and Sri Ramana, but she came into this way of seeing without knowing about any of them at all… further validating this Way of Being.

I brought her up to a friend who said 'well what about a violent act that harmed a victim? Is that not true?' Obviously I don't condone violence, but I'll just point you to her. Listen to the way she sits with victims and helps them come to a new sense of peace—through understanding, presence and compassion. It's not for everyone, but it's for everyone, you know?

Proving My Spiritual-ness

> *"When you are content to simply be yourself and don't compare or compete, everyone will respect you."*
>
> *—Laozi*

A dear friend meditator introduced me to a successful entrepreneur who created a mindfulness lifestyle app.

We all got lunch and he told us his story. He was raised Mormon and had a very driven, ambitious period in his twenties. He was an extremely successful sales rep. He made a lot of money, millions of dollars, and achieved what he set his mind to achieve.

Around that same time, I was a broke waiter reading Yogananda. My bank was in overdraft, but my heart was exploding in love.

This friend of a friend continued on. He hit that material-world emotional wall. Ultimately, he wound up in the Peruvian Andes, seeing through the fabric of reality after a few cups of ayahuasca.

This broke him out of his corporate career, careening across the globe in search of answers. He met with other teachers, shamans, guides, eventually finding one in New York, and came out of it all having created an app focused on personal transformation.

It was an impressive story and we were all captivated.

Except that while he spoke, I kept noticing the thought that I had to *prove* my spiritual-ness.

He's a little older than me. He's taller. A successful entrepreneur. Those things must've added to this awful line that came up which thankfully I did not let come out: *"while you were in sales I had been meditating for eight years!"*

That is ego, friends. There is nothing loving about that thought. But up it came.

Why was that coming up?

The ego is always comparing. After some reflection, it clearly came out of a feeling of inadequacy in comparison to his material successes.

My ego became fully inflamed when he mentioned that his final (American) shaman consultation cost him $30,000... which is hard to not pass judgment on... or discernment? (Or maybe it's exactly what he needed.) My Apache shaman friend has healed my family for decades, and while we've fed the man well, he's never charged us a cent. So when my new entrepreneur friend said "this shaman found me", I wanted to say, they found your wallet. (More judgment!) The point is, look at where he was and where he is now. He's transformed himself. And he's helping people make incremental change in their lives.

My 'spiritual egotism' was and still is unnerving. It's something I'm continually working on. If you're having trouble recognizing ego thought patterns, this is ego at its most vile:

> *"When you were making your million bucks, I was living in these traditions. I got a religion degree! I made films and made no money about these topics... but now you're the expert because you bought an app company?"*

I really sat with this.

I still am sitting with it. Even today, my ego wants to exclude this story from the book because it's so found out.

That week, feeling slimy as hell, I sat in extended meditation. What finally came up was:

I know who I am.

I don't need to list out my 'spiritual resumé' to anyone.

When I accept myself completely I have no need to be accepted by others.

I can just be.

Presence and love.

We had a follow-up lunch later that week. I decided beforehand not to criticize shaman pricing, but to stay grounded. The new thought, or mantra, I held was:

I am a compassionate brother.

Flip from comparison to collaboration.

It would've been such a joy to just hear his incredible story, without the ego jumping in, diluting the whole scene for me. And so what that new mantra helped me with was how to feel genuine compassion for his journey. To not compare myself to him, but to root for him. To support his work in helping others.

At that next lunch I shared my sincere admiration for his transformation.

I tried out his app and gave him feedback. We connected about being mystics in a corporate world... it's too rare a thing! It was lovely. And my heart was very glad that I was able to dispel the prior egotism from our initial meeting.

This story has a happy ending but it was a brutal awakening for me.

It told me to stay present, stay loving, and reminded me that despite overall increases in peace along the way, the ego continues to be a very worthy adversary.

Part Four:

The Compassionate Heart

Original sin is a lie,

because love is reciprocal.

We see the suffering around us,
which compels us to act
from a place of compassion for others,

and we gain joy ourselves.

CHAPTER 11

Turning Them into Us

How Can I Help?

As we covered earlier, the Hindus have jnanis, working through mental discipline, and also bhaktas, working through heart-opening devotion. Extending into the third path is *karma yoga,* the path of compassionate service.

We all want to help. But how do we? Where do we start?

The impoverished countries?

The eroding rainforests?

The homeless masses?

The endangered animals?

The orphans? The sick? The dying?

It's overwhelming, isn't it?

A first step in service is to realize that no single person can repair all the issues affecting our civilization. We would die trying to create that perfectly-unblemished utopian society that could only exist in a vacuum.

So what we should do, is *what we can do.*

It always bothered me seeing so many homeless people on our streets. When I joined Austin Kriya Yoga, an opportunity to help came through their partnership with E.A.T. Outreach. It's a local grassroots nonprofit that takes day-old, still-delicious, artisanal baked goods headed for a local grocer's trash, to a food bank distribution center. Our humble operation averaged about $200,000 worth of bakery items per year that we would redistribute from landfills to hungry bellies.

I can't save the whales, but that dedicated environmentalist with a speedy ship can flank illegal whaling ships, preventing an endangered pod's early demise.

I can't end homelessness, but that fiery progressive can draft bills to help end the housing crisis, enable new affordable housing initiatives and support outreach non-profits.

I can't solve world hunger, but I can spend a couple of hours a week making sure that less underprivileged families, traumatized veterans, disabled, orphaned, fellow human beings go without hunger here in my community.

When everyone does just what they are able to do, even in a humble way, the whole world improves.

In the *Bhagavad Gita,* Lord Krishna explains the ideal psychological motivation behind service:

> *"Your human right is for the activity only, never for the resultant fruit of actions. Do not consider yourself the creator of the fruits of your activities, neither allow yourself attachment to inactivity."*
>
> *—Krishna, Bhagavad Gita 2.47*

Karma yoga is a way of focusing purely on the action.

But what is karma, really?

Many people understand karma as a kind of 'what goes around, comes around' concept. Some Hindu scholars have an issue with such a simplistic understanding, but I really don't. I think that the modern Western conception of karma is actually pretty close to what Indian philosophy has been describing for so many millennia.

As articulated by Dr. Georg Feuerstein in the *Shambhala Encyclopedia of Yoga,* "Karma refers to the moral force of one's intentions, thoughts and behavior. In this sense, karma often corresponds to fate, as determined by the quality of one's being in past lives and the present life. The underlying idea is that even the moral dimension of existence is causally determined."[1]

Within Hindu philosophy, there is a further distinction between:

1) *sancita-karma,* the total accumulated stock of karmic deposits (*ashaya)* awaiting fruition;

2) *prarabhda-karma,* which has come to fruition in this life;

3) *vartamana-* or *agama-karma,* karma acquired during the present lifetime that will bear fruit in the future.[2]

A foundational text of hatha yoga, the five centuries' old *Shiva Samhita,* declares:

> *"Whatever is experienced in the world, is born of karma. All creatures enjoy or suffer, according to the results of their actions...In proportion to the force of his karma, man suffers misery or enjoys pleasure. The Jiva (individual soul) that has accumulated an excess of evil never stays in peace—it is not separate from its karmas. Except karma, there is nothing in this world."* [3]

"Good" or "bad" karma is binding, if, (and this is a massive "if",) that intention, thought, or behavior is generated from the ego. From the separate self. From the carnal, monkey mind. According to a wide variety of Hindu philosophers—those who have broken through the veil—the way out of the chains of karma is by transcending ego and living from the Self. Meaning, detaching from ego gratification alongside continued actions within the world.

Ram Dass helps us understand this ego dissolution in *How Can I Help?*:

> *"The most familiar models of who we are—father and daughter, doctor and patient, "helper" and "helped"—often turn out to be major obstacles to the expression of our caring instincts; they limit the full measure of what we have to offer one another. But when we break through*

> *and meet in spirit behind our separateness, we experience sincere moments of companionship. These, in turn, give us access to deeper and deeper levels of generosity and loving-kindness. True compassion raises out of unity."* [4]

Any action is a tightrope: on one side we should avoid the fact that we're doing good (being a do-gooder), and the other side to avoid is expectation from the results (wanting the crisis to end). The spiritual aim, as Krishna articulates, is just *doing the work*.

Many of us have seen the ego trap of being a do-gooder. The social media photo opp of the college kid with the poor children in a developing country. It's okay to take a photo, of course, but that should never be the *why*. True activism is not about the optics.

Yet it is the release of our emotional attachment to the results of the work that tends to be even more difficult. The 'We fed this many, but there are still so many more hungry bellies' stream of thoughts will drive us insane. Because we could feed a thousand people every day for years and there will be a thousand more the day after we stop.

The way to avoid the two extremes is to concentrate solely on the action. In an ideal perspective, we are the work itself. That's karma yoga.

Within a mystical context, this sole concentration on the work is a form of devotion to God, a devotion to the Essence Within All. Christ tells us that serving 'the least of these' is actually serving him. The Buddha encourages us to radiate boundless love to every being like a mother loves her child. If there is inherent divinity in all beings, then isn't helping them ultimately helping The Infinite Creator, The Rootless Root of All?

> *"I slept and dreamt that life was joy.*
>
> *I awoke and saw that life was service.*
>
> *I acted and behold, service was joy."*
>
> *—Rabindranath Tagore*

Recently, my work team went to a local soup kitchen, Caritas of Austin, for a corporate community engagement day. Two moments stand out:

I can be a chipper bastard. Like almost annoyingly-happy, to where the other volunteers teamed up with us asked me with a grin, "How the hell are you so cheerful?" (I can be a grumpy primate too, just ask my wife, but when I'm in that mental space of authentic service, genuine connection, it manifests as highly energetic friendliness.) A realization I had was that as our underprivileged friends came through the doors for lunch, the moment of service is actually an opportunity to be compassionate to someone whose receptivity to such love is a fleeting window of time. Going around saying "you are loved" to our homeless population is nice but it might not create a lasting impact, whereas feeding them gets you directly into their consciousness to shine a light into. You demonstrate that they are loved by your action. And the elimination of their hunger is the physical aspect, but the connective moments—the warm welcome, the eye contact, the heart-beam are the emotional & spiritual aspects to the service. And without the latter it's a bit thinner than this practice has the potential to be.

The other moment was based around what my friend Jeremy shared with me. We served plates of food from 11am-12:30pm. He said that he is used to eating promptly at 12pm every day. So, by about 12:15, standing over hot food for the past hour, his regimented consumption manifested as significant, uncomfortable hunger. Jeremy said, "at first I was annoyed about it because I was getting so hungry, but then I looked up and realized that the people receiving our plates *live* with this feeling." They are constantly fighting the tangible irritation that consistent hunger can be, so he shifted his perspective. He went from discomfort to gratitude. That shift is a crucial awakening moment!

Service is a win-win. You help others and you fill yourself up. It gets us one step better to the ideal harmonious society, and it provides the internal perspective shift to gratitude. These benefits of the act of sincere service really charge you up for the rest of your day, and ultimately, bring you closer to that Unity within All.

"After so much austerity I have known that the highest

> *truth is this: He is present in every being! These are all in manifold forms of him. There is no other God to seek for! He alone is worshipping God, who serves all beings!"*
>
> —*Swami Vivekananda*

The Blazing Heart

> *"Underprivileged people are my gods."*
>
> —*Amma Sri Karunamayi*

I was lucky enough to make a short film about Amma Sri Karunamayi in April 2014.[5] If you're not familiar, *Amma* (Mother) is considered an incarnation of the Divine Mother to thousands of Hindu devotees. In addition to her spiritual teachings and blessings (*darshan*) on international tours, she has created a massive humanitarian organization, the SMVA Trust, which provides free education, free healthcare, builds homes, and purifies water for some of the most underprivileged regions of India. Not to be confused with Ammachi, "The Hugging Saint", Amma Karunamayi's work for the world's poor has been recognized by the United States Congress, former U.S. president Jimmy Carter, and the United Nations where she spoke on the International Day of Peace in 2015.[6]

It started because I filmed so many yogis in Austin from 2011-2013 for *The Kingdom Within*. I became somewhat established in the local community of older "white Hindus" (as I lovingly refer to them) as the go-to spiritual video guy here in town. In 2014, a friend emailed me and asked if I would "do a video" for Amma's visit to Austin, and I said absolutely, but it'll be a "short film". (Hear the ego in that?) That weekend of shooting covered Indian, Indian-American and white American devotees contextualizing her loving nature and efforts across the world. It starts with a *homa* fire, a devotional Vedic ritual, and the grand finale is an interview with Amma herself. My footage ended up being the 16-minute documentary, *The Blazing Heart*, playing at film festivals including Tribeca's 30Under30 in New York City.

In April 2015, Amma returned to Austin, and I spoke to her closest disciples and advisors about playing the film during the weekend of her return. It played there for about a hundred people, including Amma, and it was received warmly. During *darshan,* Amma told me personally that she enjoyed the film and thanked me for making it. What an honor that was.

Afterwards, we all took a break for lunch. While I was eating in the courtyard alone, a tall charismatic guy walks over to me and introduces himself as "Kriyavan". Kriyavan wasn't a devotee of Amma, but more like a spiritual wanderer who follows saints for various periods of time, respectful of the path but ultimately disconnected from institutional attachments. He said he loved the film and we started talking about conscious cinema, and spirituality in general. While we're talking, one of Amma's closest disciples, Miles, approaches us. He smiles and listens quietly to our increasingly enthusiastic conversation.

At some point the conversation reaches "the masses" and their complacency—their stubbornness to perceive life strictly through the senses, fixated on work/sex/money, resistant to self-improvement and intellectual stimulation, unaware of metaphysical principles or even just plainly apathetic to it all! I mention my Apache teacher, Richard, and I share to Kriyavan that he refers to people like this as "mud-puppies". Because they're just "stuck in the mud". Kriyavan laughs and Miles turns his head to speak. He said, "Do you know what Amma calls them?" "What's that?" I ask.

"My children."

....

The extended commentary here is that I love Richard. He's far closer in proximity to Being / Love / Enlightenment than I am at this point in time and space, so much so that I feel ridiculous even typing that out, but (within this dream) he might be at a lower level than Amma here. Even my closest spiritual mentor can curl up a dismissive smirk at people out there who stay stuck in the wheel of birth and death.

I have to reiterate, he's an extremely compassionate human being. The man's a probation officer (not for the money!) in order to counsel ex-convicts, who can come out pretty broken from the ravages of the American justice system. And even beyond that, he volunteers his time and energy (energy in many ways) to help guide people, to assist people who are sick or in need of his guidance on the path. For all of the ceremonies, prayers, teachings, and healings my family has been so grateful to receive over the years, we've gotten charged all of zero dollars. He doesn't have a website, he doesn't have a business model. He's just doing the Lord's Work. And even he is not all the way to boundless, unconditional love!

It's a process.

Thankfully we have many gargantuan teachers of Love whose examples we can humbly strive toward!

The Bodhisattva Vow

> *"May I be a guard for those who need protection*
>
> *A guide for those on the path*
>
> *A boat, a raft, a bridge for those who wish to cross the flood*
>
> *May I be a lamp in the darkness*
>
> *A resting place for the weary*
>
> *A healing medicine for all who are sick*
>
> *A vase of plenty, a tree of miracles*
>
> *And for the boundless multitudes of living beings*
>
> *May I bring sustenance and awakening*
>
> *Enduring like the earth and sky*
>
> *Until all beings are freed from sorrow*
>
> *And all are awakened."*

—*Bodhisattva Prayer for Humanity*

Like in Christianity, in Buddhism there are a few main schools. They all follow the Four Noble Truths, and the Eightfold path that is outlined in the fourth truth. The primary Buddhists sects are:

- Theravada (The School of the Elders)
- Mahayana (The Great Vehicle)
- Vajrayana (The Diamond Way)

Theravada claims to be the oldest, and nearest to the Buddha's own life. It follows the traditional religious breakdown that a clergy of monks is spiritually more advanced than a congregation of laypeople. The focus is primarily on one's own liberation, outlining a series of meditations, practices, and rituals that allow oneself to break free of thoughts and disturbances.

As an example of Theravada's institutional rigidity, it has a more outdated relationship with women. On one hand, Buddha was radically inclusive to every being—he was explicit that enlightenment was attainable for both men and women in their current lifetime—and yet his teaching came in a culture and a time when women were extremely subordinate to men. Consequently early Buddhism established more requirements for Buddhist nuns (*bhikkhunis*). For example, ten bhikkhunis were needed to ordain a new one. Because of an 11th century conquest in southern India, all surviving monks and nuns were killed, leaving no new nuns to continue the order and forcing female Theravada Buddhists to "content themselves with lay life" for the past millennia.[7] Whereas, the Mahayana school has no shortage of female nuns, including heads of schools—Mugai Nyodai was the first female Zen master in 13th century Japan. Even the ancient teacher of Bodhidharma, Zen's emissary to the East, was Prajñātārā, the twenty-seventh Indian Patriarch of Zen. Prajñātārā was believed by many to be a woman, including Dōgen Zenji, who wrote about her teachings with great admiration.[8]

Of all the people to make a commentary on the distinction between Theravada (or "Hinayana") and Mahayana Buddhism, we have a true gem in a religious paper from one of the greatest

Americans in our humble history. A young Rev. Dr. Martin Luther King Jr. studied comparative religion in seminary. And while it was an initially surprising find for me, his understanding of the differences between institutional coldness and spiritual warmth aligns perfectly with his nearly unparalleled gifts as a spiritual teacher. A young King explains, "[Theravada] set forth a sort of world hatred as its inspiring motive. It preferred negative philosophical speculation, rather than a warm and positive religious expression. But this negative philosophy of the [Theravada] could never become a popular religion…"[9] King goes on to quote Indian scholar, S. Radhakrishnan: "The [Theravada] ignored… the spirit of man after something higher, and wronged the spiritual side of man. The philosophical atheism of [Theravada] is the skeleton in the box, the diseased worm in the beautiful flower."[10]

Mahayana is the reactive sectarian split to centuries of Theravada's dominance in Asia. It's called "The Great Vehicle" out of either the viewpoint that their system can 'carry' more people to enlightenment, or due to being named after the "Great Congregation" that took place among the earlier Mahasanghika school. They're also Buddhists, so they are certainly concerned with their own liberation, but for the Mahayana, the primary distinction from Theravada is that there is a very powerful intention to help others along the path towards awakening.[11] The term used by the Buddha is *metta* or "loving-kindness", which he defined as the ideal way to treat every being. From the *Metta Sutta,* which is cherished by all sects:

> *"May all beings be happy and secure, may they be happy-minded.*
>
> *Whatever living beings there are - feeble or strong, long, stout or medium,*
>
> *short, small or large, seen or unseen (ghosts, gods and hell-beings),*
>
> *those dwelling far or near, those who are born or those who await rebirth,*

may all beings, without exception be happy-minded.

Let none deceive another nor despise any person whatsoever in any place;

in anger or ill-will let them not wish any suffering to each other.

Just as a mother would protect her only child at the risk of her own life,

even so, let him cultivate a boundless heart towards all beings.

Let her thoughts of boundless loving-kindness pervade the whole world:

above, below and across, without obstruction, without any hatred, without any enmity."

—Buddha, Karaniya Metta Sutta (Sn 1.8)

According to the Buddha, every being is inherently capable of Buddha-nature, and can become a Bodhisattva, a fully awakened being.

This liberated being then has the obligation, no the joy, of existing in a kind of unconditional compassion, helping all other beings attain that very same degree of liberation. The Mahayana school clearly thought that the earlier Theravadans had missed the mark, failing to see the progress of others as intrinsically a part of our own advancement. For many reasons but certainly this one, Mahayana is the most widespread and popular form of Buddhism today.[12]

Vajrayana is a derivative of Mahayana but many scholars consider it a third, unique school in its own right. It has survived primarily in Tibet, being the tradition of the Himalayan Lamas. Vajrayana is called the "Diamond Way" because of the association of enlightenment with un-break-ability. According to the Vajrayana school, not only does every being inherently possess Buddha-nature and the capacity to become enlightened, we all already are—it's just a matter of shifting our awareness and having this instantaneous realization.[13]

The Vajrayana, as with the Mahayana, similarly focuses on the goal of becoming a Bodhisattva in order to help oneself and to help others. The masters of these traditions understand that our own awakening is tied to the awakening of all—gargantuan and minuscule.

> *"We make the effort to bring joy to one person in the morning and to help relieve the suffering of one person in the afternoon. When you are just beginning to be a bodhisattva, you can do this. When you are a bigger bodhisattva, you can bring joy to many people and help relieve the suffering of many others. Every word, every look, every act, and every smile can bring happiness to others. When you know how to walk mindfully, with happiness, kindness, and humility, you are already bringing joy to many people. Practicing diligently, we become a source of peace and joy to those we love and all living beings. The joy of others is our own joy. This is the wisdom of interbeing."* [14]
>
> *—Thích Nhât Hạnh*

In a 'closing of the loop' of this short section, the late great Thích Nhât Hạnh was a young Buddhist monk protesting the Vietnam War. His social activism and calls for nonviolence were admired by Rev. Dr. Martin Luther King Jr., who befriended the young monk. Risking his global reputation, as it was highly unpopular to speak out against our actions in Vietnam at that time, King listened to his heart and knew the right thing to do. He began to incorporate his message of nonviolence to include criticizing the brutality of the American military as well. This was largely due to his admiration of and new friendship with Thích Nhât Hạnh. In their fateful last meeting, a breakfast at a hotel in Geneva, the young Buddhist monk told Dr. King that the Vietnamese considered him a Bodhisattva, "out of the awareness and honoring of his tireless efforts for nonviolence, international peace and compassion in action".[15]

A Monk at Think & Drink

"Think & Drink" was a monthly philosophy night I hosted for a few years. It started because I got tired of hanging out and talking about uninteresting things, so it was a forum (at a bar) dedicated to discussing philosophical topics, and at the very least we could feign some substance for a night.

(Nowadays I have a spiritual podcast, the Be Where How? Show, that fulfills a similar purpose... all I do is blab about this stuff...)

Our nights at Think & Drink would always start off slow, with people hesitating to get real and vulnerable, then about thirty minutes in, someone would take the leap and we'd really get rolling around 8pm. There was a sweet spot from about 8-9 ripe with honest, thought-provoking exchanges. Then after 9, it would devolve into drunken rambling by all.

We talked about purpose, physics & metaphysics, the government, psychedelics, about becoming "mountain woke", and about the ultimate degradation, or advancement, of civilization. And we drank, too.

At one of them, we were joined by a monk—practicing *brahmacharya* (spiritually-motivated celibacy) and abstaining from alcohol.

Aron, now Sanjayananda, is the cousin of one of my closest friends who moved from his home state of Alaska across the ocean to Germany to live in an ashram with his guru, Paramahansa Vishwananda. He was such a pleasant addition, incorporating yogic wisdom as well as anecdotes of his guru.

The night goes on and eventually the drunks get to the point of discussing extraterrestrial life, extending into ideas like what dimension these other beings are on, what their true purpose is in regards to our civilization, etc.

We're really getting into it when our brahmachari brother has to crack a grin.

He interrupts our somewhat heated discussion and says, "In my three years at the ashram, not once have we talked about anything like this."

I laugh and ask, "But that's a good thing, right?"

Another regular Think & Drinker questions him with pilsner-influenced irritation, "Well, what are *your* thoughts on aliens?"

He replied, "The only thing that matters to me is: *would you love them?*"

Solidarity with the Persecuted

While I have been poking at the Old Testament's portrayal of God, I want to be very clear about the Jewish religion.

It is an incredibly beautiful religion, culture, and way of living life. While many modern Jews have become more secular and in some ways less connected to the theological aspects of their ancient faith, I can't help but reference a core element of Judaism that I deeply admire and appreciate.

The history of the Jews is long and carries its share of tragedies.

The ancient Israelites chronicled their conflicts with other warring tribes in stories and poems that became the Hebrew Bible. It was the time of kings and conflicts. While there is some disagreement among scholars about whether the Jews were actually enslaved by the ancient Egyptians[16] there is plenty of archaeological evidence that they were defeated by the ancient Babylonians[17] and displaced from their homeland in terror.

And there is no denying their hardships from the time of the Roman Empire to the present day. While the Babylonians sacked the Temple of Jerusalem the first time, the Roman army burnt the rebuilt temple to the ground a few centuries later. During medieval times, they were the victims of brutal anti-Semitism largely from Christian communities, and sadly such harshness was typically justified by (false reads of) Christian scripture. The Jewish people have been expelled from countless countries throughout the past three millennia.[18]

Then of course you have one of the most brutal ethnocidal attempts in all of human history a mere eight decades ago in Europe: the Holocaust and World War II, with Hitler and the Nazis being responsible for the death of over six million Jews[19] and over five million other marginalized groups—the Jews are the primary victims of the 20th century's embodiment of evil.

Because of all this suffering, we must approach Jewish culture with the awareness that as a people, they are carrying severe generational trauma. (That's how we live in brotherhood—through understanding and empathy.) But also, that with this legendary, infamous trauma comes an undeniable resilience and a timeless courage.

Despite their smaller numbers worldwide in comparison to other faith traditions, Jewish men and women are some of society's greatest innovators: from science to literature to industry. "As of 2017, Nobel Prizes have been awarded to 902 individuals, of whom 203 or 22.5% were Jews, although the total Jewish population comprises less than 0.2% of the world's population. This means the percentage of Jewish Nobel laureates is at least 112.5 times or 11,250% above average."[20] This capacity not just to withstand, but to overcome hardship, has become permanently etched into their identity. And it helps them to create solidarity with other persecuted groups—like the blistering activism of Jewish Voice for Peace, If Not Now? and other young Jewish activist organizations making new progress in advocating for the rights of the Palestinian people.[21]

This isn't a political book but Senator Bernard Sanders from the state of Vermont in the USA, is one of my highest heroes. He has been fighting for the rights of working people since the early 1960s.

While most people are familiar with Bernie thanks to his endless criticisms of "the 1%" in defense of the working people of this country, Bernie's story begins as a student community organizer at the University of Chicago, protesting racial discrimination. Unlike in the South, segregation was illegal in

Chicago by that time, but landlords were still operating in racist ways under the table. Bernie's student group discovered that when a black couple would walk in to apply for housing, they would be told that there were no available units. However when a white couple would walk in, they would be shown residences. There were also challenges within the school system. Racist bureaucrats in the City of Chicago and the board of education were placing black schoolchildren in raggedy, infested, sweltering-hot trailers while classrooms of white kids had hundreds of vacancies. It was a grave injustice. In August 1963, days before the school year began, the City of Chicago planned to install more trailers, but as journalist Shaun King writes, "a brave interracial group of local activists and organizers decided to put their bodies on the line to block the installation of those trailers. They stood in front of bulldozers. They chained themselves together."[22] A 22-year-old Bernie Sanders was arrested while chained to a black female fellow activist in protest of those injustices.

Sanders has been a consistent advocate for the have-nots in society, and he has often credited his culturally Jewish background as the backbone of his backbone. As a kid growing up in Brooklyn, Bernie saw elderly Jews with concentration camp tattoos. They survived one of history's greatest traumas. And their faith, their humanity, and their resilience in mid-century Brooklyn influenced what would become one of the most prominent and enduring populists in American history.

Befriending a Nazi

My grandfather, Tommy Rochelle, served in WWII. Like most able-bodied young men of his generation, he went overseas to fight Hitler's fascist threat to the world.

In the 1930s and 40s, Grandpa Tommy worked in the radio business as a DJ, so his army commanders put him in the communications department. He wasn't quite an action hero, but he was near the front lines helping to receive messages from the officers to the infantry units.

One night alone on the German front, he walked out of his comms tent and looked up directly into the bright, fearful eyes of a Nazi soldier.

They were both shocked.

Both full of fear seeing the enemy face-to-face.

The Nazi soldier could hardly speak English, and my grandfather knew little German. As each man realized it was just the two of them, the situation began to cool down. It was cold out, and Tommy could tell that the man had been outdoors for some time.

What else could he do?

He simply invited the German into his tent for a warm cup of coffee and a smoke. It was getting late. There were several empty bunks in the tent and my grandfather offered him a place to lay his head.

The next morning, Grandpa Tommy called his company commander, proudly exclaiming, "I have captured a Nazi, sir!" the German man sleeping peacefully nearby. The commander asked, "How many, Pvt. Rochelle?"

"One."

"One?"

Clearly it was not a strategic victory for the Allied Forces.

After a few days of rest and warm meals, the German parted ways with the handful of American radio engineers on the front. Before leaving, they traded a few things as tokens of their brief friendship. All these decades later, my mother still has the knife that the Nazi gave to my grandfather, as physical proof of her late beloved father's favorite late night drinking story in his older years.

So while yes, a murder weapon with a swastika is one of my most cherished family heirlooms, it's not because of fascism, racism, and evil. It's special in our home because it represents brotherhood and the ability to transcend violence for the sake of our common humanity.

That night, they weren't an American soldier vs. a German soldier, they were two human beings, placed in a difficult situation, coming from a place of empathy and understanding. It's a simple story but it's very dear to me. I include it in this book to honor my grandfather's profound sense of kindness, and for the reminder that if you can befriend a Nazi, you can befriend anyone.

CHAPTER 12

Jesus Despised Greed

St. Francis and the Wealthy Church Service

As most of the Western world knows, Jesus was born in a manger. Around barn animals. Trying to picture it, it had to be pretty dirty in there. Mary and Joseph just rush in and find a comfortable spot on what was essentially the equivalent of a cow's feeding trough.

You know… the Lord?

The person who Christians don't even like referring to as a man—to most of the Western world he is the literal Son of God.

The Prince of King God was born on top of where animals eat.

As I understand it, everything on the level of form is symbolic, meaning that every detail (especially) of Jesus's life was symbolic of higher truths. In this case, there is a startling lack of emphasis on materialism. A startling lack of emphasis on wealth and our perceived notions of societal stature.

The great Saint Francis of Assisi embodied Jesus's teachings of non-attachment to wealth. Emphasizing humility, he was so unconcerned with material gain that his monastic order was and is almost entirely associated around the vow of poverty.

In St. Francis' 13th century Italy, these sentiments had already been forgotten by Christian communities.

Toward the end of 1223 on a journey to Rome, St. Francis

visited wealthy churches covered in gold-plated everything, with pews full of immaculately-dressed, pompous Italian aristocrats. He got so disgusted by the extravagance that upon his returning journey home, he came up with a new idea. In a cave near the town of Greccio, Francis set up a manger filled with straw. He brought in local barn animals while his Franciscan brothers alerted the nearby townspeople to this most unusual celebration of Christmas. Francis remarked, "once in my life I want to celebrate the coming of the Son of God upon earth in a fitting way, and see with my own eyes how poor and miserable the One who was born for love of us chose to be!"[23] As the brothers stood with lighted candles, Francis got up and preached to the crowds about Jesus's non-attachment to material wealth and his overwhelming embrace of the poor. Over the course of his passionate sermon, all were left in deeply contemplative reflection.

This story tells me two things:

To not fall into the trap of "prosperity theology", a type of contemporary Christianity (adequately conned by televangelists) that encourages incorporating spirituality with material gain and abundance. There are some complete cons among them and some admirable teachers as well, but when you look at the overwhelming number of verses where Jesus condemns, not the acquisition of, but the worship of material wealth, it's hard to reconcile.

Francis' story also tells me that society quickly loses touch with these original sparks of Divine Love, but as centuries come and go, we are reignited by a wide range of teachers and mystics.

"My Son Won't Be Catholic"

There are so many parallels between Hinduism and true Christianity, and by true Christianity I mean those true teachings of Jesus often overlooked by modern Christians. As we've discussed earlier, Krishna sounds pretty similar to Christ in many ways! But if there's one thing they have absolute alignment on, it is service to others. Service to the least fortunate. Not all Christians and not all of Christianity emphasizes this, but it is the true teaching of Jesus: that we are inherently Love and that Service is Love in action.

It needs to be said that there are incredibly pure-hearted Christians. This book title has probably made some Christians mad, so maybe angry Christians aren't still here; but if any of them still are, know that I see you and I honor your sincerity.

I've been going to a local soup kitchen at a church a couple Saturday mornings a month. We serve nearly three hundred working class poor, or as Amma says "underprivileged"... a term with a bit more dignity. Volunteers begin cooking the meals around 7AM, for serving at 9. Before the doors are opened, the main outreach director explains the process (the same way every week because of the new volunteers), and his outreach would always end with this very important fact:

> *"Just as we are feeding their bellies, we are feeding their souls too. Be sure to look them in the eye and smile from your heart. While much of the world out there is telling them that they don't have value, let our kindness remind them that we do value them, and that their Creator cares for them very much."*

It is unbelievably powerful. I so enjoy doing this work... it's not work. It's a blast of energy. You smile and they smile back. I make small talk and make them feel human again, just for a moment. You leave feeling so incredible. And this all happens in a church. A Bibles in the benches, stained glass, flyers on the walls about church-y things, Methodist church.

I had been going for over a year or so by the time my wife became pregnant with our first child, my son Bobby.

My in-laws are devout Mexican-American Catholics, and despite some initial difficulty—I was a hippie-haired Kriya Yoga filmmaker then—things have long been smoothed over with an overwhelming amount of acceptance and love. My mother-in-law and I have connected about spiritual topics and authors for many years, and these days I have a wonderful relationship with my father-in-law because he's such a sweet man. He is thankful that I love his daughter, and we have shared hobbies: tequila and cigars.

They had just gone to Italy for the first time. We were out back with our drinks, puffing away (not great for pranayama I know) as he relayed his reflections on the trip.

It was beautiful, he said. Stunning in many ways. Loved the people, the food, the espresso. But the one thing that he found so particularly bizarre, was the opulence!

He said most of those old churches had a lot of gold, and they seemed to exhibit that same ostentatious indifference held in contempt by St. Francis at the Christmas service nine centuries ago. It is the heart of his religion, literally, as the Vatican is the spiritual & economic capital of the Catholic Church. And while there was extraordinary beauty thanks to the Renaissance masters, there was also uneasiness. He especially laughed about the fact that many of the 16th and 17th century patrons would have their painter depict them into the Bible scenes. Imagine these awkward creations of 2000-year-ago working-class Palestinian Jews next to 400-year-ago wealthy Italian Christians. It was a hilariously egoistic intention they had, to be thought of in that way. So holy, yet so neglectful.

It was extremely refreshing to hear Mr. Gonzalez say that about his own faith.

It was witnessing a man that I love reach an extended plateau of awareness. Not that I'm so high and mighty, trust me, but it was a beautiful realization he had.

Not only did I agree with him, after he said that, it gave me the confidence to share with him that his grandson "won't be Catholic". For a very religious grandpa, this could have been a tough thing to hear. But we were occupying a very real space—the exploration that institutional religion has a fixation on the outer instead of the inner.

And I essentially said, "Look, we love Jesus. But my son won't be Catholic." He knows me enough already to where it wasn't that much of a shock to him.

He said, "I know, or I assumed so… but I just want to get him baptized."

We won't be going to Mass on Sunday mornings and Wednesday nights but a dip in a bath one time for his allegedly eternal salvation, I'm good with that.

Worship One: God or Mammon

If it wasn't clear enough already, Jesus really despised greed.

He said zero words about original sin.

He said hundreds of words about the futility of money. Eleven of his forty parables are about money: Jesus talks about it more than any other teaching.[24]

But instead of living the truth of those teachings, many modern American preachers are flying around in private jets. Wearing luxury apparel. Building faith-domes of worship. Is it really that surprising that American church membership has dropped below 50% for the 'first time in Gallup's eight-decade trend'?[25]

My daily bread is in digital advertising, and "Q4" is our biggest time of the year. It's the 'fourth quarter' of the year, October-November-December, and advertisers the world over plan for it obsessively. Like no other time. Why? Because December is Christmas—the "Mass of Christ", the birth festival of Jesus of Nazareth. The birthday of the most anti-greed human being in history is the precise reason for the biggest explosion of consumerism and materialism every year. The paradoxes on this plane of existence never end but this is one of the most profound.

> *"No one can serve two masters. Either he will hate the one and love the other, or he will be loved to the one and despise the other.*
>
> *You cannot serve both God and money (mammon)."*
>
> *—Jesus, Gospel of Matthew 6:24*
>
> *"Do not be afraid, little flock, for your Father has been pleased to give you the kingdom.*
>
> *Sell your possessions and give to the poor.*

> *Provide purses for yourselves that will not wear out,*
>
> *a treasure in heaven that will not be exhausted,*
>
> *where no thief comes near, and no moth destroys.*
>
> *For where your treasure is, there your heart will be also."*
>
> —*Jesus, Gospel of Luke 12:32-34*

And Christ's most explicit hyperbole:

> *"Children, how hard it is to enter the kingdom of God!*
>
> *It is easier for a camel to go through the eye of a needle,*
>
> *than for a rich man to enter the kingdom of God."*
>
> —*Jesus, Gospel of Mark 10:24-25*

That 'eye of a needle' line has Gucci-wearing pastors sweating. They do an amazing job of reading around that one, despite how explicit it is. Not that the kingdom is a place, but a state of awareness of the Self, of Union, of Unconditional Love. How can a person rest in that state if they're busy worrying about metal discs, rectangular cuts of paper, and intangible zeroes underneath the computer files in a bank's data servers? AKA money.

The issue for Jesus, and for many of us, is that *greed* is inherently selfish. Money itself is not evil, it's neutral. Save some money, spend some money. Goods and services are created and paid for with money. That's fine. But it becomes blinding when the emotional attachment and desire for money matters more than anything else. We shouldn't cling so tightly.[26] That's literally idolatry. Jesus understood and taught as the great many masters did—that a fixation on material accumulation can rob others, which ultimately robs ourselves.

Of course, this view of money and the material world is not exclusive to Jesus.

> *"Be content with what you have;*
>
> *rejoice in the way things are.*
>
> *When you realize there is nothing lacking,*

the whole world belongs to you."

—Laozi, Tao Te Ching

"Little children play with dolls in the outer room just as they like, without any care of fear or restraint;

but as soon as their mother comes in, they throw aside their dolls and run to her crying, "Mamma, mamma."

You too, are now playing in this material world, infatuated with the dolls of wealth, honor, fame...

If however, you once see your Divine Mother, you will not afterwards find pleasure in all these.

Throwing them all aside, you will run to her."

—Ramakrishna

"A kind man who makes good use of wealth is rightly said to possess a great treasure; but the miser who hoards up his riches will have no profit. ...I have severed all ties because I seek deliverance. How is it possible for me to return to the world?

He who seeks religious truth, which is the highest treasure of all, must leave behind all that can concern him or draw away his attention, and must be bent upon that one goal alone. He must free his soul from covetousness and lust, and also from the desire for power."

—Buddha

"Only when the last tree has died,

and the last river has been poisoned,

and the last fish has been caught,

will we realize that we cannot eat money."

—Cree Native American Proverb

Questioning materialism is a foundational principle within spirituality: from the Hindu sadhus who live without possessions, to Buddhist monks begging daily for food and alms, to the indigenous tribal wisdom across the globe. Unlike within our capitalistic society where bottom-line revenue drives the engines of industries, of economies, and of our modern psychologies, the mystics have a reverence for other things. Nature. Service. Community. The Great Mystery.

Try to picture white (Christian) Europeans landing in America, communicating with the Native Americans. My ancestors asked the native chiefs, "Who owns this land?" The term "ownership" didn't translate. Looking out at the expanse of endless green and blue horizons, the sound of the birds, the smell of the breeze, abject harmony of creation—how could a mere person presume to preside over such majesty? We know how the story ended but we must cherish the values of the wisdom traditions in not just resisting, but transcending, our deathly thirst for ownership of all things material.

Closing out with Jesus against greed, this is one of my favorites:

> *"If you have money, do not lend it out at interest. Rather, give it to one from whom you will not get it back."*
>
> *—Jesus, Gospel of Thomas, Saying 95*

This is radical. Not in temperament, but in teaching.

Can you imagine a world without interest?

I pay my bank every month just to have an account open, let alone 3% on this loan, and 6% on that one. The entire financial industry not only survives, but thrives on interest payments! You seen how comfy the couches are inside of a Chase?

The view of the world is to give with the thought that we should be repaid with interest. 'I helped you when your family was starving, so now that you are well, come manicure my yard for me.' What Jesus tells us is the opposite: help those who cannot possibly give you anything material in return. Why? Because what mystical, spiritual philosophy reiterates throughout the traditions is that material just isn't that valuable after all. This is the understanding developed from living in a state of Christ Consciousness. Of Transcendence. Of Uniting.

In a comical moment from both *Thomas* (Saying 72) and *Luke* (12:13-14)—which again demonstrates how much of *Thomas* is in the canonical gospels—a man asks Jesus to tell the man's brother "to divide the inheritance with me."

Jesus replies, *"O man, who made me a divider?"*

He turned to his disciples.

He said to them, *"I am not a divider, am I?"*

CHAPTER 13

Self-Love is Not Ego

The Chakras in Brief

The chakras are fascinating and largely misunderstood. I had personally explained them incorrectly for several years. Apologies to anyone I talked to about them from 2011–2015, I got it now.

Chakra, meaning "wheel" in Sanskrit, represents a series of centers of energy (*prana*) in the body. While they are in the body, they're not physical centers. They could be considered "astral", "etheric", or a part of what is often referred to as our "subtle body".[27] They are on another (non-gross matter) plane of existence. I could see why "dimension" would be a term that bothers the more scientifically-minded, but I'm comfortable saying they exist on another dimension. It just means they exist but an x-ray isn't going to pick them up. Our technology isn't quite there yet... but someday it could be... scientists from the early Enlightenment era would have their minds explode looking into an electron microscope would they not? Two hundred years ago we did not have adequate equipment to detect radio waves, let alone the quantum fields at the subatomic level. Our capacity to understand phenomena is not fixed, it is constantly progressing toward a fuller truth.

The concept behind the chakras is ancient—the first mention appears in the *Rig Veda* of Hinduism, dating back to approximately 1500 BCE—some of the oldest writing in our civilization. Similar versions of the chakras are incorporated in Buddhism, Jainism, New Age systems, ancient Egyptians, ancient Greeks and even

Native Americans.[28] The Hindus hold that there are seven, and the Buddhists four, others eight, and some nine, but there is a consensus that these subtle centers of energy do exist. Although sources vary on the exact number of chakras found in the spiritual body, the following descriptions account for those about which most writers & teachers agree.

The chakras go up and down the spine, from the bottom up to just above the crown of the head. What's most fascinating to me, however, is that they each represent a step forward in evolving consciousness.[29] They are both landmarks for new discovery and placeholders where we can become "stuck". Continued spiritual practice (like yoga & meditation), study, service, contemplation, and ultimately Love (seeing the One in All) are what help us move up to the next center.

The First Chakra (*Muladhara* / Root) is at the base of the spine. It represents the most primordial aspect of a human being: our separateness; our survivalist nature. The first chakra is an ancient jungle where we kill or be killed. The first chakra is all about number one.

The Second Chakra (*Svadhisthana* / Sacral) is right above the genitals. It's the sex chakra, plain and simple. When you succeed in the first chakra, you move to the second one. The best way to explain this is that the first chakra is survival. You've already accumulated food and shelter. Now that you have excelled at survival you can enjoy the sensuality of procreation. If the first chakra is a jungle, the second chakra is Las Vegas.[30] (I have to give Ram Dass credit for that one.)

The Third Chakra (*Manipura* / Solar Plexus) is in the abdomen. It represents health of the body (located near food and our digestive system), but it also represents power and status. It is your place in society. It's related to the bottom two, because some people use the prestige from the third to go back down and be successful in the second with sex or the first with survival, but it's even beyond those two. It's big business with a board of executives. It's a power grab. It worships at the altar of the ego.

It is important to understand that these three chakras contain the majority of the human population. These three are ruled by the ego. There is a massive (and difficult) leap from the third to the fourth. The leap ultimately comes out of seeing through the futility of the bottom three. A willingness to get to the Real. In the old Hindu depictions there is typically a white light coming down on the top four, and a gray line laterally across three and four, the bright light not reaching the lower chakras. They are all that is carnal, and the fourth is the jump into the divine.

The Fourth Chakra (*Anahata* / Heart) is the chakra of compassion. Located in the heart, it's the first instance of experiencing the brotherhood of all of humanity. It's truly coming into your heart and feeling the joys and the pains of all beings. The formerly distinct boundaries of separateness from the first chakra have now become blurry lines, nebulous energy pervading through people more loosely. The fourth chakra is the true Christian woman at the soup kitchen cooking meals for the homeless for years because to her they're not strangers, they're her extended family. If she's a mystic, they are other faces of Christ himself. It is beginning to change the understanding of self in a traditional sense, moving from "us and them" to just "us".

I've only gotten a few fleeting glimpses of the fourth, and they have been extremely profound, and really they are a major reason why I bother writing and making conscious media: when you find real Love all you want to do is share it. The fifth, sixth, and seventh are much higher than my own experience but I can paraphrase from how I understand them to be conceptually.

The Fifth Chakra (*Vishuddhi* / Throat) is the chakra of communication, as it's located in your throat region. You make even more significant leaps in losing your own sense of self. Yogananda writes,

> *"Beyond the limits of the mortal frame,*
>
> *To farthest boundary of Eternity—*
>
> *Where I, the Cosmic Sea,*
>
> *Watch the little ego floating in Me."* [31]

Because of this erosion, you become a clearer vessel for

communicating higher information. This also applies to creativity and expressing truths that you learned in the fourth chakra, from feeling the essence of compassion flowing through you. You transcend technique, you become pure creative communication. Michelangelo saying he was just removing the stone around David is the fifth chakra.

The Sixth Chakra (*Ajna* / Third Eye) is the chakra of divine sight, located on the forehead in between the eyebrows. Words start to become inadequate at explaining this one: the closer you get to going beyond form, the less form (in this case words) can frame the concept. There is apparently a sense of understanding so full about the universe, that you can perfectly see the explanation behind any action. You see the cause behind each effect (the law of karma), along with a heightened sense of peace. This is the stereotypical master at the top of the Himalayas, All-Seeing, All-Knowing but still has an outburst every few years because he's not quite at the seventh. He's still in a body but there's an extremely thin line between his physical form and "The All That Is". Ruffling some scientific materialists' feathers here—there are photoreceptor cells in the pineal gland.[32] The pineal is exactly where the location of the 'third eye' corresponds to in the body. Granted, those photoreceptor neurons are "nonvisual", and they're adapted from our bodies' ancient reptilian ancestry, but it feels Vedic-ly irresponsible to not point out this undeniable connection here.

The Seventh Chakra (*Sahasrara* / Crown or "Thousand-Petaled Lotus") is the chakra hovering just slightly above your head. When your consciousness makes it up to the seventh, you merge into the One. It's Pure Awareness (*mahasamadhi*)—no subject, no object. It's "no longer a channel of reception but of radiation."[33] It's pointless to try to conceptualize it, really. You're not in a body much longer. Your chains are broken, you have liberated the cycle of birth and death and (re-)enter into Ever-New Cosmic Joy.

It's also worth mentioning that the chakras are connected by the *Sushumna*, or "central channel", or also the "Divine Road", that goes up and down the spine. This is the pathway that the energy (*prana*) travels, and with prolonged periods of meditation and yoga practice, the movement of energy on this channel is supposedly physically tangible.

The practice of *Kundalini yoga* is solely focused on using deep meditative breathing (*pranayama*) and a series of postures (*asanas*) to move energy from the first chakra at the base up to the seventh at the crown.[34] This process is considered a 'Kundalini awakening' or a 'Kundalini experience' which is apparently incredibly powerful and leads to heightened states of awareness and bliss. Prominent writers about the Kundalini experience are Gopi Krishna, Charles Leadbeater of the Theosophists, and Swami Sivananda Saraswati, although there are many more who claim to have had this experience in recent decades.

In *The Evolutionary Energy in Man* (1970), Gopi Krishna writes:

> *"Entirely unprepared for such a development, I was completely taken by surprise; but regaining my self-control, keeping my mind on the point of concentration. The illumination grew brighter and brighter, the roaring louder, I experienced a rocking sensation and then felt myself slipping out of my body, entirely enveloped in a halo of light. It is impossible to describe the experience accurately. I felt the point of consciousness that was myself growing wider surrounded by waves of light. It grew wider and wider, spreading outward while the body, normally the immediate object of its perception, appeared to have receded into the distance until I became entirely unconscious of it. I was now all consciousness without any outline, without any idea of corporeal appendage, without any feeling or sensation coming from the senses, immersed in a sea of light simultaneously conscious and aware at every point, spread out, as it were, in all directions without any barrier or material obstruction. I was no longer myself, or to be more accurate, no longer as I knew myself to be, a small point of awareness confined to a body, but instead was a vast circle of consciousness in which the body was but a point, bathed in light and in a state of exultation and happiness impossible to describe."* [35]

The chakras are not just pretty tattoo designs. They are steps forward in our consciousness—a ladder to a higher, fuller understanding of reality.

Richie Flores, the Ex-Convict Turned Yoga Master

Richie Flores, the ex-convict turned yoga master, had such a compelling story that I continued to follow him around with a camera for the next three years.[36] As his probation was coming to a close, we filmed inside the courtroom along with a few contemplative nature scenes where he reflects on what went wrong and what went right.

According to an April 2011 report by the Pew Center on the States, the average national recidivism rate for released prisoners is 43%. But according to a report by the Bureau of Justice Statistics (BJS), about 68% of 405,000 prisoners released in 2005 were arrested for a new crime within three years of their release from prison, and 77% were arrested within five years.[37] Conquering this extreme trend is an incredible feat. It is a personal accomplishment to celebrate and a beautiful pathway out for others stuck in the darkness of the system.

The main point of the film we made, *Asanas in the Yard,* is to try to understand Richie's transformation: how did he break the cycle?

While Richie certainly got immensely lucky (or karmically intertwined) with Geoff O'Meara and Community Yoga Austin; there was another, deeper component to his success.

Richie concludes the film with the following lines:

> *"There's never a day in my life that I don't look back on the different times that I wanted to change, that I wanted to be somebody else, and how many times I promised myself or my family that I'd do it for this person or I'd do it for that person.*

But what Geoff taught me was to love myself.

And until that happened I couldn't do it."

Love Yourself, with Humility, without Ego

> *"If you want to awaken all of humanity, then awaken all of yourself.*
>
> *If you want to eliminate the suffering in the world, then eliminate all that is dark and negative in yourself.*
>
> *Truly, the greatest gift you have to give is that of your own self-transformation."*
>
> —*Hua Hu Ching*

Love yourself.

Most people are kind to others, or at least neutral, but we beat ourselves up.

Be gentle with yourself. You're doing your best.

We create an absolute hell every minute of every day by constantly criticizing our past actions, being inattentive in the present, and looking idly to the future.

Sink into this present space.

Inhale gratitude.

Exhale forgiveness.

When you start to look at your life, instead of focusing on failures, look at all your successes too. Examine your greatest failure, and then look at what you did afterwards. Look at what you learned from your mistakes.

This doesn't mean to pretend everything is amazing and perfect all the time, either. That's called "spiritual bypassing"[38] which is an unfortunate development from New Age spirituality's focus on love & light. Focusing on love and light is good! But it doesn't mean we push away traumas or cover them up in a forced happiness. On one end is spiritual bypassing, on another end is excessive trauma-fixation—which we see across our culture in a kind of romanticizing of sadness, disappointment, and despair. I don't think either end of that spectrum is the way to live. The aim of true spirituality is to shine the light of love deeply within, underneath the crevices of our minds and our emotions in order to fully understand and release our issues in a healthy way.

We are all growing. Life isn't a ladder, it's a spiral. When you're here in this moment you can start to see that you are deserving of love. It's a profound realization worth sitting with. And in that love you start to accept other, formerly unlovable parts of yourself in a new, sincere way.

> *"I have been meditating, doing yoga, chanting, doing strict devotional practices, studied under a Hindu guru, Buddhist meditation teachers, all of this for the past twenty-five years, and I haven't gotten rid of a single neurosis. What has happened though, is where they used to be these overwhelming, massive monsters... now they're like little goblins. 'Oh hi there Anger, how are you doing? Oh hey Sexual Perversion, been awhile since I've seen you!"*
>
> *—Ram Dass*

Laughing at our own mental tendencies is a brilliant antidote. This is humility, AKA ego dissolution! That laughter can come from a place of real love.

> *"He who laughs at himself never runs out of things to laugh at."*
>
> *—Epictetus*

As we continue along the path, we start to have sincere self-love deep down underneath the seeming surface of our place in the world. We become more and more detached from our personality-identity, yet we are firmly rooted in the Self. This grounding into the Self can help us eliminate the need for external validation.

When a person feels inadequate, they're always seeking approval outside themselves, and consequently people disapprove. It creates the antithetical outcome to the original intention.

> *"Half of life is lost in charming others. The other half is lost in going through anxieties caused by others.*
>
> *Leave this play, you have played enough."*
>
> —*Rumi*

Whereas when you're detached from the perception of others, that's usually considered a highly positive trait! Not in an ego-maverick way but in a confident way. We're still compassionate, empathetic, but we're less outwardly needy, bothersome. And as you become more detached from the separate ego-identity, your heart opens, generating even more compassion for yourself and others. It becomes a self-assured, or (capital S) Self-assured, way to live our lives.

There are misconceptions around detachment in the West—that it's selfish, apathetic and generally an undesirable trait. But it's the combination of self-love and detachment of our own separate identity that generates a real force for good, in ourselves, and those around us. There's a term called "engaged detachment", which gets across the paradox.

Vivekananda explains:

> *"With everything we do in life we identify ourselves. Here is a man who says harsh words to me. I feel anger coming on me. In a few seconds anger and I are one, and then comes misery. Attach yourselves to the Lord and to nothing else, because everything else is unreal. Attachment to the unreal will bring misery. There is only one Existence that is real, only one Life in which there is neither object nor [subject]. ...*
>
> *But unattached love will not hurt you. Do anything — marry, have children. ... Do anything you like — nothing will hurt you. Do nothing with the idea of "mine". Duty for duty's sake; work for work's sake. What is that to you? You stand aside.*

> *When we come to that non-attachment, then we can understand the marvelous mystery of the universe; how it is intense activity and vibration, and at the same time intense peace and calm; how it is work every moment and rest every moment. That is the mystery of the universe — the impersonal and personal in one, the infinite and finite in one. Then we shall find the secret. He who finds in the midst of intense activity the greatest rest, and in the midst of the greatest rest intense activity, he has become a Yogi."* [39]

Self-love is not ego, it's humility.

Non-attachment is not apathy, it's freedom!

CHAPTER 14

Maharajji

"Meditate like Christ."

In addition to the Avatars, there are occasionally highly-advanced human beings who become fully realized (*jivanmukta*). And if they meet a series of criteria, I trust them. I don't put all of my certainty in their claims, but I see where my experiences line up with what they're getting across and if they teach what Truth I understand in my heart (our Inherent Unity), I listen.

Neem Karoli Baba was one such beautiful Hindu saint in the 20th century.

There are many miracle stories about him, but miracles are surface-level. They're not the real miracle. The *real miracle* is living in a state of Love and Oneness, whereas "miracles stories" are showy. They're just designed to give you a double-take in regards to reality and perception.

Neem Karoli Baba, known affectionately as Maharajji, didn't have a "teaching". He didn't give long lectures or write philosophical books. He lived in love, emphasizing truth and service to others.

Many famous Westerners studied under him, the most influential being former Harvard psychology professor Dr. Richard Alpert who took the name Ram Dass (meaning servant of God), as well as Dr. Larry Brilliant, Dr. Daniel Goleman, Lama Surya Das, Bhagavan Das, Krishna Das, and many others. Ram Dass's book *Be Here Now* (1971) was, and is, a stunning, spectacular introduction to the essence of this legendary guru.

> *"Of course Maharajji loved everybody, that's what saints do. But what was so profound was that when I was sitting by Maharajji, I loved everybody."*[40]
>
> *—Dr. Larry Brilliant, epidemiologist with WHO, former executive at Google*

This is the goal! To radiate love so strongly that it must go outward, making it contagious to all who come into your presence.

> *"What struck me was how utterly at peace and how kind Maharajji was. He took an equal interest in everyone who came – and they ranged from the highest-ranking government officials to beggars. There was something about his ineffable state of mind that I had never sensed in anyone before meeting Maharajji. No matter what he was doing, he seemed to remain effortlessly in a blissful, loving space, perpetually at ease. Whatever state Maharajji was in seemed not to be some temporary oasis in the mind, but a lasting way of being: a trait of utter wellness."*[41]
>
> *—Dr. Daniel Goleman, psychologist, author of Emotional Intelligence*

Maharajji also shared my admiration for that radically-loving teacher from Galilee.

One day his American disciples asked him how to meditate. His unexpected response was,

> *"Meditate like Christ."*

The devotees were quite surprised to hear this. They had traveled across the oceans, away from Western culture, miles up in the Himalayas at a secluded ashram listening to a guru who was a devotee of Hanuman, the monkey god of ancient India.

The last thing they expected was to hear anything about Jesus.

They asked further, "How did Christ meditate, Maharajji?" He replied:

> *"He lost himself in love…*

He was one with all beings and he had great love for all in the world. He was crucified so that his spirit could spread throughout the world. He was one with God. He sacrificed his body for the dharma. He never died. He is atman living in the hearts of all.

See all beings as the reflection of Christ." [42]

"Spleen."

One word, "spleen", changed the lives of tens of millions of people. It's hard to quantify how many people's lives will never be the same because one man said one word to one other man.

Dr. Richard Alpert had just been fired from Harvard University.

Before he was fired, Dr. Alpert had been an influential professor of psychology, teaching Freudian analysis, submitting interesting research proposals, and achieving worldly fame among the intelligentsia—a combination of accolades only reserved to select members of our society.[43]

He had a private jet, he hosted dinner parties, and he was brutally unhappy.

Until one day another professor moved into the wing of his building, Dr. Timothy Leary. Dr. Leary was intelligent, but also joyful. He had a lightness to him that was extremely appealing to people like Dr. Alpert. When Dr. Leary returned from one of his travels south of the border, he suggested that Dr. Alpert join him on an excursion to Mexico to enjoy the sights, and to experiment with a psychedelic substance, called psilocybin, that grows there naturally.

Richard was a scientist in a field about our thinking mind. He was interested in understanding other states of consciousness. He agreed and while his "trip" didn't occur on that trip, it certainly did happen soon thereafter back in New England. The "magic mushrooms" he tried with Tim forever altered his understanding of self. He had a "shamanic death", watching each layer of his outward personas rise and dissipate. He would see 'Richard the son' arise and melt away; then 'Richard the scientist', then 'Richard the professor', then lastly, he thought: *"I can always get a new social identity. At least I have my own body… But I spoke too soon."* [44] He witnessed the progressive disappearance of limbs and torso, erasing everything except the "I"—independent of his social and physical identity. Initially this experience was beyond horrifying, until eventually he settled into an awareness and recognition of this Observer perspective as the Sole Reality, creating a profound calmness beyond any prior experience or understanding.

Dr. Leary and Dr. Alpert started to research these psychotropic chemicals in an academic setting. This was the early 60s, before *Sgt. Pepper,* before much of the counterculture, and before any real taboos around these drugs existed in American culture. While Leary was an undeniable trailblazer, both Leary & Alpert were influenced by the renowned British author Aldous Huxley's psychedelic guidebook *Doors of Perception*; the same author of the science fiction commentary *Brave New World* and universalism textbook *The Perennial Philosophy*—Huxley's influence on 20th century thought is truly boundless. The newly starry-eyed pair designed scientific experiments, including the "Good Friday Experiment", and co-wrote *The Psychedelic Experience,* all of which culminated in the both of them getting tossed out of Harvard, one of the most prestigious centers of education in the globe.[45]

Now what?

Richard Alpert had been faced with a crippling sense of dissatisfaction. He had embarked on a new journey of the mind, which took him to new heights of awareness, but that ultimately led him to being unemployed. Defrocked. Publicly shamed as a bad influence on American society.

After his firing, he parted with Tim, and began to travel the world.

He wanted to see if anyone, anywhere, knew more about the states of mind that these chemicals were allowing him to explore. He took some of them with him, offering them to various holy men and saints in an attempt to know more, to know anything about the layers of self, and the Awareness of What Is.

After months of searching, from North Africa through the Middle East to all over India, he was sitting in an Indian cafe, frustrated.

> *"And it got frighteningly clear that there might be a possibility that we knew as much as anybody knew that was alive. And we didn't know. And that was a very unpleasant feeling to have. Because that made it all... a little too irresponsible whoever was planning it!"* [46]

Nobody really knew, and Richard was giving up.

He knew a friend in Japan that would be a good way to get back to the States, and his final journey home.

Sitting with a few other hippies in a Katmandu cafe called The Blue Tibetan, he looked up and saw a very tall, bearded, blonde American man walk into the cafe.[47] He was younger, with a surfer-look, but very hairy, wearing a traditional dhoti and beads, and he had clearly been in India for some time. His name was Bhagavan Das. Richard later described him as being "someone who knew." They hung out for a few days and Richard decided to follow this young American devotee across India... meeting various sages and monastics across traditions. From Tibetan Buddhists to Hindu Vaishnavas, to practically every spiritual community along the way, Bhagavan Das was greeted with much enthusiasm.

Richard became more exhausted and wanted to explain his woes to the young man, who was generally unempathetic. Richard would start explaining some neurotic detail and Bhagavan Das would respond:

> *"Don't worry about the past. Just be here now."*
>
> *"Don't worry about the future. Just be here now."* [48]

After several weeks of this traveling, it came up that Bhagavan Das needed to see his guru. They had access to a Land Rover, and Richard agreed to go with him, despite never hearing about a "guru" in the time they'd been together.

The January before, Richard's mother had passed away. She

had spleen cancer, which took her quickly, enlarging her stomach. One night in the middle of absolutely nowhere, Richard walked outside and under a beautiful blanket of stars, thought of his late beloved mother. "What am I doing?", he thought. Following this strange white Hindu boy around the jungle… 'if only you could see me now.'

The next day, the two finally made it to their destination. Bhagavan Das stopped the car, and excitedly ran up to see "Maharajji". Richard walked behind him, more anxiously, unsure of the unfolding situation as the two came upon a grassy hill near a temple at the foot of the Himalayas. Bhagavan Das could hardly contain himself as he greeted the man at the center of the group, a grinning bald man with a full frame sitting under a blanket. It was an idyllic scene. The focus soon turned to the defrocked professor.

> *"What kind of car is that?" the guru asked him through a translator.*

Richard explained it was a Land Rover but it wasn't even his.

> *"Are you going to give it to me?"*

The nerve of this guy. Who asks something like that within minutes of meeting? Richard was the only one in the entire group who looked out of place. He had no beads, he had no Indian clothing, just a confused man thousands of miles from home.

The guru asked Richard to come closer.

> *He leaned into him very gently and said, "Last night you were under the stars, thinking of your mother."*

Richard started to become very warm.

His hands started to get sweaty.

Pretty strange coincidence, that this man knew that.

How could he know?

Not even his traveling companion knew that—Bhagavan Das was asleep last night and he didn't tell him.

Then in English, Maharajji articulated:

"Spleen. She died of spleen." [49]

Dr. Alpert later explained that it was like when a computer is computing too much data all at once and it shuts off. His scientific rational mind was asking a thousand questions at once, trying to connect the dots on how this strange mustached man could know that. No one could know this. 'Is this man connected to his alma mater?' The thought "Is a CIA operative going to walk out of the bushes?" even popped up in his head.

Very simply, there's no rational way, from a material point of view, that Neem Karoli Baba could've known that Mrs. Alpert died of spleen cancer. The only explanation is that he was able to access a superconscious state of information, beyond the material.

This was not the only fact that he knew that he shouldn't have known over the course of their friendship, but it was the most impactful moment of sharing such a truth, because it was in their first few minutes together.

Richard was eventually given the name "Ram Dass" by Maharajji, which means "servant of God". He lived in that temple ashram for another seven months. Over the next few years he would go back and forth to the States as a Hindu devotee of Hanuman, becoming a "Johnny Appleseed of Eastern spirituality"[50] throughout the West... a role he played all the way until his death in 2019.

"Don't You See It's All Perfect?"

There are many guru stories of Ram Dass & Maharajji and they're all wonderful. There's even a book called *Miracle of Love: Stories about Neem Karoli Baba* that RD helped compile after Maharajji's death. Some are long tales like their initial meeting, and others are short glimpses into truth for a devotee. One of my favorites goes like this:

Baba was sitting with a disciple and they were both listening to another man reading the newspaper out loud in a dull monotone. The disciple tells us that he couldn't bear to hear this man go on and on endlessly. It was a seemingly pointless story without any regard for his listeners. The disciple could hardly take it anymore, and then suddenly he started to feel "the most incredible love welling up in [his] being, greater and greater love" that was about to burst his heart open.[51] He looked over at Baba who was smiling gently, so full of compassion for both of them. The devotee immediately realized how much farther he had to go in embodying the loving state that Maharajji was constantly expressing to all.

On another occasion, a devotee asked Maharajji, "How do I get enlightened?"

He famously said,

"Feed people." [52]

Neem Karoli Baba wrote zero books. He never gave lectures or taught from scriptures, but he taught through incidents and situations.[53] He was the embodiment of love, helpfulness, and lightness… flipping consciousnesses all over India.

And yet while he was compassionate, he was also aware.

Ram Dass tells a story about the time when there was great suffering in nearby Bangladesh. He was especially distraught and planning on how to get over to the border to help the refugees. His frustration kept bubbling up in the ashram and Maharajji looked at him and said,

"Ram Dass, don't you see it's all perfect?" [54]

RD clarifies by saying that his guru was a dedicated humanitarian. Neem Karoli Baba lived in an earthly body: he wept, he laughed, he fed the hungry, he consoled those in sadness. Maharajji lived a richly vibrant life.

But at the same time, he rested in a place of seeing that perfect, karmic harmony of the way things are—what's also been called the *Tao*, the natural cosmic unfolding of it all.

My wife had a traumatic medical experience as a child. During that time, and years following, she endured such immense pain, both physically and emotionally. But in reflecting on that experience now, it made her stronger, fuller, more aware of herself.

She often reminds me—I get so caught up in evangelizing this material but I can't forget this fact—that everyone is going through their own obstacles in a deeply formative way.

So there's a real balance, in that dance of karma yoga, the path of service. We act out of a place of compassion, without letting that same fiery passion burn us up if we let the suffering overwhelm us. True compassion must include our own peace, as it is only in that state of awareness and compassion that we can share any peace in the first place.

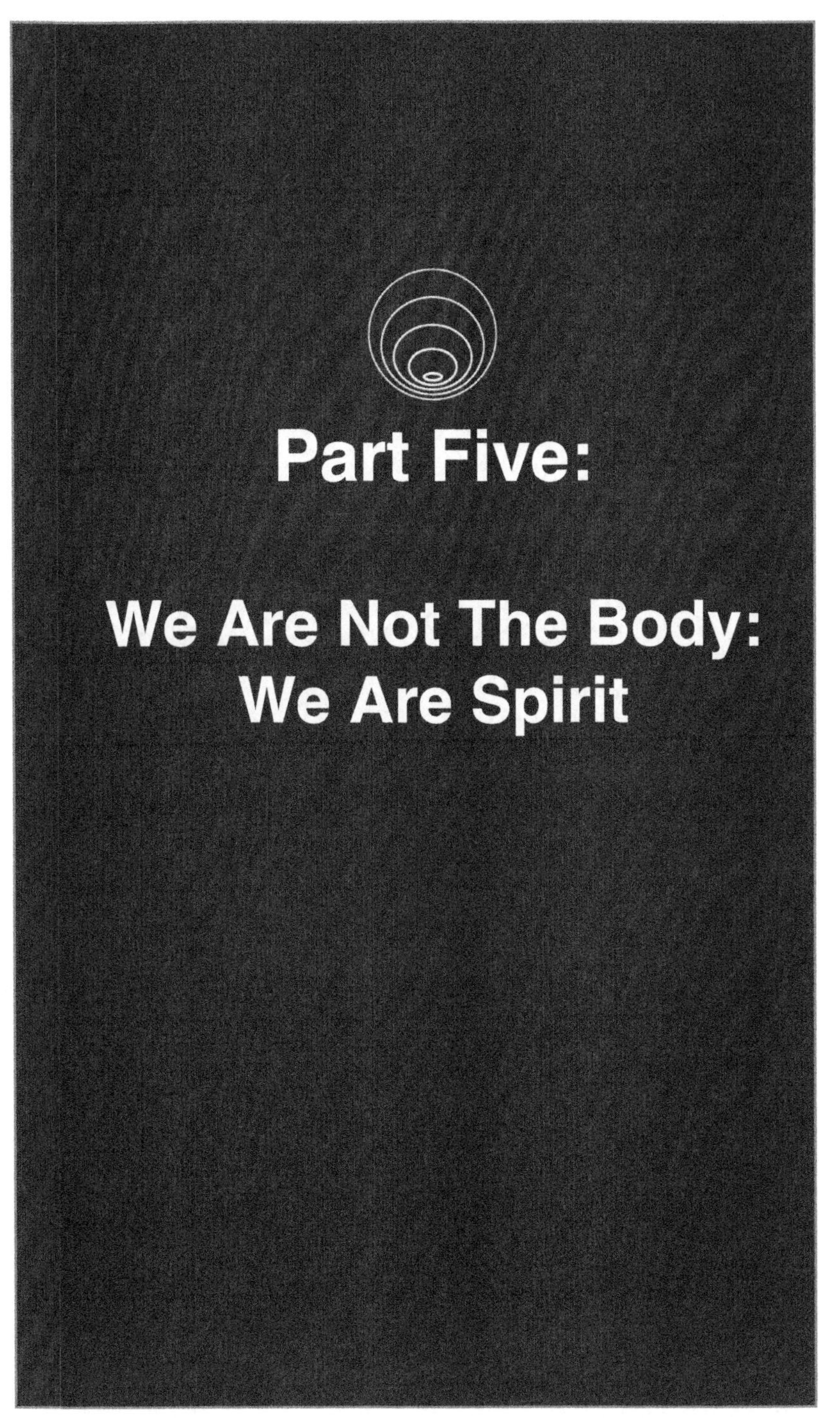

Part Five:

We Are Not The Body: We Are Spirit

Original sin is a lie,

because there are so many layers
to the human experience.

How can we be stamped with
badness when That Which Is, is
always unfolding?
Always growing?
Always expanding?

CHAPTER 15

What Happens To Us Is For Us

The Wheel of Samsara

"The world is a gymnasium, we come here to get strong."

—Swami Vivekananda

We've all heard this idea before: that life is a test. A classroom. According to the mystics, it's true. We are all unraveling through a transitory cosmic carousel of experiences until we once again merge with the Divine. We are in the perfect playground, where the law of cause and effect is an undeniable physical reality.

Our growth or our descent, is entirely up to the everyday choices we make in this universe. We are all entranced in this grand journey, inevitably leading to one common destination:

Heaven,

Enlightenment,

Nirvana,

Moksha,

Satori,

Atonement,

Unity with the One...

Transcendence!

[Nondualism disclaimer: to the nondualist, there is a play on using the term "destination", because **we are already there**; we're just not aware of it yet. But within the dimension of time, it takes us lifetimes of experiences to realize our inherent, inescapable union.]

The famous American Buddhist, Dr. Robert Thurman, father of actress Uma Thurman, quipped in a TED talk:

> *"The Buddhists think that, because we've all had infinite previous lives, we've all been each other's relatives, actually. Therefore all of you, in the Buddhist view, in some previous life, although you don't remember it and neither do I, you have been my mother… for which I do apologize for the trouble I caused you."* [1]

Reincarnation is discussed by the ancient Hindus, the ancient Greeks, the Buddhists, the Jains, and a whole host of mystical sects and thinkers. From Plato's *Republic* to the *Tibetan Book of the Dead*. The atman, the core essence ("soul") of an individual, travels throughout all of its lifetimes. The framework of all of these lifetimes exist within the "wheel", samsara, that keeps spinning until we make the choice to stop it, by waking up. As Huston Smith articulates:

> *"The mystic vision at-one-ment is not a state to be achieved but a condition to be recognized, for God has united his divine essence with our inmost being. Tat tvan asi. That thou art. Atman is Brahman; samsara, Nirvana."* [2]

Yogananda writes that we have all been both rich and poor thousands of times over. Fat, thin. Beautiful, ugly. Famous, unknown.

We identify so strongly with our current bodily state when it's only a temporary consequence of past choices in previous lifetimes…

> *"Unfulfilled desires are the root cause of reincarnation. You don't have to be a king in order to have complete*

> *fulfillment. Nor do you end desires by giving up everything and becoming a poor man. You have your own self-created destiny with its lessons to be learned, and you must play well that part for which you were sent here."* [3]
>
> —*Paramahansa Yogananda*

This body's existence will soon transpire (death), and your soul will once again resume living (rebirth into a new body). And over again. So instead of focusing on external scenarios, bring that attention inward. This metaphor holds up with a wheel analogy: don't get trapped in the perimeter of the wheel (externals), through spiritual practices we can work our way inward, down the spokes, into the center. There's less movement there, we are confronted by less frantic energy than on the outside of the wheel. That stillness is where we can find our peace.

A close yogi friend of mine and I have talked about how reincarnation is what we believe, because it's the only thing that makes sense to us.

To the materialists, look, there's too much importance, purpose, and underlying effects in the cosmic web of life by every living being to have it all evaporate into dust after one measly lifetime. There's more to it all than one and done.

But I'm also (relatively) self-aware, I know that some materialists accuse spiritual thinkers of creating the meaning ourselves. And in a way, they're right. The ego is very good at inflating itself and its own importance.

However for me, there are just too many puzzle pieces that fit perfectly into the explanations brought forth by the *Vedas*, the Gnostics, and the world mystics who themselves have experienced this understanding of our existence beyond the body with such intimacy, such clarity. The accounts of these sages resonate deeply within my heart. Who's to doubt them? And that connection? And now we have extremely reputable scientists talking about consciousness as a fundamental phenomenal layer underneath matter?[4] Come on down the rabbit hole. Read the texts, try these practices. See for yourself.

So if scientific materialism, AKA 'when the body dies you die', ain't it; what about the orthodox religious? The 'single-life straight to afterlife' crowd?

What about babies that die within days or hours of being born? That was their only shot?

I mentioned Dr. Ian Stevenson earlier. He was a methodical researcher of reincarnation in a clinical setting. Stevenson was a researcher at the University of Virginia School of Medicine for over forty years, writing over three hundred papers and fourteen books on the topic.[5]

While both the environment and genetic makeup can account for certain diseases, his initial interest in reincarnation was based on an attempt to explain what those two variables cannot.

> *"Reincarnation, at least as I conceive it, does not nullify what we know about evolution and genetics. It suggests, however, that there may be two streams of evolution—the biological one and a personal one—and that during terrestrial lives these streams may interact."* [6]
>
> *—Dr. Ian Stevenson*

Dr. Stevenson studied nearly 3000 cases of previous life memories, near-death experiences, and related phenomena. Although not completely accepted by the scientific community at this time, he contributed greatly to a phenomenon called "xenoglossy"—where children from a certain cultural background could inexplicably speak the language of a completely foreign culture. In other instances the children would explain various details about their previous lifetime when they existed as a person in a completely unfamiliar culture to the person they are in this life.

> *"I found that the children often talked with strong emotions about the previous lives, and they sometimes behaved as if still living in the past life. For them it seemed still present, not past. For example, a child of low-caste parents who said that he remembered the life of a Brahmin would show snobbish behavior toward his own family and might even refuse to eat their food: from his perspective it*

> *was polluted. A child remembering a previous life as a person of the opposite sex might dress for that sex and play its games. One who remembered being shot would show a fear of guns and loud noises."* [7]
>
> *—Dr. Ian Stevenson*

Stevenson retired in 2002, (and died in 2007, moving onto his next incarnation), and Dr. Jim B. Tucker took over this research at the University of Virginia School of Medicine. Tucker has since implemented a 'strength-of-case scale' framework for analyzing the empirical evidence of past life phenomena.[8] It is as follows:

1) whether it involves birthmarks / defects that correspond to the supposed previous life;
2) the strength of the statements about the previous life;
3) the relevant behaviors as they relate to the previous life; and
4) an evaluation of the possibility of a connection between the child reporting a previous life and the supposed previous life

Dr. Jonathan Edelmann and Dr. William Bernet examine this framework and propose an even more ironclad research protocol—collecting the information from trained professionals, data evaluation, medical record review, and integrating an additional party of professionals to investigate the child's supposed previous life to collect data.[9] The point is, we can build on Stevenson's work and others, to conduct an even more ideal level of rigorous research within this field of study.

One of the most striking stories about reincarnation comes from Trutz Hardo's *Children Who Have Lived Before.* In one of many fascinating tales in that book, a boy from Syria told his parents that he had been murdered by a man with an ax. [10]

He was born with a large red birthmark scar on his head, and explained to them that he was murdered in a nearby community. They ultimately took him before the village elders, sharing several details about his past life. The group decided to travel to neighboring villages to understand if this identity could be established. Dr. Eli Lasch, MD, a prominent physician in Israel, was invited to come along because he was interested in reincarnation.

The first two villages conjured no memories for the child, but the third village, familiar names and places were named. Eventually, they came upon members of the community, and he pointed at one man, saying:

> *"I used to be your neighbor. We had a fight and you killed me with an ax."*

Dr. Lasch then observed that this man's face suddenly became white as a sheet. The 3-year-old then stated:

> *"I even know where he buried my body."*

The boy then led the group, which included the accused murderer, into fields that were located nearby. The boy stopped in front of a pile of stones and reported:

> *"He buried my body under these stones and the ax over there."*

Excavation at the spot under the stones revealed the skeleton of an adult man wearing the clothes of a farmer and on the skull, a linear split in the skull was observed, which was consistent with an ax wound. The man confessed and they found the ax buried nearby.[11]

It's just changing the clothes that you're wearing.

You wear one set of clothes today, and another tomorrow. Consciousness, or the soul, or the atman, continues on beyond these lifetimes.

> *"Worn-out garments are shed by the body.*
>
> *Worn-out bodies are shed by the dweller."*
>
> —*Krishna, Bhagavad Gita 11.22*

A Kriya Yoga teacher of mine explained it like moving apartments.

You're in one for a while, dating some person living a certain life, and then things change and you move to another place. But we take most of our stuff with us.

> *"All the world's a stage,*
>
> *And all the men and women merely players;*
>
> *They have their exits and their entrances;*
>
> *And one man in his time plays many parts."*
>
> —*William Shakespeare, As You Like It*

Yogananda himself claimed to remember his own past experiences with a sense of cosmic vision:

> *"I also recall my own past incarnations, beyond all doubt. In the Tower of London, for example, I found many places that I remembered from a past life, places the present caretakers didn't know anything about. Because I was once an Englishman, in my childhood in India I preferred to eat with a fork and knife. When my family asked why I wanted to use these instead of my fingers, as is the Indian custom, I said, 'I remember this from the past'."* [12]

Your actions from your past are influencing you at this very moment.

We know this is true from our own one-life perspective. We live in a universe of cause and effect. It's not just our actions, but our reactions, to events in our lives that determine which set of possibilities we hurtle into next.

> *"Nothing ever goes away until it teaches us what we need to know."*
>
> —*Pema Chödrön, American Tibetan Buddhist, author of When Things Fall Apart*

Your current incarnation in this body is exactly where you need to be to grow. Our flaws are our tickets here, and they are also what we have to overcome. We've already overcome many, many others.

Everything is a vehicle for getting liberated.

And our reaction determines our freedom. We can either have

the Monkey Mind in charge (carnal desire) or let the Self come through (be an instrument of the Lord's Peace).

Each lesson, each event in our life will continue to show up until we learn it. Until we transcend it. There is a finite number of lessons but an infinite number of ways each lesson can manifest. So as Yogananda and the great masters tell us: we were sent here to undo. Let us release our negative tendencies and habits that we keep holding onto life after life. May they be dissolved into the Truth of our Inherent Oneness with the Divine, with the Source, with All.

Which cosmic door do we walk through?

We progress through a series of experiences in unique lifetimes that offer distinct lessons for our maturation and development, until ultimately, class is over. After that, we either assist others still learning (as bodhisattvas), or we plunge into an Endless Transcendental Reality of Ever-New Joy for Eternity. It's a win-win.

Nil and Sam Harris

I met a quantum physicist, Nil, at the soup kitchen preparing food for our city's working poor. He said that he had recently come into spiritual thinking, which was new for him, and it led him to feeding the hungry.

I learned that Nil is from the state of Bengal in India, and that he grew up resistant to spirituality and metaphysics.

For context, Bengal is somewhat ironically the ancestral home to a healthy variety of authentic Hindu saints—particularly the great Ramakrishna and his disciples, most prominently the earth-shattering force, Swami Vivekananda. However in contemporary India, the excesses of guru-worship-culture have created the same moral atrocities and abuse that the Catholic Church hides within its ranks.

So as a young man, Nil was searching for truth in laboratories, not temples.

After undergraduate in India, Nil made his way to Texas to complete his study for his Ph.D. in quantum physics. In Austin, he stumbled across *Waking Up* by Sam Harris, the neuroscientist atheist author of *The End of Faith*.

Harris came into my view many years ago thanks to him publicly debating (and humiliating) spiritual teachers like Deepak Chopra, antagonizing Islam, and conflating religious thinking with outdated tribalistic belief.[13] Despite his intelligent and justifiable critiques of institutionalized religion, I wrote off Sam Harris to be close-minded to the beauty of authentic spirituality.

Years after his initial celebrity tidal wave as one of the militant "New Atheists", Harris began to encourage the practice of meditation—the secular kind, veering into agnostic Buddhist techniques that he had practiced personally for decades—which prompted his authorship of 2014's massive hit, *Waking Up: A Guide to Spirituality Without Religion*.

Imagine my face when I asked Nil what it was that got him interested in spiritual thinking, and my new Calcuttan friend replied: "Sam Harris."

We all have our own way in.

For me it was the Bengali saints. For Nil it was the Western scientists—from the early quantum physicists, to one of the world's most famous atheists—that led him to question his own views of reality and discover a deeper meaning underneath it all.

Katyayana's Laughter

Lama Surya Das shares the following story of a fully liberated Buddhist named Katyayana.[14]

One day an old sage, Katyayana, walked into a village begging for alms. He saw a woman enjoying her daytime meal of fish, while holding her baby on her lap. There was a dog close by who was very interested in her fish bones. As Katyayana neared the scene, the dog got a bit too close and the woman kicked the dog out of frustration.

Katyayana started laughing uproariously. The woman turned to him in a state of confusion. He said, between laughter:

> *"Devouring the flesh of one's father,*
>
> *kicking one's mother;*
>
> *chewing the bones of one's father*
>
> *while nursing one's enemy upon one's breast –*
>
> *What a gigantic melodrama, what a spectacle*
>
> *is this magical illusory wheel of Samsara!"*

Due to his higher cosmic awareness, the sage was able to perceive the previous existence of everything present before him.

Her baby was a recently killed enemy.

The fish was her late father reborn.

And the dog had existed before as her beloved mother.

The saint concluded:

> *"The wondrous wheel of cyclic existence, like a waterwheel, endlessly turns–refilling its buckets again and again, ceaselessly emptying and replenishing itself."*

Don't get caught in these finite roles. Realize the constantly changing nature of this universe. Lama Surya Das reminds us to consider:

> *"Who knows from whom the meat on our table has been butchered, whose bones we chew upon?"*

A dear friend asked me, "Why? Why are you so certain of all this?"

Because I have had a thimbleful of experiences that are un-come-back-able.

So if I've had a drop and I'm already at fervor, there are saints who have had many oceans' worth of experiences...!

At some point, “certainty” doesn’t even describe what it is. It’s innate.

The more you practice compassion and non-judgment, the more frequently and easily you see instances of Oneness. It's not much more complex than that.

A few fleeting glimpses have brought me too far down the rabbit hole!

CHAPTER 16

Psychedelia: A Glimpse but Impossible to Stay Up

Shamans Melting Boundaries

Human beings have been consuming psychoactive plants for tens of thousands of years.

Botanist, writer and futurologist philosopher Terence McKenna thought it was the psychedelic mushroom that jumped humanity forward so significantly. We went from apes holding spears overlooking the grasslands, to introspective beings at the forefront of a mighty civilization in a very short period of time. He called this the "Stoned Ape" hypothesis based on his own experiences with psychedelics alongside citing studies by researcher Roland Fischer and others.[15] Despite his initial outright rejection from the scientific community, highly reputable mycologists like Paul Stamets D.Sc. are starting to re-examine the plausibility of McKenna's theory—primarily due to the "extraordinary expansion" of the human brain size 200,000 years ago. According to Stamets, there is *"no explanation for this sudden increase in the human brain"* ... which makes him point to the magic mushroom as a plausible hypothesis.[16]

McKenna talked about *"the Goddess, the Cow, and the Mushroom"* and how much of what has been discovered about our ancestors associates those three things together: the Divine Feminine, the beginning of agriculture, and increased brain capacities to organize information... an expansion into a new plateau of consciousness.[17] He explained that this was because when you're herding cattle, and you're walking behind them for so long, you'll start to find fungi growing in their dung. Cow manure creates a fertile soil for mushrooms containing psilocybin. Psilocybin is one of many psychoactive chemicals that powerfully affect our ability to cognize our surroundings and ultimately our reality. And if you eat enough, the Mother will show up.

The fundamental component of the psychedelic experience is the dissolution of boundaries. This includes altering our sense perception, but also the dissolving of conceptual ideas, and even erasing the ego itself. You might notice two previously disconnected ideas come together in striking new ways. McKenna himself would relate the mathematical stylings of the ancient Chinese text, the *I Ching* (*Book of Changes*) to sociological commentaries and predictions. He had a fascinating way of interconnecting our psychological understanding with our history, our culture, and our ego. McKenna also made many accurate hypotheses about the potential of the internet and the frightening direction our consumerist culture was headed. A typical Terence McKenna passage is as follows:

> *"The 20th century mind is nostalgic for the paradise that once existed on the mushroom dotted plains of Africa where the plant-human symbiosis occurred that pulled us out of the animal body and into the tool-using, culture-making, imagination-exploring creature that we are. And why does this matter? It matters because it shows that the way out is back and that the future is a forward escape into the past. This is what the psychedelic experience means. It's a doorway out of history and into the wiring under the board in eternity.*
>
> *...When psilocybin is regularly part of the human experience the ego is suppressed and the suppression of the ego means the defeat of the dominators, the materialists, the product peddlers. Psychedelics return us*

> *to the inner worth of the self, to the importance of the feeling of immediate experience—and nobody can sell that to you and nobody can buy it from you, so the dominator culture is not interested in the felt presence of immediate experience, but that's what holds the community together. And as we break out of the silly myths of science, and the infantile obsessions of the marketplace what we discover through the psychedelic experience is that in the body, IN THE BODY, there are Niagaras of beauty, alien beauty, alien dimensions that are part of the self, the richest part of life."* [18]

Consuming psychoactive plants is a core ritual among the shamanic traditions. The word "shaman" comes from the Tungusic word *saman*, meaning "one who knows".[19] From an academic perspective, "shaman" is a broad term used to group together beliefs and activities across the world. Scholars have studied indigenous cultures in Asia, Africa, Australasia and the Americas, and while I can't help but point out the continually unfolding commonalities, it is unscholarly, and even culturally insensitive, to deny the nuanced variety among indigenous cultures.[20] I appreciate the almost indescribable complexity, however this is not a thorough exploration of indigenous diversity, it's a mere glimpse at consciousness-altering flora: plants & fungi whose use by ancient wisdom traditions offers substantial validation of their value in the modern world.

Where scholars agree, is that shamans are known for their traversing of the spiritual realms.

The Oxford English Dictionary defines a shaman as: *"A person regarded as having access to, and influence in, the world of good and evil spirits, especially among some peoples of northern Asia and North America. Typically such people enter a trance state during a ritual, and practice divination and healing."* [21]

A distressed member of the community would come to them, explaining their problems in a way not too unlike patients of modern psychotherapists, and depending on the situation, a shamanic ritual would be performed in accordance with the person's issue. The shaman would use contemplative, mystical practice to obtain useful information that would be beneficial. They would often use medicinal plants and herbs as healing pastes and ointments for physical ailments, as well as entheogenic (AKA sacred-psychedelic) plants for their own journeys through astral and subtle planes of consciousness.

> *"Of all the techniques used by the shaman to induce ecstasy and visionary voyaging—fasting, prolonged drumming, breath control, and stressful ordeals—I now feel confident that the use of hallucinogenic plants is the most effective, dependable, and powerful. I believe that rational exploration of the enigma of the Other is possible and that the shamanic approach to hallucinogenic plants, especially those containing psilocybin and dimethyltryptamine (DMT), will be absolutely central to achieving that end."* [22]
>
> —*Terence McKenna*

"Set and Setting", as popularized by Tim Leary, rings true. We must treat these powerful tools with a sacred reverence, and be highly conscious of both *the intention* and *the environment* of psychedelic use. In the modern West, we tend to take psychedelics either at a big party or an outdoor music festival. There really aren't two worse places to do them. Instead try a field of flowers alone, or the shade of a giant oak tree with a close friend, or Terry's favorite: a calm fire in a backyard as the sun begins to set. And within a more controlled environment, be sure to set the intention to cultivate growth, connection, understanding, and love.

Since McKenna's passing in 2000, a 'psychedelic renaissance' has occurred. While most psychedelics are still federally illegal in America, as of the time of this writing, psilocybin mushrooms are now currently legal in Brazil, Bulgaria, Jamaica, the Netherlands, Samoa, Portugal, and the state of Oregon.[23]

A helpful push for this renaissance was the highly respected journalist Michael Pollan writing his sixth New York Times bestseller in 2018 on psychedelics called *How to Change Your Mind: What the New Science of Psychedelics Teaches Us About Consciousness,*

Dying, Addiction, Depression, and Transcendence. Pollan calls himself a 'reluctant psychonaut', in that this was not his cup of mushroom tea, but as an immersive journalist, it was an obligation to have psychedelic experiences. He writes about losing his ego-identity, and the sense of ineffable peace that came with that dissipation... but he also chronicles the fascinating scientific research currently taking place regarding the use of psychedelics as alternatives for more traditional pharmaceutical prescription drugs.[24] Pharmaceutical drugs have their own benefits certainly, but they have also brought forth the modern opioid epidemic—specifically Methadone, Oxycodone (such as OxyContin®), and Hydrocodone (such as Vicodin®)—creating generations of addicts, killing hundreds of thousands of Americans and absolutely ravaging rural America. [25]

Psychedelics are only addictive in exceptional cases[26] and both psilocybin and LSD have extremely low toxicity rates.[27] The term is "LD-50", meaning lethal dose-50%. So LSD's danger is not from the chemical itself, but rather by doing something outrageous while under its influence. That is not the case however for mescaline (derived from the peyote cactus), which although rare, can be lethal from over-ingesting.[28] Research is critical before traversing psychoactive highways, combined with guidance from a more experienced traveler who can provide the right "set and setting".

All this is to say, I encourage diligent research on the effects of these chemicals on the body and the mind. Like most open-minded millennials, I've had a few beautiful experiences on psychedelics.

They've shown me that our senses are wholly incapable of interpreting reality. They've shown me that the ego is afraid of being found out, and that my True Self is a limitless source of Love and Forgiveness behind the ego's fickle, frightened, false identity. I've felt so much Love for every being it was almost unbearable. Every one of us is doing the best we can, trying to get by, working through our flaws with heavy difficulties and humble victories. It may sound trite, but when you really sit in that space it can be unimaginably profound.

Pollan writes about how this new science of psychedelics is

finding cases of people who can completely relinquish a past addiction after one psychedelic experience: quitting smoking cold turkey for example. And even beyond kicking nicotine, they are opening up to a fuller way of being and understanding oneself. He tells a story of a woman who had cancer, and was in remission, but was paralyzed by her fear of the cancer returning.[29] In her psychedelic experience, under the aid of a skilled therapist-researcher, she was able to confront not the cancer, but the fear itself, manifesting in her vision as a black cloud in the center of her body. She screamed at it, "*Get the f out of here!*" and… it did. After her trip she was able to live without the fear that had previously consumed her life. She went into complete remission shortly afterwards.

Psychedelics can also trigger discomfort. The altering of consciousness can be a lot to handle.

I had a close friend who was a musician. At the end of his mushroom trip, he was in his room holding his guitar for what felt like hours. He finally put it down forcefully and later told me that his experience helped him see how surface-level his musical efforts had been. He wanted the fame & influence that comes from being a successful musician, as opposed to the creation of the musical work itself. Despite his incredible talent, he was in it for the wrong reasons. And he hasn't played a note since.

The Concord Prison Experiment

Can the psychedelic experience truly change human behavior in a positive way for the long-term?

One of Dr. Timothy Leary's most famous experiments was to test this hypothesis on prisoners. From 1960-1963, Leary's team of Harvard researchers worked in a maximum-security prison for young offenders, in Concord, Massachusetts. They offered psilocybin to a group of prisoners to understand how it would affect their recidivism rate—which means coming back to prison post-release. Sitting with a group of remorseful prisoners, guiding them through a profound psychedelic experience: would they be more or less likely to commit another crime after serving their sentence?[30]

Leary has been spoken about at length. There are dozens of biographies, and plenty of cultural opinions. He was a polarizing figure, and for many, sadly his reputation seems to endure as a drug-crazed wacko. And that's a reductive view. He was not an avatar, but Leary was inarguably a pioneer with a sincere intention. A hilarious bit of history is that John Lennon originally wrote "*Come Together*" to be a theme song for Leary's California gubernatorial campaign against Ronald Reagan. We might have had Governor Leary if he wasn't interrupted by a prison sentence for cannabis possession.[31]

In the writeup for the "Concord Prison Experiment", Leary describes his early social work in orphanages, counseling and teaching children in the low-income slums of Boston suburbia:

> *"All this, of course, was very déclassé at Harvard. Universities are supposed to be research institutes and if you get too involved in service functions or helping people, you're considered a bleeding heart. I was able to justify the work in the orphanage, the work with alcoholics, the work in the slum projects, by using the phrase 'methodology'. We weren't really trying to help these people. No sir, not us. We were trying to develop new techniques and scientific methods for changing psychotherapeutic theory. Of course, if people enjoyed it and got help, that was an interesting by-product which supported the method and the theory..."* [32]

Unfortunately, what Leary had in a positive intention to help the prisoners, he lacked in rigor as a researcher for this experiment. While the study originally reported a considerable improvement (32% reduction) to the recidivism rate among the 32 prisoners offered psilocybin group psychotherapy, in the decades following, additional research analyses were made that determined that the initial experiment was closer to 1%, not 32%. The prisoners exposed to the group psychedelic psychotherapy were certainly affected in profound ways, as was reported in the follow-up research, but the test group's rate of recidivism was ultimately insignificant.

Rick Doblin, Ph.D., the founder of the Multidisciplinary Association for Psychedelic Studies, writes:

> *"The 71% recidivism rate of the sample of 21 is just one percentage point below the mid-point of the range of possible values (72%)... suggesting there was ultimately no treatment effect, in terms of reduced recidivism rates…"* [33]

In addition, however:

> *"The failure of the Concord Prison Experiment to generate a reduction in recidivism rates should not be interpreted as proof of the lack of value of psychedelics as adjuncts to psychotherapy in criminals. Rather, the failure of the Concord Prison Experiment should finally put to rest the myth of psychedelic drugs as magic bullets, the ingestion of which will automatically confer wisdom and create lasting change after just one or even a few experiences. Personality change may be made more likely after a cathartic and insightful psychedelic experience, though only sustained hard work after the drug has worn off will serve to anchor and solidify any movement toward healing and behavior change."* [34]

Doblin tracked down several of the former convicts three decades later and interviewed two:

> *The subject who did not return to jail speculated that he was able to stay out of jail primarily because he had a family to return to post-release. [He] credited the psilocybin experiences with helping him to stay out of jail, saying, "I know this thing [the psilocybin experience] was great for me in my life for about two years after I had taken it. You know, my wife and I would discuss it every once and a while, and she'd ask me, 'How do you feel?' And I'd say, ' I feel great; you and I are together, so I got something out of it.'" He reflected on the content of his psilocybin experience by saying, "You tear your life down*

and you put it back together." [35]

Both Leary and Doblin conclude that a combination of both a pre-release administration of psilocybin-assisted group psychotherapy along with a comprehensive post-release follow-up program, similar to an Alcoholics Anonymous-type support group, would ensure a better success rate for prisoners released from prison.

Psychedelics are not instantaneous eternal enlightenment.

> *"If the only thing to say about psychedelics was that they seem on occasion to offer direct disclosures of the psychic and celestial planes as well as (in rare instances) the Infinite itself, we would hold our peace. For though such experiences may be veridical in ways, the goal, it cannot be stressed too often, is not religious experiences; it is the religious life."* [36]
>
> *—Huston Smith*

Psychedelics can offer us profound experiences & realizations that are highly useful throughout our growth, but there is real, hardened behavioral work that goes into the process of human betterment, when you come back down.

Maharajji's LSD Story

The morning after Ram Dass met Neem Karoli Baba, there's a famous story of "the yogi medicine" and the great guru.

Not only was Professor Richard Alpert unhappy, unsatisfied, and unfulfilled; he recently came off of several years of experimenting with an intense amount of psychedelics. At the peak of his experiments with other researchers, artists, musicians & philosophers, they locked themselves in a room for two weeks and they all took 400 micrograms of LSD every four hours.[37] It was profound, and comically maniacal, but as Ram Dass emphasized throughout his life: they all came down.

So after he and Leary were kicked out of Harvard, as he was

searching the globe for answers, one of those questions was: does anyone know more about this consciousness-altering chemical?

The first day he met Maharajji was a blur. After his future guru told him how his mother died ("Spleen"), he just broke down. Ram Dass said it was this powerful heaviness in his chest that gave him the feeling, *"I'm home"*. There was no need to keep searching after meeting that smiling man under the blanket. The other devotees gave him food and some necessary emotional support so that he could regain his senses. The next morning at the temple, the first thing Maharajji said to him was *"Do you have a question for me?"* 'Question?' he thought… 'no I'm just fine… you've already proved to me that you know everything' …beginning to float into this new level of appreciation and love for his guru.

Maharajji repeated it another way: *"Where's the medicine?"*[38]

Again, Richard (in the process of becoming Ram Dass) was unsure. His traveling companion, Bhagavan Das, reminded him of the LSD he'd brought. 'OH yes, *that.*'

Maharajji held out his hand.

This particular type of acid was called "White Lightning"—it was given to Dr. Alpert specifically, an experienced user, as a kind of 'going away present'. He gave the old Indian man one pill.

Typically a "hit" of LSD is 275 micrograms, but this special batch was 305mg. The guru asked for more: two, making it 610mg. For a normal seventy-year-old man, 150mg would be suitable to affect the consciousness quite substantially. Then he asked for a third: 915mg… *"that's really gonna do it"* thought the doctor. And Maharajji downed all of them.[39] The scientist in him thought, *"Well, this is going to be interesting."*

All day they hung around, but ashram life continued as normal. Every now and then the guru would twinkle softly at his new disciple.

And nothing happened at all.

In Ram Dass' later reflections about this event he said that the best way to understand this is that there are levels of consciousness.

Neem Karoli Baba was at, or near, the peak of the human mind's ability to transcend external stimuli. For most of us mortals, we are significantly affected by mind-altering chemicals, but for those who have had such profound spiritual realizations and attained new heights of human potential, psychedelics are a lower level—these 'gateways' are in-between most humans and those rare masters, as a true guru is a gateway incarnate.

Richard the Apache shaman has shared with me that he's not affected by the peyote tea. When he goes to the spiritual ceremonies, and drinks with the elders, he feels nothing. And when my dad accompanied him to an Oklahoma powwow, Dad confirmed with me that Richard was treated with considerable tribal reverence. Even Dad got love merely for being the friend of a powerful medicine man.

As Ram Dass shared to American audiences in the following decades, *"When you're in Detroit, you don't need to take a bus to Detroit."*

Being immersed in Hindu guru miracle stories, and understanding that we're all a seeming projection of mind for a blink of an eye, I've never questioned this extraordinary acid story. Yogananda tells far more spectacular tales that defy space-time in *Autobiography*. But several friends have asked me after my now-stereotypical late-night retelling: do you, Bob, really think that happened? Even Terence McKenna, an admirer of Ram Dass, told science journalist John Horgan that he thought no one, including Maharajji, would be unaffected by 915mg of LSD.[40]

Well even Ram Dass began to doubt this extraordinary feat of his guru. Upon his return to America in 1968 he told the story so much that he started to question if Maharajji had actually thrown the pills over his shoulder or performed some sleight-of-hand parlor trick, not uncommon for Hindu sadhus attempting to impress gullible Westerners. While the Part 1 of this story is world-famous thanks to *Be Here Now*, the follow-up as reported in *Miracle of Love*, is almost unknown, but just as important:

> *"Three years later, when I was back in India, he asked me one day, 'Did you give me the medicine when you were in*

> *India last time?'*
>
> *'Yes.'*
>
> *'Did I take it?' he asked. (Ah, there was my doubt made manifest!)*
>
> *'I think you did.'*
>
> *'What happened?'*
>
> *'Nothing.'*
>
> *'Oh! Jao!' [Go!] and he sent me off for the evening.*
>
> *The next morning I was called over to the porch in front of his room, where he sat in the mornings on a tucket. He asked, 'Have you got any more of that medicine?'*
>
> *It just so happened that I was still carrying a small supply of LSD for 'just-in-case,' and this was obviously it. 'Yes.'*
>
> *'Get it,' he said. So I did. In the bottle were five pills of three hundred micrograms each. One of the pills was broken. I placed them on my palm and held them out to him. He took the four unbroken pills. Then, one by one, very obviously and very deliberately, he placed each one in his mouth and swallowed it…"* [41]

The guru addressed the doubt of the disciple directly, in as controlled of a setting as he could offer to the former research psychologist. After this explicit consumption, Maharajji called over an older devotee with a watch and they all waited over the next hour to see if it would affect the great saint. Yet again, nothing happened. He even joked that he was being overwhelmed for a moment, only to become completely normal when a panicked Ram Dass glanced back at him.

Maharajji concluded:

> *"These medicines were used in Kulu Valley long ago. But yogis have lost that knowledge. They were used with fasting. Nobody knows now. To take them with no effect, your mind must be firmly fixed on God."* [42]

CHAPTER 17

Transcending What the World Offers

We Are Tourists

"I am a spark from the Infinite. I am not flesh and bones. I am Light. In helping others to succeed I shall find my own prosperity. In the welfare of others I shall find my own well-being.

*****

I am infinite. I am spaceless, I am tireless; I am beyond body, thought, and utterance; beyond all matter and mind. I am endless bliss." [43]

—Paramahansa Yogananda

A penetrating spiritual experience, caused either by psychedelic plants or transcendental influences, can affect the way we see ourselves and the world. True saints caution us that these experiences are not the end-goal, but that they can help to establish a firmer realization that *things are not quite as they seem.*

These are ape bodies. If you've ever watched *Planet Earth* on too many spliffs, you'll hear Attenborough describe yourself in the ape scenes. One time on the *Jungles* episode, my friends were all sitting around the room watching and the apes were all sitting around in eerily similar postures. They rest their head on their curled fist with a bent elbow. They make peculiar thoughtful faces.

We ain't that different. As I told friends and family about my newborn son asking for updates: he's eating and sleeping, which is pretty much all we adults do too.

Of course, the mystics tell us we are beyond this silly limiting form. Gurdjieff called it "a prison", Pradhupada called it "an embarrassment", and ACIM calls it the "ego's masterpiece". Our bodies are perfectly designed to engender the perception of separateness. But even science tells us our perceptions are wrong. Or less right that we think we are.

I'm not saying don't honor the body and don't take care of it. I wash my car once a week. My body is the same way, washing more often than once a week. My car needs gas and oil, and my body needs water and nutrients. It's an '88 model.

But to reiterate, we know that light extends far beyond what the human eye can process visually.[44] There are audio waves both higher and lower than what the human ear can detect. Our body systems work pretty well, and yet they are not the peak of existence. I have gratitude for my body and for the work it does in letting me inhabit this plane, but ultimately, all of these spiritual traditions, philosophies, and now scientific research are coming together to suggest that we are not merely the body.

We are spirit, we are the atman, we are consciousness extending far beyond this mortal visitation. We are not this frail form.

We are tourists.

We have a duty to serve others, and this planet, but we're not from here.

Jesus says in the *Gospel of Thomas*, saying 42:

> *"Be passersby."*

Continuing this idea is a saying attributed to Jesus, in an Arabic inscription, on a mosque in Fatehpur-Sikri, India:

> *"Jesus, Son of Mary (on whom be peace) said:*
>
> *The World is a Bridge, pass over it, but build no houses*

> *upon it. He who hopes for a day, may hope for eternity; but the World endures but an hour. Spend it in prayer, for the rest is unseen."*[45]

And even in canonical *Matthew* (8:2), he tells us:

> *"The foxes have holes and the birds of the air have nests, but the Son of Man has nowhere to lay his head."*

The wisdom traditions echo this idea... Eastern views on temporality are embraced by the contemplative Abrahamic religions too. There's a very similar idea within the *Hadith*, a complementary scripture to the Muslim *Quran* containing additional insights from Muhammad's actions:

> *"Be in this world as though you were a stranger or a wayfarer."*
>
> —*Hadith 40*

There is a famous story of an American tourist visiting a 19th century Jewish rabbi, Hofetz Chaim. Bewildered by the rabbi's simple room containing only books, a table and a bench, the man asked:

> *"Rabbi, where is your furniture?"*
>
> *"And where is yours?"*
>
> *"Mine?" The American asked, confused. "I'm only passing through, I'm a visitor here."*
>
> *Rabbi Chaim replied: "So am I."*

And lastly, Hafez, that giant of Sufi poetry, declares:

> *"Listen:*
>
> *This world is the lunatic's sphere,*
>
> *Don't always agree it's real,*
>
> *Even with my feet upon it*
>
> *And the postman knowing my door,*
>
> *My address is somewhere else."*

Cremation Luncheon

My mom said she's going to a cremation luncheon.

My initial surprise quickly receded into laughter at the absurd, morose humor of the situation:

"Jesus, Mom, a lunch? Is it buy-one-cremation, get-one-free?"

She said, "No! ...It's $500 off."

I nodded, and she clarified, "We paid too much for Mom... plus I love La Madeleine."

I smiled, my punchline-inspiration evolving into sincere admiration for her self-acceptance.

"You're very Buddhist right now about this whole impermanence thing."

She said, "Yeah, and there's a 7-day cruise giveaway!"

The Middle Way and The Narrow Gate

It takes some precision, and some intention. Some awareness.

There is some urgency.

The Buddha tells us to really use this birth.

It's all here right now in the present, but why delay our own peace? Why delay our own true happiness?

When we realize that the external world does not have what we're searching for, its fleeting pleasure dissipates time and again, it's time to get real. It's time to really dive into our own thoughts, our own habitual patterns, our own hesitations, anxieties and fears. What's underneath them?

The spiritual path is often misperceived as being a joyful skip through the meadow and while I do believe the end goal has that type of feeling, truly all the time, I know that the way from the state of desire-full suffering can be difficult. It can be painful to deeply investigate at first, but over time, it becomes more natural and more liberating.

> *"Unless you have made a clear decision to turn your back on samsara, then however many prayers you recite, however much you meditate, however many years you remain in retreat, it will all be in vain. You may have a long life, but it will be without essence. You may accumulate great wealth, but it will be meaningless. The only thing that is really worth doing is to get steadily closer to enlightenment and further away from samsara. Think about it carefully."* [46]
>
> *—Dilgo Khyentse Rinpoche*

The sensual world of material phenomena is utterly fascinating and captures my attention constantly. But I can always come back to stillness. I can always come back to forgiveness, and love—for myself and others.

The Buddha's path is called "The Middle Way", because he refused both sides of the spectrum of the material world.

First, he was a rich prince with every carnal comfort of life.

Then when he left the palace he became a spiritual ascetic, renouncing everything, rejecting all. His sole corner of the cosmos was a humble seat in a cave and barely enough nutrition to survive.

Both were wrong.

As he eventually discovered under that famous Bodhi tree, the way through it all is to live in the world naturally, in moderation, while detaching from our mental association with either the pleasure or the pain. It's a tightrope we're walking across. Gently. With compassion. In order to not fall off into either side of this duality.

Buddha used the metaphor of a stringed instrument. If the string is not tight enough, you can't pluck it. It won't make any noise at all. But if the string is too tight, it'll snap. When the string is neither too loose nor too tight, you hear the music.

I've heard many Christian fundamentalists quote this saying of Jesus from *Matthew*:

> *"Enter by the narrow gate; for wide is the gate and broad is the way that leads to destruction, and there are many who go in by it.*
>
> *Because narrow is the gate and difficult is the way which leads to life, and there are few who find it."*
>
> —*Jesus, Gospel of Matthew 7:13-14*

The typical context associated with this line is that the narrow gate is Christianity. It's the exclusive gateway to heaven, even though this institution didn't exist at all in the same capacity during the teacher's own lifetime.

What Jesus is really saying here isn't that far off from his Indian brother and predecessor: the way of the world is alluring! You can easily fall off into either side of this dualistic tightrope. There are extremes in terms of pleasure or pain and both can hook you, unless you have some discernment, some self-awareness about yourself.

The Middle Path through the gate is narrow.

It is difficult, but a few do find it. And they've been telling us how to find it, and walk through it, for millennia.

Part Six:

The Love of Our Creator is Inescapable

Original sin is a lie,

because when we reduce
our ego perceptions of the world around us,
boundaries between nature,
other beings,
and previously unknown parts of ourselves melt away…

Leaving a blinding sense of connective Love and Unity underneath it all.

CHAPTER 18

Piercing the Illusory Veil

Experience Rather Than Theology

"God wills no one suffer.

He does not will anyone to suffer for a wrong decision, including you.

That is why He has given you the means for undoing it."

—*A Course in Miracles, T.8.III.7:5-7*

After graduating from the University of Texas with my shiny new Religious Studies bachelors, I realized I needed to catch up with Richard. Our family had lost touch with our shaman friend. My dad still had his number, but the last time I saw him was at my high school graduation party. It's so fun to see him at a big gathering... you'll be walking through a crowd of people and see him in the corner advising the most needful person... the aunt who got a divorce, the friend whose mother just passed... Richard is always on the clock.

We reconnected on the phone and met up for dinner. I excitedly told him about my college studies and increasing embrace of the 'perennial philosophy'. I had become 'initiated' into Kriya Yoga and was now meditating daily. He asked me throughout the evening if I wanted to begin the spiritual path. As I vocally affirmed for the third time in our conversation (somewhat unknown by me and intentional by him), I cemented my spiritual-door-opening status.

Richard said that if I really wanted to begin the spiritual path in earnest—while there are many ways to God, one of the clearest, most uncorrupted teachings on earth at this time is a book called *A Course in Miracles*. He received confirmation from his guides that it is comparable to Christ's original instruction to his apostles, alongside the Buddha, Moses, Shankara, and other authentic sages and saints throughout history. The advantage is that it was published in 1976.[1] It has yet to become watered-down. Much of the older faith teachings have become victim to centuries of dogmatic, doctrinal, and sectarian issues—not entirely, but they have been diluted in a way. Humanity hasn't tried to manipulate *A Course*'s undeniable power yet. We'll corrupt it in a few centuries too, but for now it's a highly useful tool in the process of spiritual self-actualization.

A Course in Miracles (often stylized as *ACIM*) is a 1333-page book containing a self-study curriculum of spiritual transformation. There's a "Text", a "Workbook" of 365 daily lessons, and a "Manual for Teachers", structured not unlike academic material.

> *"The curriculum the Course proposes is carefully conceived and is explained, step by step, at both the theoretical and practical levels. It emphasizes application rather than theory, and experience rather than theology. It specifically states that 'a universal theology is impossible, but a universal experience is not only possible but necessary.' (C-In.2:5) Although Christian in statement, the Course deals with universal spiritual themes. It emphasizes that it is but one version of the universal curriculum. There are many others, this one differing from them only in form. They all lead to God in the end."* [2]

It was received by an "inner voice" in the mind of a research psychologist named Helen Schucman. In the 1960s, Schucman was an atheist-leaning researcher at the Columbia University College of Physicians and Surgeons in New York City.[3] She was working directly under Dr. Bill Thetford, a former graduate student of the world-famous psychologist Carl Rogers.[4]

Bill & Helen's research center was a challenging environment. It was a university, a hospital, and a predoctoral training program with divided authorities... a complex bureaucratic maze of confrontational power struggles and reputational politics.[5] After the two could no longer stand the difficulty, Bill said to her:

"There must be another way."

To his surprise, Helen agreed completely. She said:

"I agree. And I'll help you find it."

This now-famous decision for human betterment brought about a series of symbolic dreams and even waking images that came to Helen, totally foreign to her background and personality. She writes:

> *"Although I had grown more accustomed to the unexpected by that time, I was still very surprised when I wrote, "This is a course in miracles." That was my introduction to the Voice. It made no sound, but seemed to be giving me a kind of rapid, inner dictation which I took down in a shorthand notebook. The writing was never automatic. It could be interrupted at any time and later picked up again. It made me very uncomfortable, but it never seriously occurred to me to stop. It seemed to be a special assignment I had somehow, somewhere agreed to complete. It represented a truly collaborative venture between Bill and myself, and much of its significance, I am sure, lies in that. I would take down what the Voice "said" and read it to him the next day, and he typed it from my dictation."* [6]

There's no church, no institution, no leader, no scheme to get your money. There is a publisher, because we're in contemporary civilization. It's simply a book that helps us remember Who We Truly Are. As stated in the intro, its purpose, and ours, is to "remove the blocks to the awareness of love's presence" (T-In.1:7).

Whenever I learn about a new philosophy, I like to read about what its critics think. Unsurprisingly, extremist fanatical Christians have referred to *A Course* as demonic scripture.[7] That's never scared me because those are the same close-minded folks who think yoga is of the devil, remember? They aren't crazy about gay people either. A lot of beautiful things are disliked by those thoroughly confused human beings. Peace to them.

To my great satisfaction, some critics of *A Course* have referred to it as "Hindu Christianity". Bill Thetford himself called it the "Christian Vedanta".[8] The Christian association is because the 'inner voice' intuited by Schucman claims to be the enduring spirit of a liberated Jesus. While much of the *Course* is dedicated to piercing the illusory ego mind, occasionally Jesus will clarify a lesson from the Bible that has been misunderstood for millennia.[9]

The resurrection, for example, is reinterpreted not as a message of a sacrificial clearing away of sin, but as a symbol of reawakening, and an ability shared by all of God's children. It's a striking parallel to the title of Yogananda's voluminous Bible commentary, *The Second Coming of Christ: The Resurrection of the Christ Within You*. From *A Course's Manual for Teachers*:

> *"Very simply, the resurrection is the overcoming or surmounting of death. It is a reawakening or a rebirth; a change of mind about the meaning of the world. It is the acceptance of the Holy Spirit's interpretation of the world's purpose; the acceptance of the Atonement for oneself. It is the end of dreams of misery, and the glad awareness of the Holy Spirit's final dream. It is the recognition of the gifts of God. It is the dream in which the body functions perfectly, having no function except communication. It is the lesson in which learning ends, for it is consummated and surpassed with this. It is the invitation to God to take His final step. It is the relinquishment of all other purposes, all other interests, all other wishes and all other concerns. It is the single desire of the Son for the Father."*
>
> *—ACIM, M-28.1:1-10*

So within ACIM, Christian terminology is used ("the Holy Spirit", "God", "sin") but these terms are presented within a nondualist theology. It closely resembles Advaita Vedanta,

Shankara's 'the-world-is-an-illusion' branch of Hinduism. This close proximity to "the jewel of Indian philosophy" only furthered fascination and gratitude:

> *"Simply do this: Be still, and lay aside all thoughts of what you are and what God is; all concepts you have learned about the world; all images you hold about yourself. Empty your mind of everything it thinks is either true or false, or good or bad, of every thought it judges worthy, and all the ideas of which it is ashamed.*
>
> *Hold onto nothing. Do not bring with you one thought the past has taught, nor one belief you ever learned before from anything."*
>
> *—ACIM, W-189.7:1-4*
>
> *"Stillness is the aim of the seeker. Even a single effort to still at least a single thought, even for a moment, goes a long way to reach the state of inactivity. Your duty is to be: and not to be this or that.*
>
> *'I AM that I AM' sums up the whole truth.*
>
> *The method is summed up in 'Be still'.*
>
> *What does 'stillness' mean? It means "destroy yourself". Because any form or shape is the cause of trouble. Give up that notion that 'I am so and so.'"*
>
> *—Ramana Maharshi*
>
> *"Nothing real can be threatened. Nothing unreal exists. Herein lies the peace of God."*
>
> *—ACIM, T-in.2:2-4*
>
> *"The impermanent has no reality; reality lies in the eternal. Those who have seen the boundary between these two have attained the end of all knowledge."*
>
> *—Krishna, Bhagavad Gita 2.16*
>
> *"The real does not die, the unreal never lived."*
>
> *—Nisargadatta Maharaj*

> *"Hold no one prisoner. Release instead of bind, for thus are you made free.*
>
> *...You are not free to give up freedom, but only to deny it.*
>
> *...As long as a single 'slave' remains to walk the earth, your release is not complete."*
>
> *—ACIM, W-192.9:1-2; T-10.IV.5:1; T-1.VII.3:13*
>
> *"A dreamer dreams that all the other characters in his dream must wake up before he can."*
>
> *—Ramana Maharshi*

We are at a fascinating place in history with this material because it is so young.

Now that the original co-scribes, editor, and publisher (Dr. Helen Schucman, Dr. Bill Thetford, Dr. Ken Wapnick, and Dr. Judith Skutch-Whitson) have died (Wapnick passed in 2013, a psychologist & extraordinary philosopher in his own right; psychologist & spiritual pioneer Skutch-Whitson passed in 2021—while writing this book), there are only a few ACIM teachers who knew Helen & Bill personally. Rev. Jon Mundy is one such author. Jon comes from a Methodist background, a mystically minded preacher for decades until fully embracing his role as a *Course* teacher in the early 90s. What Jon articulates so beautifully is that the *Course*'s core content resonates with every mystical tradition throughout history:

> *"What the Course says is not new. How could the eternal be new? Mystics, masters, saints, and sages from all over the world and throughout the ages have talked about that which goes beyond perception. We find "themes," "songs," and "representations of the Course in the world's oldest philosophies—the Advaita Vedanta philosophy of Hinduism, Buddhism, Gnosticism, Christian Mysticism, Sufism, German Idealism, American Transcendentalism, The New Thought Movement, Unity, Religious Science, Christian Science, and many more thousands of forms."* [10]

The primary message of *A Course,* and all the above systems, is that God is not some distant entity. She lives within us completely and is fully knowable once we begin to "wake up".

So why is ACIM different than these centuries-old faith traditions? The format itself is different because of its directness. Every sentence is another addition to the curriculum of mind training. There are parallels to Buddhism in that way—they're both more of a practical psychology than a religion.

And like Christ's original teaching, this 20th century teaching is also a radical philosophy.

> *"Temptation has one lesson it would teach, in all its forms, wherever it occurs.*
>
> *It would persuade the holy Son of God he is a body, born in what must die, unable to escape its frailty, and bound by what it orders him to feel. It sets the limits on what he can do; its power is the only strength he has; his grasp cannot exceed its tiny reach.*
>
> *Would you be this, if Christ appeared to you in all His glory, asking you but this:*
>
> *'Choose once again if you would take your place among the saviors of the world, or would remain in hell, and hold your brothers there.'*
>
> *For He has come, and He is asking this."*
>
> —*ACIM, T-31.VIII.1:1-6*

The *Course* says that our current perception (the ego's) is upside down and backwards. In order to get free, we have to undo the way we see the world, and the way we see ourselves.

As you might begin to appreciate, the writing of the *Course* itself is incredibly beautiful. The verses are given in iambic pentameter, also called Shakespearean blank verse.[11] It's poetry. You can flip to any page and feel the truth of its message in your core. In that sense it's like no other book I've ever read in my life.

But most importantly, all of these external details don't

actually matter.

They are mere trivialities of form. The path that it lays before us is experiential. Even if it's the voice of Jesus or not, let the material into your heart and watch it expand for yourself. The evangelicals think that they can persuade people with their words… and while their efforts can be in earnest, true knowledge only comes through experience. And so I do the same. May we all find the peace within.

"Teach only love, for that is what you are."

—ACIM, T-6.I.13:2

"You have no idea of the tremendous release and deep peace that comes from meeting yourself and your brother totally without judgment."

—ACIM, T-3.VI.3:1

"The holiest of all the spots on earth is where an ancient hatred has become a present love."

—ACIM, T.26.IX.6:1

"This Is A Table."

"This place is a dream.

Only a sleeper considers it real.

Then death comes like dawn, and you wake up laughing at what you thought was your grief."

—Jalaluddin Rumi

Towards the end of a lovely family dinner, after hours of wine, funny stories and entertaining yet trivial small-talk; my aunt, dad and I snuck off. We passed around our dessert: a hurried bowl of cannabis, the great unifier of counterculture-era boomers and tree-hugging millennials. Predictably, the discussion took a significant turn from surface to substance. Bob III and I had a passionate discussion about many of our standard topics of conversation…

that night we were gabbing about yet another mystic parallel... how this line from Meister Eckhart sounds like Zhuangzi or something equally transcendental.

After patiently listening to our seemingly endless dialogue, my beloved aunt thoughtfully jumped in.

She said that as a fellow spiritual person she understands and appreciates the vast majority of what we're talking about: the value in being inclusive to others, the underlying parallels across major faiths, the positive effects of meditation, etc.

"I get all that...

What I struggle with is 'the illusion'," she said.

She knocked on the table and declared, *"This is a table. ...Isn't it?"*

Dad smiled at me and I smiled at them, realizing that it was now preposterously on me to attempt to explain in a few sentences the metaphysics behind nonduality. Fortunately in that moment, my expectations of my own capacity to explain away what is nearly unexplainable, were quite low.

Nonduality means "not two": that everything we see, hear, smell, taste, and touch is merely another appearance of the One. While Shankara and modern masters like Sri Ramana and Nisargadatta helped to articulate this elusive philosophy, it ultimately stems from the *Vedas.* Although nonduality, or "not-two-ness", does appear across many traditions, from Zen Buddhism to even the Gospels:

> *"The light of the body is the eye: if therefore thine eye be single, thy whole body shall be full of light."*
>
> *—Jesus, Gospel of Matthew, 6:22 KJV*

Because of its ancient progeny, it's important to understand that the Vedic definition of "real" differs a bit from the English translation. Within Indian philosophy, "Real" does not mean "perceptible to the senses", but rather:

- Permanence

- Unchangeability
- Self-luminosity

So the question contemplated by Advaitists (Indian nondualists) and mystics the world over really is: "Is this perceived world permanent, unchangeable and self-luminous?"

According to the sage of Arunachala, Sri Ramana Maharshi, that answer is a definitive "no". The names and forms appear in Brahman (God), the underlying substratum of all material phenomena. So it's not necessarily that this world is "unreal" but rather, that, as David Godman summarizes Sri Ramana:

> *"The world is known and directly experienced to be a mere appearance in the underlying Brahman, it can be accepted as real, since it is no longer perceived as a separate entity. If one knows oneself to be Brahman, one knows that the world is real because it is indistinguishable from one's own Self. However, if one merely perceives external names and forms, without experiencing that substratum, those forms have to be dismissed as unreal since they do not meet the strict definition of reality."* [12]

Bhagavan Ramana himself further contextualizes this nuance:

> *"Shankara was criticized for his views on maya without understanding him. He said that (1) Brahman is real, (2) The universe is unreal, and (3) Brahman is the universe. He did not stop at the second, because the third explains the other two. It signifies that the universe is real if perceived as the Self, and unreal if perceived apart from the Self. Hence maya and reality are one and the same."* [13]

The Buddhists have some interesting conceptual overlap with Advaita. Unlike the Hindus, they're typically indifferent to the presence of God, but they similarly don't give the world of form much solidity either.

Their sense of the "illusion", or maya, is based on our tendency to misperceive time. Buddhism considers this world transitory, because it is always in motion—which intersects with recent findings in cognitive neuroscience.[14] (Our neural processes are fluctuating as much as the cosmos.)

A Buddhist monk might respond to my aunt in the following way:

> *This is a table, as we're looking at it tonight.*
>
> *But if you step back far enough, it was a tree before that, and a seed even earlier.*
>
> *Someday it will be scraps in a wood pile.*
>
> *It could be burned for a fire, and then it will be ash.*

This world is constantly changing forms so don't be fooled by what it seems to be at this moment.

One unfortunate aspect of nondual talk is that it can be perceived as being dismissive or cold to the problems affecting this world. This is a common misconception I hear often: "If it's all illusory then why should we bother doing anything? There are people suffering the world over who need help, and we need to help them!"

Damn right we do. Illusion or otherwise.

That "uncle of the counterculture" Ram Dass spent his life harmonizing Eastern spiritual philosophies with passionate social action.[15] He talked about how accessing a place of Oneness can generate empathy and radical compassion to address suffering. His humanitarian work took him to helping cure blindness in Nepal, supporting refugees in Guatemala, and teaching prisoners meditation in San Quentin.

> *"I was in Guatemala and one of the women, widows whose husbands had been murdered before their eyes, one of these women said to me through a translator, 'Thank you so much for leaving your home and family to come and help us.'*
>
> *And I said 'I didn't. You're my home and family.' Who's leaving what?*
>
> *And I felt that, the truth of that at that moment.*

> *Because she was defining it as though she was Them, but I didn't see her as Them, she was Us."* [16]
>
> —*Ram Dass*

All of this would've been a better explanation for my dear auntie. But what I said that night was that while acknowledging its conceptual difficulties, the best analogy for the world as we know it, is a dream.

When you're really in a dream, it feels like you're really in that environment.

I waited tables in college and after you work a few double-shifts in a row, when your mind is thoroughly consumed by the job, it's common to have a "wait-mare". They are dreams where you are the only waiter in the restaurant: it's a packed house with every table trying to get your attention, livid customers are yelling at you, some are walking out cursing the whole establishment. You write down orders furiously but you can't read them back (because it's a dream) but you try to anyway. Then you go to the computer to put in all the orders that you can't read. Their collective anger rises to a crescendo, waking you up... opening your eyes, exhausted, from working all throughout your dream. Then you head into work for the morning shift.

> *"The world, like a dream full of attachments and aversions, seems real until the awakening."*
>
> —*Adi Shankara*

Most dreams are frustrating because you want to get to a certain place, or tell a certain person something, and you can't. You are captivated by its dream figures, you are bound by its imaginary rules.

Then you wake up. And realize.

Well, according to the mystics you woke up back into another dream. This table is just an image in this one.

Flipping Desire Is All It Takes

> *"Wrath springs only from thwarted desires. I do not expect anything from others, so their actions cannot be in opposition to wishes of mine. I would not use you for my own ends; I am happy only in your own true happiness."* [17]
>
> *—Sri Yukteswar Giri*

What do we really want?

Do we want the next worldly thing, or do we want to get free of worldly things?

What the spiritual traditions suggest is that you might not see the futility of worldly phenomena quite yet, but ultimately you will. As long as our desire points outward, we will be in pain, if not now then soon. The Buddha was clear: 'Desire (in Pali: *taṇhā*) is suffering.' Taṇhā means thirst, or craving, based in ignorance; and for the Buddha there are three major categories[18] to undo:

- *Kama tanha*: sense desires — the most far-reaching and familiar to all of us; any pleasure of sensual comfort as well as our thoughts and beliefs
- *Bhava tanha*: existential desires — the struggle of becoming something beyond what we currently perceive ourselves to be; the pain of ambitious striving
- *Vibhava tanha*: nonexistence desires — the wanting of a situation or attitude to end so badly that we prefer our own annihilation; a needful release often associated with unbearable suffering, shame or humiliation

I haven't transcended any of the three, really. They're all fundamentally relatable to the human experience. It's a process of undoing. But I do know that the first step is unquestionably the noticing of these phenomenal desires. From Jungian psychoanalysis to the self-inquiry of jnana yoga, we have to 'see' the tendencies of the mind before we can do anything about them. The observational power of the mind is the first opening to peace.

And the secondary step is to then flip our wanting, from the outer to the inner. From the carnal to the divine. Ramakrishna tells us:

> *"So long as these passions are directed towards the world and its objects, they behave like enemies. But when they are directed towards God, they become the best friends of man, for then they lead him unto God. The lust for the things of the world must be changed into the hankering for God: the anger that man feels in relation to his fellow man should be turned towards God for not revealing Himself to him. One should deal with all the passions in the same manner. These passions cannot be eradicated but can be educated."* [19]

According to these luminaries, we can pull a judo move on ourselves. We can transmute the fires engulfed in the physical towards the Transcendent. There's a helpful image attributed to Yogananda, Ramakrishna, and so many Eastern masters that it even gets credited to Zen Buddhism:

> *A student asks the master, "How can I see God?"*

(Or in Zen, it's 'become liberated'.)

> *The master says, "A man is being held under the water, and he is struggling to break free.*
>
> *The man wants air more than anything.*
>
> *When you want God as much as a drowning man wants air, He will reveal Himself to you."*

Or liberation. Or ego dissolution, or atonement, or the kingdom of heaven, or transcendence from the Many into the One. The ancient scriptures agree that our external desires are obstacles.

> *"The Lord is my shepherd; I shall not want."*
>
> —*Psalm 23*

Krishna tells us in the *Gita* (6.23-27):

> *"When the mind of the yogi is in peace, focused on the Self within, and beyond all restless desires, then he experiences Unity. His mind becomes still, like the flame*

of a lamp sheltered from the winds. When the mind rests in the prayerful stillness of yoga, by the grace of the One, he knows the One, and attains fulfillment... The yogi whose heart is still, whose passions are dissolved, and who is pure of sin, experiences this supreme bliss and knows his oneness with Brahman."

Even Augustine of Hippo, our friend from the beginning of this book due to his invention of our original sinfulness, understood this transformation:

> *"How sweet all at once it was for me to be rid of those fruitless joys which I had once feared to lose! You drove them from me, you who are the true, the sovereign joy. You drove them from me and took their place, you who are sweeter than all pleasure, though not to flesh and blood, you who outshine all light, yet are hidden deeper than any secret in our hearts."*
>
> —*Augustine, Confessions*

A Course in Miracles explains this process as simply having "a little willingness" to let the Holy Spirit remove all fear and hatred. (T-18.V.2:5) The Holy Spirit is fairly enigmatic within the Christian religion, but the Third of the Trinity is defined specifically by ACIM as a "Bridge": "God's Answer to the separation", and the "Communication Link between God and His separated Sons".[20]

Ultimately, reconfiguring our desire is the key (T-20.VIII.2-5):

> *"Truth is restored to you through your desire, as it was lost to you through your desire for something else. Open the holy place that you closed off by valuing the "something else," and what was never lost will quietly return. It has been saved for you. Vision would not be necessary had judgment not been made. Desire now its whole undoing, and it is done for you."*

Or don't. Desire 'something else' over and over again and stay in hell.

CHAPTER 19

Hell Is A State of Mind

The Samurai and The Monk

A big, tough samurai once went to see a little monk.

"Monk," he said, in a voice accustomed to instant obedience, "teach me about heaven and hell!"

The monk looked up at this mighty warrior and replied with utter disdain,

"Teach you about heaven and hell? I couldn't teach you about anything. You're dirty. You smell. Your blade is rusty. You're a disgrace, and an embarrassment to the samurai class. Get out of my sight. I can't stand you."

The samurai was furious.

No one talks to a samurai like this! He shook, got all red in the face, was speechless with rage. He pulled out his sword and raised it above the monk, preparing to cut off his head.

And right before he did, the monk said calmly, "That's hell."

The samurai was overwhelmed.

The compassion and surrender of this little man who had practically just risked his life to give this teaching! He slowly put down his sword, filled with gratitude, he bowed in reverence and appreciation to the monk.

"And that's heaven."

—Zen fable, author unknown, styled by Ram Dass

"Gehenna" and the "Gnashing of Teeth"

Coming full circle here... bringing Jesus back (resurrecting him?) by discussing more Bible scholarship in these last moments together.

Let's be perfectly clear:

Jesus of Nazareth does talk about "hell" in the Gospels. That's true.

But there's a very important distinction between the separate words used for "hell" in the Bible: "Hades" (Greek), "Sheol" (Hebrew), and "Gehenna" (Aramaic).

"Hades" is the Greek word for a dark underworld where evil people go. The fiery burning location predates Christianity. You might recall images from Greek mythology. Orpheus trying to find his bride who had passed to the underworld. Plato wrote about the *Myth of Er,* set in a fiery underground world that the hero traverses.[21] The Hellenistic world had a massive influence on Judaism and formative Christianity.[22] It is clear to scholars that the image of the Christian hell is heavily colored by a wide variety of influences (Greek, Roman, and even Egyptian)[23]; little of which has to do with the central figure of what later became Christianity, that Galilean big brother of humanity. "Hades" is used eleven times in the Bible, but only four times by Jesus himself (*Matthew* 11:23, 16:18, *Luke* 10:15 and *Luke* 16:23). It also occurs in *Revelation,* the final chapter of the New Testament, a spooky end-times book with little historical significance in terms of its closeness to Jesus' teachings. The "Lake of Fire" in *Revelation* closely resembles Plato's imagery in *Phaedo.*[24]

The word "Sheol" is the Hebrew word translated as "hell" in the Old Testament. It was the earlier Jewish tradition's word for "afterlife", not just "grave", but it was more of a generic 'abode of all dead' without ethical context.[25] For example, a late great king

Samuel wakes up from Sheol sleepy and annoyed when a medium contacts him on behalf of Saul, asking: *"Why have you disturbed me by bringing me up?"* (1 *Sam* 28:15) Sheol is clearly different from the modern conception of hell if one of the most famous, beloved kings of Israel belongs there.

In the entire New Testament, the word "hell" appears twenty-three times. Fifteen of these were spoken by Jesus and were translated from the Greek word "Gehenna" (*Matthew* 5:22, 5:29, 5:30, 10:28, 18:9, 23:15, 23:33, *Mark* 9:43, 9:45, 9:47, and *Luke* 12:5). Jesus uses the word Gehenna when he's discussing the opposite of the kingdom of heaven. And he's the only person in the Bible to use the term.[26]

Gehenna is an Aramaic word for the "Valley of Hinnom": a trash dump. It was a smelly landfill outside of Jerusalem where trash was burned. While there was human sacrifice in that area centuries prior, during the time of Jesus it was just a bunch of garbage.[27]

It's fair to conclude that his usage of the term "hell" is symbolic, like so much of his teachings. It's not a literal description of endless eternal torture and suffering, it's an experiential state of mind. Jesus is simply saying "that way of thinking is garbage". Similar to the verse the "kingdom of heaven is within you" (*Luke* 17:21)—so is the suffering of hell. Hell is when we live our lives off the path of Love and Unity. It's like living in filth. It's not pitchfork demons poking you forever. Thanks Hieronymus Bosch(!)—a 15th century Dutch painter largely responsible for nightmarish depictions of a literal hell.

Admittedly there is a commentary from Jesus on the "everlasting fire" of Gehenna in *Matthew.* But like his uniquely-scorching criticism of the Pharisees, this characterization is exclusive to *Matthew*. In *Mark,* Jesus has a single reference to hell, *John* talks about judgment without elaborating much on the consequences, and *Luke* has a solitary parable involving hell with a rich man and Lazarus[28]—typical of the Lukan author advocating for the poor.

The late Pope John Paul II spoke about notions of hell in 1999:

> *"It is not a punishment imposed externally by God but a development of premises already set by people in this life.*
>
> *The very dimension of unhappiness which this obscure condition brings can in a certain way be sensed in the light of some of the terrible experiences we have suffered which, as is commonly said, make life "hell"."* [29]

But Bob, and Pope John Paul II, what about that 'gnashing of teeth' line?? Doesn't it prove Jesus was warning us about a cruel eternal damnation? That strange description used primarily in *Matthew* where Jesus warns people about what takes place in hell / the trash dump...?

Six times in *Matthew*, once in *Mark* and once in *Luke*, Jesus uses the phrase "where there is weeping and gnashing of teeth", to add to the suffering image of "hell". Here's why I believe it's a later invention of the Gospel writers and has nothing to do with Jesus' actual teaching. Remember the *Gospel of Thomas*? That mysterious collection of sayings?

Within the scholarly debates around how early *Thomas* is, the *Thomas*-is-the-earliest-Gospel crowd point out that *Thomas* has no narrative.[30] It's merely a hundred short sayings. From a literary development standpoint, wouldn't it make sense that a simple collection of verses came before a more complex narrative of plot points like in every one of the four gospels (*Mark, Matthew, Luke* & *John*)?

Again, *Thomas* has dozens of sayings that made their way into the other gospels in the Bible, and one such parable is "The Great Banquet".

This parable told by Jesus appears in *Matthew, Luke,* and *Thomas*. For context, not all parables are in every gospel—a story is either unique to one, present in two, or three. Very few are in four, let alone five. What's useful about understanding this, is that the differences between each version give us a fuller understanding of the texts themselves. Here is the "Great Banquet" parable in each version:

> *Gospel of Thomas, Saying 64:*

"Jesus said: A man had guests; and when he had prepared the dinner, he sent his servants to invite the guests. He went to the first, and said to him: My master invites you. He said: I have money with some merchants; they are coming to me this evening. I will go and give them my orders. I ask to be excused from the dinner. He went to another (and) said to him: My master invites you. He said to him: I have bought a house, and I am asked for a day. I shall not have time. He went to another (and) said to him: My master invites you. He said to him: My friend is about to be married, and I am to arrange the dinner. I shall not be able to come. I ask to be excused from dinner. He went to another, he said to him: My master invites you. He said to him: I have bought a farm; I am going to collect the rent. I shall not be able to come. I ask to be excused. The servant came back (and) said to his master: Those whom you have invited to dinner have asked to be excused. The master said to his servant: Go out to the roads, bring those whom you find, that they may dine. Traders and merchants [shall] not [enter] the places of my Father."

Gospel of Luke, 14:15-24, NRSV:

"...Then Jesus said to him, "Someone gave a great dinner and invited many. At the time for the dinner he sent his slave to say to those who had been invited, 'Come; for everything is ready now.' But they all alike began to make excuses. The first said to him, 'I have bought a piece of land, and I must go out and see it; please accept my regrets.' Another said, 'I have bought five yoke of oxen, and I am going to try them out; please accept my regrets.' Another said, 'I have just been married, and therefore I cannot come.' So the slave returned and reported this to his master. Then the owner of the house became angry and said to his slave, 'Go out at once into the streets and lanes of the town and bring in the poor, the crippled, the blind, and the lame.' And the slave said, 'Sir, what you ordered has been done, and there is still room.' Then the master said to the slave, 'Go out into the roads and lanes, and

compel people to come in, so that my house may be filled. For I tell you, none of those who were invited will taste my dinner.'"

Gospel of Matthew, 22:1-14, World English Bible:

"Jesus answered and spoke again in parables to them, saying, "The Kingdom of Heaven is like a certain king, who made a marriage feast for his son, and sent out his servants to call those who were invited to the marriage feast, but they would not come. Again he sent out other servants, saying, 'Tell those who are invited, "Behold, I have prepared my dinner. My cattle and my fatlings are killed, and all things are ready. Come to the marriage feast!"' But they made light of it, and went their ways, one to his own farm, another to his merchandise, and the rest grabbed his servants, and treated them shamefully, and killed them. When the king heard that, he was angry, and sent his armies, destroyed those murderers, and burned their city. "Then he said to his servants, 'The wedding is ready, but those who were invited weren't worthy. Go therefore to the intersections of the highways, and as many as you may find, invite to the marriage feast.' Those servants went out into the highways, and gathered together as many as they found, both bad and good. The wedding was filled with guests. But when the king came in to see the guests, he saw there a man who didn't have on wedding clothing, and he said to him, 'Friend, how did you come in here not wearing wedding clothing?' He was speechless. Then the king said to the servants, 'Bind him hand and foot, take him away, and throw him into the outer darkness; there is where the weeping and gnashing of teeth will be.' For many are called, but few chosen."

The main point of the story is that a wealthy man / king (God) invites people to dinner, and they refuse his invitation.

Symbolically, this is quite clear.

It's God's invitation for salvation / enlightenment / Unity

with All that is refused by human beings (the host's friends, analogous to God's children) because we are caught up by our worldly obligations. Our focus is on our business responsibilities, our relationship responsibilities, and just general to-do's that prevent us from enjoying this 'divine feast' of bliss and harmony with God.

In *Thomas,* the story is the most basic and clear. After the invitees decline, the host invites everyone his servants can find, with a little line at the end suggesting that 'traders & merchants' are no longer invited to this dinner. Their focus is on money, not God, (a consistent theme throughout the entire New Testament) and their preoccupation with worldliness prevents them from knowing their true selves, their true connection with the divine.

In *Luke,* the host responds by inviting 'the poor, the crippled, the blind, and the lame'. Inclusivity with all, as again, the Lukan author tends to be more concerned with the poor than the other gospel authors. Otherwise, it's pretty close to *Thomas*!

In *Matthew,* the ending takes a wild turn. Not only do the invitees become murderers who miss the RSVP, after they decline, the servants fill the house with many guests, including one who didn't have on "wedding clothing". Exclusivity. The king is outraged, telling his servants to *"bind him hand and foot, and throw him into the outer darkness... where the weeping and gnashing of teeth will be."* This ending is not in *Thomas* or *Luke,* the two simpler, likely earlier versions of this story.

Why would the Matthean author add this ending?

In an early section of this book I discussed how we know that the *Gospel of Matthew* was written in Galilee, around 70-80 CE, where there were tense sectarian divisions among Jewish groups at that time. The Temple was sacked by the Romans which created an environment of existential questioning for a large amount of the Jewish religion. So in this time and place, the Jesus-following Jews were competing with the Pharisees for new believers. The 'many are called, few are chosen' theme of exclusivity is glaring in *Matthew,* and simultaneously it's where the image of "hell" (Gehenna, the trash dump) is accentuated by the 'weeping and gnashing of teeth': a reference to the Old Testament. *Matthew* 8:11-15 even discusses a new group within Judaism 'taking their place at the feast with Abraham'; and those on the outside (competing sects) can look forward to getting their teeth gnashed.[31]

When we comb through scripture with both an academic understanding of the history and a spiritual understanding of the symbolism, fear-based concepts like 'burning in hell' start to fall off. You see them for what they are: silly little fictions of fearful separateness that got added on top of original mind-altering truths of love & unity.

Plato's Cave Points to Transcendence

While traditional Christianity offers us hell, Greek philosophy offers us transcendence. One of the most famous images in all of philosophy is Plato's "Cave": a dialogue between his teacher Socrates and a fellow student, described by Plato in the seventh book of his *Republic*.

"Imagine," says Socrates to Glaucon and a few others at the house of Polemarchus, *"a number of men living in an underground den…"*[32] They have been bound by chains to prevent them from leaving since childhood. Fires are lit, their communication consists of confusing echoes, and their movements cast shadows on the cave walls.

Suppose one of the men is freed from his predicament—entering (or re-entering) the world of daylight. After recovering from initially painful glares, would he not ultimately be filled with profound joy and peace at the sight of the natural world? Asks Socrates, would he not contemplate the beauty of this upper reality: "the light of the moon and the stars and the spangled heaven"?[33]

Ecstatic with this new understanding of existence, he heads back down into the cave to explain to the rest of his community what he has encountered. We can break our chains, brothers! We can emerge from this hellish cavern of fires and shadows! It's right outside of where we've been stuck for so many years of agony!

In Plato's narrative, not only do the underground men not believe him, they kill him for spreading such preposterous fiction. The cave is the reality for the chained.

There have been as many interpretations as there have been years since this ancient piece, but it's safe to conclude that the hero of the story is the awakened being: the philosopher, the sage, the spiritual teacher who comes into the understanding of Reality As It Is. *"The sights of the cave are human, and those outside in the sun are divine."*[34] The community is us: trapped in our carnal system of thought, bound by our own chains to the limited perceptions of primordial impulses and sensual reactivity.

The ending to the story is too perfect because death has been the historic ending of so many great teachers. Plato's own mentor Socrates was sentenced to death by the governing body of Athens. *"The charge was one of corrupting the youth and impiety, or specifically - of introducing new gods in place of those recognized by the city."*[35] This false world doesn't want the Truth of the Real, and has no problem reacting accordingly.

But Plato's main point is that there is another plane of awareness, another realm, another existence. It is attainable for all human beings by breaking the chains of hellish ignorance and advancing upwards.

CHAPTER 20

Our True Nature Is Love

Who Are We, Really?

> *"Before there was anything there was the One.*
>
> *When the universe came into being,*
>
> *The One became many."*
>
> —*Rig Veda*

If "original sin" is a lie, then what's our true nature? Where did we come from?

We've already gone through what the ancient rishis of India tell us. The Hindus' "namaste" means *"the divine in me, recognizes the divine in you"*. We are an infinite expression of the Cosmic Creator, cycling through mortal lifetimes until we re-emerge back from the Many into the One. Meanwhile the Buddhists are meditating to help undo our false notions of self (*anatta*) to reveal our inherent Buddha-nature (*tathāgatagarbha*) or Buddha-Mind.

The East doesn't call us dirty sinners.

Scientific materialism thinks we're meat machines with great thumbs and a neocortex, but even the great humanist astronomer Carl Sagan put it eloquently:

> *"The cosmos is within us. We are made of star stuff."*

But what does the Bible really say? I've spent a good amount of time demonstrating the human side of the Bible. And yet again, I do consider it a profound spiritual document. There is some real wisdom under the surface and so it's important for me to examine what the Bible really thinks of us... beyond that eviction from the Garden.

The first book of both the Jewish Tanakh and the Christian Old Testament—the Book of Genesis—is especially lucid:

> *"God said, "'Let us make mankind in our image, in our likeness ...' So God created mankind in his own image, in the image of God he created them; male and female he created them."*
>
> *—Genesis 1:26-27, NIV*

What does "His image" and "likeness" mean in this context? How solid is that connection?

Very shortly after the above description, *Genesis* continues:

> *"When Adam had lived 130 years, he had a son in his own likeness, in his own image; and he named him Seth."*
>
> *—Genesis 5:3, NIV*

The same phrases "image" and "likeness" describe Adam's relationship to his son, Seth. So there you have it. That's what it means. The oldest text in the Bible, where we were 'kicked out of the Garden', is quite clear about our inherent identity as *children of God*. A perfect, endless, infinite, loving God creates children that are... inherently evil? Sorry Augustine, sorry colonial era American pastors, sorry Westboro Baptist Church. Not sorry. Our True Nature is Eternal Love, as is Our Infinite Creator's.

In case *Genesis* isn't clear enough, we have *Luke* finishing his genealogy with this line:

> *"...the son of Enos, the son of Seth, the son of Adam, the son of God."*
>
> *—Gospel of Luke 3:38*

Okay so it's quite clear. We're children of the divine.

But what about our mistakes? Our "sins"? The original translation of "sin" ("*hamartia*" in Greek) means "missing the mark" from archery and spear-throwing.[36] Not staining your soul with an unredeemable evil.

In one of the best *A Course in Miracles* commentaries, *Disappearance of the Universe* by Gary Renard, Gary's ascended friends explain to him that the most important story in the entire Bible is the Parable of the Prodigal Son.[37] If you got rid of every other story in the Bible, just keep that one. That's how revealing it is.

It goes like this.

> *He said, "A certain man had two sons. The younger of them said to his father, 'Father, give me my share of your property.' So he divided his livelihood between them. Not many days after, the younger son gathered all of this together and traveled into a far country. There he wasted his property with riotous living. When he had spent all of it, there arose a severe famine in that country, and he began to be in need. He went and joined himself to one of the citizens of that country, and he sent him into his fields to feed pigs. He wanted to fill his belly with the husks that the pigs ate, but no one gave him any. But when he came to himself he said, 'How many hired servants of my father's have bread enough to spare, and I'm dying with hunger! I will get up and go to my father, and will tell him, "Father, I have sinned against heaven, and in your sight. I am no more worthy to be called your son. Make me as one of your hired servants."'*
>
> *"He arose, and came to his father. But while he was still far off, his father saw him, and was moved with compassion, and ran, and fell on his neck, and kissed him. The son said to him, 'Father, I have sinned against heaven and in your sight. I am no longer worthy to be called your son.'*
>
> *"But the father said to his servants, 'Bring out the best robe, and put it on him. Put a ring on his hand, and sandals on his feet. Bring the fattened calf, kill it, and let's eat, and celebrate; for this, my son, was dead, and is alive*

> *again. He was lost, and is found.' Then they began to celebrate.*
>
> *"Now his elder son was in the field. As he came near to the house, he heard music and dancing. He called one of the servants to him, and asked what was going on. He said to him, 'Your brother has come, and your father has killed the fattened calf, because he has received him back safe and healthy.' But he was angry, and would not go in. Therefore his father came out, and begged him. But he answered his father, 'Behold, these many years I have served you, and I never disobeyed a commandment of yours, but you never gave me a goat, that I might celebrate with my friends. But when this your son came, who has devoured your living with prostitutes, you killed the fattened calf for him.'*
>
> *"He said to him, 'Son, you are always with me, and all that is mine is yours. But it was appropriate to celebrate and be glad, for this, your brother, was dead, and is alive again. He was lost, and is found.'"*
>
> *—Gospel of Luke 15:11-32*

There's so much to this story but of course the main point is that not only does the father forgive his son for leaving him, by accepting him… he ***celebrates*** his son's return. The son thinks that the father will reject him. He ran away and squandered his wealth, returning poor and broken. Not only does he embrace his son fully, he kills the most valuable calf for a grand feast. It is the best possible scenario. Because: *"he was lost and now is found".*

The mistakes of the prodigal son, meaning "wasteful", don't determine the father's reaction, but rather it is the identity of the son—the fact that they have a supreme, unalterable bond of family—that paves the way for this joyful reunion.

The son is humanity.

The father is our Infinite Creator.

We ran away into this world of material objects, sensual pleasures that become futile; a misdirection that ultimately creates pain and suffering for ourselves.

We think we can never return to our true, divine inheritance. We've made mistakes. We've wronged others and caused harm. We've judged others, and judged ourselves. So we must not be worthy.

Jesus in this parable assures us: the Cosmic Creator's Love is endless for his earthly children. There is nothing… nothing(!) we can do to escape His Infinite Love and Forgiveness and Union. It is inevitable… it is only ourselves who keep us from Him.

There's another brother in the parable who reflects the do-gooders of the world. They can sometimes see lost souls as less deserving. There's an aspect of that older brother in all of us too. When we do the right thing, we can look down on others doing the 'wrong thing' and we might think either directly or indirectly that we deserve more than others. Christ adds in that contextual layer here as well, in that both brothers are equally deserving of the father's love. Pretty good storyteller.

In a beautiful twist of scriptural fate, there's an almost identical parable in the *Lotus Sutra*.[38] The *Lotus Sutra* is a sacred Buddhist text containing the last of Buddha's teachings to his disciples.

Essentially, the story has the same message.

A son runs away from his powerful father for many years. The father searches endlessly, always holding his son in his heart. The son, poor and downtrodden, assumes he can never return, and even when they are reunited, the son doesn't even recognize the father. The wealthy father recognizes his son immediately, of course, and pretends to be a poorer man to be more approachable! He hires the son under this guise for many years. On the father's deathbed, he gathers everyone and tells them all to much surprise that this man is actually his son and heir.

The theme of who we are and what brought us to where we are at this moment is very clear.

We exist temporarily in these mortal frames, until we reunite with the All That Is. We are deluded, momentarily, in that we think we have no value. In Christianity we think we're sinners, in

Buddhism we think we're ignorant, in Hinduism, and *A Course in Miracles,* we think we're separate. We are the poor, prodigal Son, unaware, until we realize our true inheritance.

A Course has a helpful cosmology describing what brought us here. There seems to be a moment where the Child decided to split from the Father. The text describes this moment as *"the tiny mad idea"* which created our separateness:

> *"Into eternity, where all is one, there crept a tiny, mad idea, at which the Son of God remembered not to laugh. In his forgetting did the thought become a serious idea, and possible of both accomplishment and real effects. Together, we can laugh them both away, and understand that time cannot intrude upon eternity. It is a joke to think that time can come to circumvent eternity, which means there is no time."*
>
> *—ACIM, T-27.VIII.6:2-5*

Unsurprisingly at this point, the term *"pragyapradh"* from the Hindu *Vedas* is hilariously similar to this idea. It means *"mistake of the intellect"*, an underlying causal decision behind incoherence in ourselves and creation.[39] We have simply chosen incorrectly.

A 'tiny mad idea' or a 'mistake of the intellect'... same thing, right?

Sri Ramana elaborates on creation:

> *"The Vedanta says that the cosmos springs into view simultaneously with the seer. There is no detailed process of creation. This is said to be yugapat srishti [instantaneous creation]. It is quite similar to the creations in dream where the experiencer springs up simultaneously with the objects of experience. When this is told, some people are not satisfied for they are so rooted in objective knowledge. They seek to find out how there can be sudden creation. They argue that an effect must be preceded by a cause. In short, they desire an explanation for the existence of the world which they see around them. Then the Srutis try to satisfy their curiosity by such*

theories of creation. This method of dealing with the subject of creation is called krama srishti [gradual creation]. But the true seeker can be content with yugapat srishti - instantaneous creation." [40]

We have simply chosen the misperception of separateness, weakness, limited-ness, springing up the false dream around us. And all this spiritual work is about helping us to "choose again, dear brother". (ACIM, T-31.VIII.3:2)

We are 'lost children' who were never lost. See your Inherent Oneness and reclaim your True Inheritance as Infinite, as Loved, as Love Itself.

A Father and Son: Human and Divine

I do deep breathing Kundalini-style in the morning. Heavy inhales. Powerful exhales.

I can feel the spinal fluid coming up into the upper half of my body. I am connecting with Source.

Formerly dormant Shakti at the base is rising upward. It hits my chest organs, then it comes up into the head, into the crown, approaching liberation… and then Bobby walks by smelling like an overflowed toilet.

Photograph: Bob Peck IV and Bob Peck V. (2021)

Source: Author's personal collection

An Emptying of the False, A Stilling of the Mind, A Transforming of the Self

After all this deconditioning, we get further away from that toxic false image that we are, as 18th century American pastor Jonathan Edwards infamously preached to a frightened colonial crowd, *"sinners in the hands of an angry God"*. Instead, we start to see how much power we truly have.

Look, God was, is, and always will be. His Love is constantly shining on us, and in us, fuller than we can ever conceptualize. And in the mystic's view, there is an undoing that takes place. Call it the "removal of sin"—(or "removal of mark-missing") without the implication of an inherent stain—but I prefer an "emptying of the false".

> *"The secret of Buddhism is to remove all ideas, all concepts, in order for the truth to have a chance to penetrate, to reveal itself."* [41]
>
> —*Thích Nhất Hạnh*

This 'clearing out' is a core component of Buddhism, contemplative Christianity and Judaism as well:

> *"Have mercy on me, O God,*
>
> *according to your steadfast love;*
>
> *according to your abundant mercy*
>
> *blot out my transgressions.*
>
> *Wash me thoroughly from my iniquity,*
>
> *and cleanse me from my sin."*
>
> —*Psalm 51:1-2*

Experientially, I believe that our true nature is love, because when I get very still, and I have rooted out vices and temptations from my mind, at least for a short time, there is a feeling of boundless love that comes up in me.

If we were originally sinful, wouldn't our stillness and

presence generate weakness? Fear? If that's who we truly are? Then why does being still with ourselves generate love? Compassion, gratitude, and happiness? Because it's our true nature.

> *"To know the self as the only reality and all else as temporal and transient is freedom, peace and joy. It is all very simple. Instead of seeing things as imagined, learn to see them as they are. When you can see everything as it is, you will also see yourself as you are. It is like cleansing a mirror. The same mirror that shows you the world as it is, will also show you your own face. The thought 'I am' is the polishing cloth. Use it."* [42]
>
> *—Nisargadatta Maharaj*

We get beyond the falseness of the physical world, and ourselves, by making the decision to relinquish the false. By consciously choosing the Truth. ACIM says that's the only real decision that matters out of all the thousands of worldly decisions every day (W-138.4:1).

> *"It is your nature to crave for the revelation of That Which Is, for the Eternal, for Truth, for limitless Knowledge. This is why you do not feel satisfied with the evanescent, the untrue, with ignorance and limitation. Your true nature is to learn for the revelation of What You Are."* [43]
>
> *—Anandamayi Ma*

Divine Love is the sun, and we perceive it *"through a glass darkly."* (*Corinthians* 13:12) Our window is full of dirt, dust, and mud, and if we want the happiness of the divine, we clean our own window. We're not turning the sun on and off, the sunlight is always hitting this planet. By doing spiritual work (whichever path—inquiry, devotion, service, compassion to ourselves and others), our window becomes clear and we experience more and more of the light. The darkness is dispelled, but it's our job, our duty, our dharma to undo our ego tendencies to make way for the light.

That's it.

It can seem like a lot or it can seem like hardly anything at all.

Buddha said:

> *"Why do what you will regret? Why bring tears upon yourself? Do only what you do not regret, and fill yourself with joy."*

Sri Ramana said:

> *"Since you are awareness there is no need to attain or cultivate it. All that you have to do is to give up being aware of other things, that is of the not-Self. If one gives up being aware of them then pure awareness alone remains, and that is the Self."*

The great British poet and painter, William Blake writes:

> *"If the doors of perception were cleansed everything would appear to man as it is, Infinite. For man has closed himself up, till he sees all things thro' narrow chinks of his cavern."*

The world is saved by our own inner advances and realizations that take us beyond the body. Beyond the ego. Into a fuller sense of who we are, and of All That Is. The 'Second Coming of Christ' is the 'Resurrection in You'. We are not the body, we are not this fragmentary, momentary frame. The more we break out of this role, the lighter everything around us becomes. May we carry that aspect into all that we do.

A friend asked me recently if I believed in Jesus' resurrection on Easter Sunday.

Yes I do. However, as you may assume by now, not in the traditional sense.

After we read *Autobiography of a Yogi*, *The Gospel of Ramakrishna*, and so on, we become more aware of the ability of great masters to manipulate the physical world. Dozens of devotees of Sri Ramana have claimed that they saw him in the flesh after his passing in 1950. Sri Yukteswar came back to Yogananda in a complete bodily form months after he was buried beneath the sands at Puri.[44] They spoke for hours, with the guru answering Yogananda's enthusiastic questions about heavenly, astral worlds and the deeper laws of existence. Google "Hiranyaloka". After this Q&A and a long soulful embrace, his master's consciousness-presence dissipated back into light. It's just not that big of a deal. We're an eternal soul-consciousness momentarily occupying a bunch of electrons bouncing around. While we have no physical proof of Yogananda's guru's resurrection, we do have something interesting from the end of Yogananda's own incarnation. This beacon of Light in the 20th century died of a heart attack in 1950 moments after delivering a powerful lecture on the unity between his two loves: India & America. Fascinatingly, weeks after Yogananda had left his body, his body remained preserved. The mortuary director of Forest Lawn Memorial-Park (not a devotee) wrote a three-page letter explaining this phenomenon, which was notarized and preserved by the Self-Realization Fellowship:

> *"The absence of any visual signs of decay in the dead body of Paramhansa Yogananda offers the most extraordinary case in our experience... The physical appearance of Paramhansa Yogananda on March 27th, just before the bronze cover of the casket was put into position, was the same as it had been on March 7th. He looked on March 27th as fresh and as unravaged by decay as he had looked on the night of his death. On March 27th there was no reason to say that his body had suffered any visible physical disintegration at all. For these reasons we state again that the case of Paramhansa Yogananda is unique in our experience."* [45]

Echoing Yogananda and so many other highly realized human beings, Christ's resurrection was not to "forgive the sins of the world". Rather, it was to prove to his disciples that the ***human being is not a body***. To demonstrate the transcendence of the material world—and that this is possible for every human being.

> *"The resurrection demonstrated that nothing can destroy truth. Good can withstand any form of evil, as light abolishes forms of darkness."*
>
> *—ACIM, T-3.I.7:6-7*

Easter is a true celebration. Rejoice! Transcendence is an attainable state for all. Clean your window—with any path you like! Any religion will get you there. Any method will get you there.

It starts with intention, then practice, then some results, and ultimately awakening. Be gentle with yourself, but take heart, other human beings have left this asylum of separateness and lived in a place of love and acceptance, forgiveness and unity.

> *"Are the mystics and sages insane? Because they all tell variations on the same story, don't they? The story of awakening one morning and discovering you are one with the All, in a timeless and eternal and infinite fashion. Yes, maybe they are crazy, these divine fools. Maybe they are mumbling idiots in the face of the Abyss. Maybe they need a nice, understanding therapist. Yes, I'm sure that would help.*
>
> *But then, I wonder. Maybe the evolutionary sequence really is from matter to body to mind to soul to spirit, each transcending and including, each with a greater depth and greater consciousness and wider embrace. And in the highest reaches of evolution, maybe, just maybe, an individual's consciousness does indeed touch infinity—a total embrace of the entire Kosmos—a Kosmic consciousness that is Spirit awakened to its own true nature. It's at least plausible.*
>
> *And tell me: is that story, sung by mystics and sages the world over, any crazier than the scientific materialism story, which is that the entire sequence is a tale told by an idiot, full of sound and fury, signifying absolutely nothing? Listen very carefully: just which of those two stories actually sounds totally insane?"* [46]
>
> *—Dr. Ken Wilber*

Unconditional Love Is Fearlessness

When Byron Katie first realized the true nature of her

thoughts, it took a few years to readjust. She had to relearn everything about being human: how to function in this thing called time & space, how to break apart her experience of reality into nouns and verbs so that she could communicate with other people, and how to pretend that past and future were real.[47] She had seen through it all, and had to 'come back' in a sense.

The radically otherworldly space of Katie's presence drew people to her like a magnet. Before she had fully ironed out "The Work" and its four questions, before any books or speaking tours, she had lost souls coming to her for answers—not unlike the never-ending crowds to catch a glimpse of Sri Ramana at Ramanasramam, or the queue that began forming at a newly awakened Eckhart Tolle's park bench. Bees find the honey.

During those early years, Katie was helping a woman directly who was beginning to drastically improve her life. This woman was coming to see her regularly, practicing Katie's original process of self-inquiry and making new leaps in undoing her suffering.

Until one day her husband showed up at Katie's front door in a fit of rage. He screamed at her to stop meeting with his wife. His wife's rapid transformation had upset him severely. A police officer by day, he pulled out a gun, pointed it at Katie's chest and screamed, *"I'm going to f-n kill you!"* [48]

In reflecting on this experience, Katie said that the thought that came up for her in that moment was:

"I hope he doesn't do that to himself."

The implication being that murdering another person would create a massive amount of self-guilt, and that guilt would be very difficult for him to bear emotionally.

I keep thinking about it.

Living in that space of purity and compassion creates absolute fearlessness.

Really sit with that.

A man points a gun at your chest, ready to pull the trigger, and you're peacefully sending them well-wishes. 'Dear brother, may this act of confusion not create more emotional suffering for you in the future.'

The end of the story is that the power of her calm, loving presence generated an outburst of regret in the man. He broke down, started weeping and she offered him some comfort in that moment. The man got up, left, and was never seen again.

This is the kind of incident that takes place with an enlightened human being.

> *"When another person makes you suffer, it is because he suffers deeply within himself, and his suffering is spilling over. He does not need punishment. he needs help. That's the message he is sending."* [49]
>
> —*Thích Nhất Hạnh*

As an aside, Katie doesn't claim to be "enlightened", rather, simply someone who knows how to end her own suffering. But what Katie's story teaches us is that when we can accept ourselves and others so deeply, we become the embodiment of love. We no longer have walls built up by the ego in an attempt to be perceived in a way that's different from who we truly are. We no longer have expectations or demands of others. We're just here. In a state of clarity. Acceptance. Forgiveness.

And this is the potentiality of all human beings.

A Course in Miracles Lesson 153 is, *"In my defenselessness my safety lies"*:

> *"You who feel threatened by this changing world, its twists of fortune and its bitter jests, its brief relationships and all the "gifts" it merely lends to take away again; attend this lesson well. The world provides no safety. It is rooted in attack, and all its "gifts" of seeming safety are illusory deceptions. It attacks, and then attacks again. No peace of mind is possible where danger threatens thus.*
>
> *...Defenselessness can never be attacked, because it recognizes strength so great attack is folly.*
>
> *...Be not afraid nor timid. There can be no doubt that you*

> *will reach your final goal. The ministers of God can never fail, because the love and strength and peace that shine from them to all their brothers come from Him. These are His gifts to you. Defenselessness is all you need to give Him in return. You lay aside but what was never real, to look on Christ and see His sinlessness."*
>
> *—ACIM, W-153.1:1-5; 6:4; 20:2-7*

Liberation Is True Forgiveness

All of the major religions emphasize forgiveness.

From Rabbi Hillel to the *Koran,* to Jesus on the cross forgiving *"those who know not what they do"* (*Luke* 23:24)... again, one of the most penetrating utterances in human history. Forgiveness is profoundly important, as even modern scientific research suggests that forgiveness is good for our mental, emotional and physical health.

There are incredible stories throughout cultures of instances where a human forgave the actions of an 'evil-doer', and they are some of the most beautiful expressions of enlightened action in our civilization.

In 2015, a young white man named Dylann Roof walked into a historic African-American church in Charleston, South Carolina. The Sunday worshipers did not know his intention was to kill them all. The white man amongst a room full of black congregation members, Roof sat through a peaceful Sunday Bible study. They treated him with such kindness, he later recounted, that it made him almost reconsider his plan.[50] As the session began to close, Roof opened fire in the church, killing nine beloved members of the local black community. He was arrested the following day, and later sentenced to life in prison. His intentions were nothing short of trying to start a race war in America.

At his first court appearance, in a moment of insurmountable courage and love, Nadine Collier, the daughter of her departed mother Ethel Lance, told the young killer:

> *"I forgive you.*
>
> *You took something very precious from me. I will never talk to her again. I will never, ever hold her again.*
>
> *But I forgive you. And have mercy on your soul."* [51]

This is truly the height of humanity.

My country's beacon of the true Christian understanding, MLK, writes:

> *"Now there is a final reason I think that Jesus says, "Love your enemies."*
>
> *It is this: that love has within it a redemptive power. And there is a power there that eventually transforms individuals. Just keep being friendly to that person. Just keep loving them, and they can't stand it too long. Oh, they react in many ways in the beginning. They react with guilt feelings, and sometimes they'll hate you a little more at that transition period, but just keep loving them. And by the power of your love they will break down under the load.*
>
> *That's love, you see. It is redemptive, and this is why Jesus says love.*
>
> *There's something about love that builds up and is creative. There is something about hate that tears down and is destructive. So love your enemies."* [52]

A Course in Miracles tells us: *"Fear binds the world, forgiveness sets it free."* (ACIM, W-332) While *A Course* discusses forgiveness at length, there is an additional layer through its nondual lens.

The traditional view of forgiveness in the world is that 'you wronged me, and until you express regret and apologize, then and only then, I'll consider forgiving you for the wrong you did.' Occasionally the so-called abuser will express remorse and both parties can move on in a certain way.

But not always. Sometimes it has no effect on the 'wrong-doer', and they continue to act in ways that are harmful to themselves and others.

Or when there's no remorse, we can carry that anger onwards, allowing it to shape the future of our relationship and ourselves.

On top of this ego-world variety, forgiveness is typically considered a gift to the so-called abuser, not even to the so-called victim—although most spiritually-minded folks understand the benefit to both parties.

ACIM takes it an illusory-step further.

> *"Forgiveness recognizes what you thought your brother did to you has not occurred. It does not pardon sins and make them real. It sees there was no sin. And in that view are all your sins forgiven. What is sin, except a false idea about God's Son? Forgiveness merely sees its falsity, and therefore lets it go."*
>
> *—ACIM, W-pII.1.1:1-6*

I really struggled with this one. For many years.

How did it *not happen*? That doesn't make any sense. I was wronged, and I understand that forgiveness is liberating for me, but how was there "no sin"?

It took my adoration of Byron Katie to begin to start to grasp this one.

Nondual aspect #1. The present is all there is. There is no future, no past. Only now. One thing Katie says to people about the past is *"where's your proof?"* The past only exists in our memory.

Nondual aspect #2. Expand your limited perspective. Zoom out into a grander, cosmic perspective of our personal belief systems. In another interview, Katie gave an example of a hate group making bombs. *"If you believed what they believed, wouldn't you be making bombs too?"* The actions of every human being in this world are caused by our beliefs. So we're all just going through life acting on these false beliefs—our false identities of separation, of being in need of something from others outside of ourselves—all of our actions unraveling from this state of confusion.

Nondual aspect #3. The Self is the Sole Reality and all else is temporal; created from an ignorance of this true understanding. The world is a reflection of ourselves in which we are constantly finding faults, which we can eliminate in our own mind, and nowhere else.

> *"An unforgiving thought does many things. In frantic action it pursues its goal, twisting and overturning what it sees as interfering with its chosen path. Distortion is its purpose, and the means by which it would accomplish it as well. It sets about its furious attempts to smash reality, without concern for anything that would appear to pose a contradiction to its point of view.*
>
> *Forgiveness, on the other hand, is still, and quietly does nothing. It offends no aspect of reality, nor seeks to twist it to appearances it likes.*
>
> *It merely looks, and waits, and judges not.*
>
> *He who would not forgive must judge, for he must justify his failure to forgive. But he who would forgive himself must learn to welcome truth exactly as it is."*
>
> *—ACIM, W-pII.1.3:1–4:5*

This is why Katie says: *"There's nothing to forgive."*

This is why Nisargadatta says: *"It is always the false that makes you suffer."*

This is why Christ says: *"Resist not evil."*

When you can step back far enough, and see it all happening...

This awareness of our Infinite Identity expanding beyond this confined form, beyond our past stories and our future plans...

Beyond the concept of lifetimes coming and going, being born and dying, for thousands, for millions of years...

Knowing our True Self as:

Present.

Timeless.

Loving.

...Who's harming who?

We start to see every being from a place of absolute compassion.

Despite the outward condition, loving anyway. This is Unconditional Love.

This is liberation.

This is the way out of the asylum.

It's our True Nature—Love not fear, Oneness not separation, Innocence not sinfulness—beneath it all, inherent in the Self.

EPILOGUE

The Experiencing:
The Parable of the Poisoned Arrow

What I've tried to do here is shed some light on comparative religion and scriptural scholarship, from the ancient to the contemporary.

At the same time I've tried to avoid getting too deep into textual analysis which can lead us to miss the symbolic. The feeling!

Most scholars aren't mystics. And most mystics don't give a damn about the intellectual analyses. It's a balance between both worlds and I've done my best.

I'm fairly certain that some of the academic crowd will think I haven't been as thorough, and some of the spiritual crowd will think I've spent too much time splitting textual hairs.

That's how this world works. (Buddha has a great line about haters:)

> *"They blame those who remain silent,*
>
> *they blame those who speak much,*
>
> *they blame those who speak in moderation.*
>
> *There is none in the world who is not blamed."*
>
> *—Buddha, Dhammapada, Verse 227*

(He's stating the same thing as the forgiveness vs. judgment piece in the last chapter—the tendency of the ego mind to judge. It's all connected. I am redundant.)

Regardless of my anticipated reception, all these concepts are just words on pages or sounds in headphones.

We can read every scripture in the world, and the similarities are strikingly beautiful, but living out our paths on this plane of existence will always be experiential.

Concepts can help prime our mind for a larger experience of love, of connection, of openness, but that is on the experiencer.

Meister Eckhart, a medieval inspiration for the modern master, writes,

> *"Spirituality is not to be learned by flight from the world, or by running away from things, or by turning solitary and going apart from the world.*
>
> *Rather, we must learn an inner solitude wherever or with whomsoever we may be. We must learn to penetrate things and find God there."*

I love reading the lines of these sages because I get into a place of peace that I can then live out of. It's not about intellectualizing everything, it's about translating their wisdom into usefulness—into a life free(r) from suffering, with more peace, and hey maybe even transcendence beyond this fragmentary mortal role? Mentally intellectualizing can really get in the way of our progress. The mind that is constantly analyzing can prevent us from loving ourselves and others.

Ramakrishna pointed out the inadequacies of intellectualism by likening it to counting every tree in a mango orchard.

Don't waste time counting every tree, branch, and leaf of the orchard.

Eat the mangoes.

All that data processing is not in any way comparable to enjoying the sweetness of a fresh fruit plucked from a tree in the sunshine. This is religious theology vs. spiritual mysticism. The experience is what matters, not the cognizing.

I would tell a parable so often at Think & Drink it became cliché.

We would cover the most outrageous speculative philosophies… you have to understand we were drinking too much, and blabbing about explicitly detailed cosmology. The most bizarre futurology predictions and hypotheses. They would get pretty far out… and when our conversations would get to the unanswerable, I would tell the *"Parable of the Poisoned Arrow"* from the life of the Buddha:

A monk asked the Buddha,

> *"Because you're the Awakened One:*
>
> *How many heavens are there?*
>
> *How many realms are there?*
>
> *How many beings in the cosmos?"*

and he responded with this parable:

> *"A man fighting in a war is shot by an arrow.*
>
> *A doctor is called to heal the man.*
>
> *The doctor is not concerned with what the war is being fought over,*
>
> *which generals oversee each side,*
>
> *or even who shot the arrow;*
>
> *the doctor is only concerned with removing the arrow and saving the man's life."*

Similarly, we shouldn't let ourselves be overwhelmed by exhaustive analyses of the cosmos and all of its complexities. This world, this universe, this 'multiverse'... our form in time and space is far too unendingly baffling to fully codify.

It's a nearly perfect trap to prevent us from experiencing Reality As It Is. Spiritual teacher and mystic, David Hoffmeister, referencing *A Course*, says:

> *"The graven image is the entire cosmos, you see?*
>
> *It's not like making a golden calf or something and worshipping it. The graven image is all of it, all of the images."* [1]

So all we have to do is remove the arrow.

Remove our suffering, remove our own obstacles to peace—to awareness of the Love deep within ourselves.

So that's it.

Use this birth.

Use this incarnation and all that it provides for our learning.

Notice the present, forgive, and don't get caught in these fear-based lies that keep us stuck in spiritual stagnation. Our truest essence is not fear. It's not pain.

Original sin is a lie.

We are Love.

. . . .

Vivekananda was the most famous disciple of Ramakrishna. His work influenced not only Hinduism at large, but religious dialogue in 19th century America, Gandhi & the Indian nationalist movement, and countless other seekers on the path. He quoted from the *Gita*, the *Bible*, and the *Koran*. He was the first swami to lecture in universities the world over, blowing Ivy League brains out of their skulls in the late 1800s. He spoke about the beauty of every faith, and of the form and Formlessness of it all.

He sums up pretty much everything I've tried to put into these humble pages… aptly reassuring us of how it all works in five sentences:

> *"Each soul is potentially divine.*
>
> *The goal is to manifest this divinity by controlling nature, external and internal.*
>
> *Do this either by work, or worship, or mental control, or philosophy—by one, or more, or all of these—and be free.*
>
> *This is the whole of religion.*
>
> *Doctrines, or dogmas, or rituals, or books, or temples, or forms, are but secondary details."* [2]

Citations

Part One: Debunking Fearful Institutions: Original sin is a lie, our true nature is Love

1. Scheck, Thomas P. (2012). "Pelagius's Interpretation of Romans". In Cartwright, Steven (ed.). *A Companion to St. Paul in the Middle Ages*. Leiden: Brill. pp. 79–114.
2. Timpe, Kevin, "Sin in Christian Thought", *The Stanford Encyclopedia of Philosophy* (Summer 2021 Edition), Edward N. Zalta (ed.), https://plato.stanford.edu/archives/sum2021/entries/sin-christian/.
3. Augustine, and Peter Holmes. *The Anti-Pelagian Works of Saint Augustine, Bishop of Hippo*. T. & T. Clark, 1872.
4. Adolf von Harnack, Carl Gustav. *Encyclopedia Brittanica*, Volume 17., "Marcion". 1917
5. Haardt, Robert, and J. F. Hendry. *Gnosis: Character and Testimony*, E.J. Brill, Leiden, 1971, p. 341.
6. "In the Beginning--': a Catholic Understanding of Creation and the Fall, by Pope Benedict", Wm. B. Eerdmans Publishing, 1995, p. 72.
7. "The First Jewish Revolt and Its Aftermath." *From Jesus to Christianity: How Four Generations of Visionaries & Storytellers Created the New Testament and Christian Faith*, by L. Michael White, HarperCollins, 2016, pp. 217–238.
8. "The Blackwell Companion to the New Testament." The Blackwell Companion to the New Testament, by David Edward Aune, Wiley-Blackwell, 2010, pp. 9–10.
9. "Forgery and Counterforgery: the Use of Literary Deceit in Early Christian Polemics", by Bart D. Ehrman, Oxford University Press, 2014.
10. "Domesticating Paul: The Pastoral Epistles." *From Jesus to Christianity: How Four Generations of Visionaries & Storytellers*

Created the New Testament and Christian Faith, by L. Michael White, HarperCollins, 2016, pp. 426-438.

11. "Jesus As the Culmination of Apocalyptic History." *Jesus in History: An Approach to the Study of the Gospels*, by Howard Kee, Harcourt Brace Jovanovich, 1977, pp. 143–148.

12. Ehrman, Bart D. *Misquoting Jesus: The Story Behind Who Changed the Bible and Why*. HarperSanFrancisco, 2007.

13. Ehrman, Bart D. "Are the Gospels Historically Reliable? The Problem of Contradictions." YouTube, © Defenders Media 501(c)(3), 27 June 2020, www.youtube.com/watch?v=AymnA526j9U.

14. "Christianity." The World's Religions, by Huston Smith, HarperOne, 2009, pp. 317–320.

15. Robert Wall, *New Interpreter's Bible Vol. X* (Abingdon Press, 2002), pp. 373.

16. Koester, Helmut. *Ancient Christian Gospels: Their History and Development*. SCM Press, 1990.

17. Eta Linnemann, "The Lost Gospel Of Q—Fact Or Fantasy?," Trinity Journal 17:1, Spring 1996.

18. Clement, *Hypotyposes*; Eusebius, *Ecclesiastical History*, 6.14.7.

19. Livingstone, E. A.; Sparkes, M. W. D.; Peacocke, R. W., eds. (2013). *The Concise Oxford Dictionary of the Christian Church*. Oxford University Press. p. 92.

20. "Lamb of God." *Scripting Jesus: The Gospels in Rewrite*, by Michael L. White, Harper One, 2011, p. 15.

21. Dass, Ram. "Ram Dass Here and Now." Episode 159: "Stuck In-Between Stories", Apple Podcasts, March 6, 2020. Lecture original recording, 1993.

22. Josephus, *Antiquities* 13.10.5-6.

23. "One Church and Their Synagogue: Matthew's Jewish Sect." *From Jesus to Christianity: How Four Generations of Visionaries & Storytellers Created the New Testament and Christian Faith*, by L. Michael White, HarperCollins, 2016, pp. 243–247.

24. A. Roy Eckhardt, *Elder and Younger Brothers:The Encounter of Jews and Christians*, Scribner New York, 1967.

25. "Justice and Good Sinners." *The Storytelling God: Seeing the Glory of Jesus in His Parables*, by Jared C. Wilson, Crossway, 2014, p. 88.

26. "The Samaritans—Religious Intolerance." *Greek Testament Lessons: Consisting Chiefly of the Sermon on the Mount, and the*

Parables of Our Lord with Notes and Essays, by John Hunter Smith, William Blackwood & Sons, 1884, pp. 133–136.

27. Marshall, I. Howard. *The Gospel of Luke*. Wm. B. Eerdman, 1978, pp. 449-450.
28. Stuber, Stanley I., and Thomas Curtis Clark. *Treasury of the Christian Faith; an Encyclopedic Handbook of the Range and Witness of Christianity*. Association Press, 1949, pp. 43.
29. "Chapter I. The Doctrine of Non-Resistance to Evil by Force Has Been Professed by a Minority of Men from the Very Foundation of Christianity." *The Kingdom of God Is Within You*, by Leo Tolstoy, Barnes & Noble Books, [1893] 2005, pp. 2-6.
30. Savastio, Rebecca. "KKK Member Walks up to Black Musician in Bar-but It's Not a Joke, and What Happens Next Will Astound You." *Guardian Liberty Voice*, 21 Nov. 2013, guardianlv.com/2013/11/kkk-member-walks-up-to-black-musician-in-bar-but-its-not-a-joke-and-what-happens-next-will-astound-you/.
31. Friedersdorf, Conor. "Talking About Race With the KKK." *The Atlantic*, Atlantic Media Company, 27 Mar. 2015, www.theatlantic.com/politics/archive/2015/03/the-audacity-of-talking-about-race-with-the-klu-klux-klan/388733/.
32. "Marking the Passion." *Scripting Jesus: The Gospels in Rewrite*, by Michael L. White, Harper One, 2011, p. 136-137.
33. Eubank, Nathan. "A Disconcerting Prayer: On the Originality of Luke 23:34a." *Journal of Biblical Literature*, vol. 129, no. 3, 2010, pp. 521–536., doi:10.2307/25765950.
34. Vivekananda, Swami. "The Absolute and Manifestation." Volume 2: Jnana Yoga. *The Complete Works of Swami Vivekananda*, 1896, London.
35. "Anti-Institutionalism." *Jesus Is Still Speaking Through the Gospel of Mark*, by Jimmy R. Watson. 2011, pp. 40–44.
36. "I AM THAT I AM." *The Mystic Christ: The Light of Non-Duality and the Path of Love as Revealed in the Life and Teachings of Jesus*, by Ethan Walker, Devi Press, 2003, pp. 19–21.
37. "Discourse 41: Matthew: 1034-39." *The Second Coming of Christ: the Resurrection of the Christ Within You: a Revelatory Commentary on the Original Teachings of Jesus*, by Paramahansa Yogananda Self-Realization Fellowship, Los Angeles, CA, 2004, p. 792.
38. Moyers, Bill. "Masks of Eternity." *The Power of Myth*, interview with Joseph Campbell, season 1, episode 6, Public Broadcasting Service, 26 June 1988.

39. Yogananda, Paramahansa. *Autobiography of a Yogi.* Self-Realization Fellowship, Los Angeles, California. Reprinted with permission. 1946.

40. Yarow, Jay. "The Only Book Steve Jobs Downloaded To His IPad." Business Insider, 21 Oct. 2011, www.businessinsider.com/the-only-book-steve-jobs-downloaded-to-his-ipad-2011-10.

41. "The Cauliflower Robbery." *Autobiography of a Yogi,* by Paramahansa Yogananda, Self-Realization Fellowship, Los Angeles, ,California, pp. 132–141. Reprinted with permission.

42. Ramelli, Ilaria. "Luke 17:21: 'The Kingdom of God Is inside You' The Ancient Syriac Versions in Support of the Correct Translation." *Hugoye: Journal of Syriac Studies* (Volume 12), 2009, pp. 259–286., doi:10.31826/9781463220631-011.

43. Harris, Stephen L. (2006). *Understanding the Bible* (7th ed.). McGraw-Hill.

44. "The Story of Jesus as Mystical Participation: The Gospel of John." *Jesus in History: An Approach to the Study of the Gospels,* by Howard Clark Kee, Harcourt Brace Jovanovich, 1977, pp. 203–214.

45. CBN News. "Tim Tebow's Shocking Story About John 3:16 'Coincidence' Goes Viral." CBN News, 8 Jan. 2018, www1.cbn.com/cbnnews/entertainment/2018/january/tim-tebow-rsquo-s-nbsp-shocking-story-about-john-3-16-lsquo-coincidence-rsquo-goes-viral.

46. "Discourse 15: God's Love Gave to the World His Only Begotten Son." *The Second Coming of Christ: the Resurrection of the Christ Within You: a Revelatory Commentary on the Original Teachings of Jesus,* by Paramahansa Yogananda, Self-Realization Fellowship, 2004, pp. 273–274.

47. Clement, *Excerpta ex Theodoto 6:3.*

48. "John, Thomas, and Docetism: The Evidence of 1 John." *From Jesus to Christianity: How Four Generations of Visionaries & Storytellers Created the New Testament and Christian Faith,* by L. Michael White, HarperCollins, 2016, pp. 314–315.

49. De incarnatione 54,3, cf. Contra Arianos 1.39

50. "The Story of Jesus as Mystical Participation: The Gospel of John." *Jesus in History: An Approach to the Study of the Gospels,* by Howard Clark Kee, Harcourt Brace Jovanovich, 1977, pp. 228.

51. Haygood, Lisa. "The Battle To Authenticate 'The Gospel of Thomas'." *LUX,* vol. 3, no. 1, 2013, pp. 1–31., doi:10.5642/lux.201303.06.

52. Hippolytus of Rome, *Refutation of All Heresies*, Book V, translated with an Introduction and notes by M. David Litwa, Atlanta, SBL Press, 2016.

53. "Nature and Structure." *Gnosis: The Nature and History of Gnosticism*, by Kurt Rudolph and Robert McLachlan Wilson, HarperSanFrancisco, 1987, p. 55.

54. Hoeller, Stephan A. *Gnosticism: New Light on the Ancient Tradition of Inner Knowing*. The Theosophical Publishing House, 2002.

55. Perrin, Nicholas, and Christopher W. Skinner. "Recent Trends in Gospel of Thomas Research (1989–2011). Part II: Genre, Theology and Relationship to the Gospel of John." Currents in Biblical Research, vol. 11, no. 1, 2012, pp. 65–86., doi:10.1177/1476993x12458067.

56. Haygood, Lisa. "The Battle To Authenticate 'The Gospel of Thomas'." *LUX*, vol. 3, no. 1, 2013, pp. 1–31., doi:10.5642/lux.201303.06.

57. "The Secret of Judas Thomas." *Thomas: Seeking the Historical Context of the Gospel of Thomas*, by Risto Uro, T & T Clark, 2003, pp. 12–13.

58. "Mystics of the Ancient Past." *History of Mysticism: The Unchanging Testament*, by Swami Abhayananda, Watkins, 2002, p. 75.

Part Two: The Perennial Philosophy: It's All True

1. Peck, Bob. *Tribute to an Angel: How a Former Altar Boy Turned Devout Atheist Finally Found God, Love, and Happiness.*, unpublished.

2. Ibid.

3. Abhedananda, Swami and Sri Ramakrishna Paramahansa. "Right Attitude To Religious Differences." *Sayings of Ramakrishna*, by Ramakrishna, Ramakrishna Vedanta Math, 1968, p. 134.

4. Buonarroti, Michelangelo. *The Creation of the Sun and the Moon*. 1511, Sistine Chapel ceiling.

5. "The Healing of the Dream." *A Course in Miracles*, Foundation for Inner Peace, 1985. T-27.VIII.6:2

6. "Religious Responses." *Living Religions*, by Mary Pat Fisher, Pearson, 2017, pp. 5–9.

7. Yousef, Jinan. *Reflecting on the Names of Allah*. Al Buruj Press, 2021.

8. Smart, Ninian. "Polytheism." *Encyclopædia Britannica.* 1999, www.britannica.com/topic/polytheism#ref420550.

9. Hartshorne, Charles. *Man's Vision of God and the Logic of Theism.* Archon Books, 1964.

10. Peck, Bob, director. *The Kingdom Within.* Be Where How? Channel, Mind Heart Lens Films, 2015, www.youtube.com/watch?v=shw0Dvm8JBk.

11. "Chapter 25 (第二十五章)." Tao Te Ching, by Lao Tzu and William Scott Wilson, Shambhala, 2013.

12. Sankaracharya, Adi. *Atma Bodha (The Awakening of Self).* Translated by Swami Chinmayananda, Chinmaya Mission, Sankaracharya.org - Your Gateway to Advaita Vedanta, www.sankaracharya.org/atmabodha.php.

13. 'ANTL-WEISER W, 2009: The time of the Willendorf figurines and new results of Palaeolithic research in Lower Austria. *Anthropologie* (Brno) 47, 1-2: 131-141'.

14. Godman, David. "An Introduction to Sri Ramana's Life and Teachings - Page 3 of 5." David Godman, 12 July 2019, www.davidgodman.org/an-introduction-to-sri-ramanas-life-and-teachings/3/.

15. Reade, William W. *Martyrdom of Man.* University Press of the Pacific, 2004, 1872.

16. "The Rigveda and the Indus Civilization." *Discovering the Vedas: Origins, Mantras, Rituals, Insights,* by Frits Staal, Penguin, 2017, pp. 7–11.

17. "Hinduism: Philosophical and Metaphysical Elements." *Living Religions,* by Mary Pat Fisher, Pearson, 2017, pp. 71–75.

18. Minar, Edwin L., and Herbert Strainge Long. "A Study of the Doctrine of Metempsychosis in Greece: From Pythagoras to Plato." *The American Journal of Philology,* vol. 71, no. 4, 1950, p. 447., doi:10.2307/292397.

19. Kinsley, David. "Avatar." *Encyclopedia of Religion.* Mercia Eliade, ed. New York: MacMillan Publishing, 1987. 14-15.

20. Hein, Norvin. "A Revolution in Kṛṣṇaism: The Cult of Gopāla: History of Religions, Vol. 25, No. 4 (May, 1986), pp. 296-317". **25**: 296–317.

21. Yogananda, Paramahansa. "The Supreme Science of Knowing God." *The Bhagavad Gita: God Talks with Arjuna: Royal Science of God-Realization,* Self Realization Fellowship, 1995, p.440.

22. Pasles, Chris. "'Mahabharata'--in Condensed Form." *Los Angeles Times,* 5 Oct. 1999, www.latimes.com/archives/la-xpm-1999-

oct-05-me-18924-story.html.

23. "Introduction." *Alternative Krishnas: Regional and Vernacular Variations on a Hindu Deity*, by Guy L. Beck, State University of New York, 2005, pp. 4–5.

24. Hayden, Bethany. "Is There Any Similarity between the 'Trimurti' in Hinduism and the 'Holy Trinity' in Christianity?" *Spirit Restoration*, 12 Sept. 2020, www.spiritrestoration.org/religion/is-there-any-similarity-between-the-trimurti-in-hinduism-and-the-holy-trinity-in-christianity/.

25. Yogananda, Paramahansa. "Introduction." *The Bhagavad Gita: God Talks with Arjuna: Royal Science of God-Realization*, Self Realization Fellowship, 1995, p. xxx.

26. "Buddhism." *The World's Religions*, by Huston Smith, Harper One, 1995.

27. "The First Noble Truth – Dukkha - The Buddha and His Teachings - OCR - GCSE Religious Studies Revision - OCR - BBC." *BBC News*, BBC, www.bbc.co.uk/bitesize/guides/zj4g4qt/revision/3.

28. Crossan, John Dominic (1995). *Jesus: A Revolutionary Biography*. HarperOne. p. 145.

29. Yogananda, Paramahansa. "Spiritual Symbolism of the Mahabharata Story." *The Bhagavad Gita: God Talks with Arjuna: Royal Science of God-Realization*, Self Realization Fellowship, 1995, p. xxxiv-xxxix.

30. "XXV. JETAVANA." *The Gospel of Buddha: Compiled from Ancient Writings*, by Paul Carus, Pacific Publishing Studio, 2011, p. 36. (First published 1894.)

31. "Volume 1: Lectures & Discourses - Krishna." *The Complete Works of Swami Vivekananda*, by Swami Vivekananda, Advaita Ashrama, 2016.

32. "What Bahá'ís Believe." *Manifestations of God | What Bahá'ís Believe*, www.bahai.org/beliefs/god-his-creation/revelation/manifestations-god.

33. Ram, Arun. "US Pastor Says Yoga 'Demonic', Sparks Row." *The Economic Times*, 18 Oct. 2010, economictimes.indiatimes.com/news/politics-and-nation/us-pastor-says-yoga-demonic-sparks-row/articleshow/6766880.cms.

34. Peck, Bob, director. *The Kingdom Within*. Be Where How? Channel, Mind Heart Lens Films, 2015, www.youtube.com/watch?v=shw0Dvm8JBk.

35. Davids, Paul. "Jesus' Lost Years May Finally Have Been Found." *HuffPost*, 25 May 2011, www.huffpost.com/entry/jesus-lost-years-may-fina_b_179513.

36. Case, Shirley Jackson. "Jesus and Sepphoris." *Journal of Biblical Literature*, vol. 45, no. 1/2, 1926, pp. 14–22., doi:10.2307/3260163.

37. Notovich, Nicolas. *The Unknown Life of Jesus Christ.* Indo-American Book Co., 1894.

38. Younghusband, Francis Edward. *The Heart of a Continent: A Narrative of Travels in Manchuria, Across the Gobi Desert, Through the Himalayas, the Pamirs, and Hunza (1884-1894)*, John Murray, 1896.

39. Chaitanya, Brahmachari Bhairab; *Swami Abhedananda's Journey into Kashmir and Tibet*; Ramakrishna Vedanta Math, Calcutta, 1987 (first published in Bengali in 1929) pp.119-121, 164-166

40. Burke, Abbot George. *The Christ of India: The Story of Original Christianity*. Light of the Spirit Press, 2018.

41. Cayce, Edgar, and Jeffrey Furst. *Edgar Cayce's Story of Jesus.* Berkley Books, 1987.

42. Bhavishya Maha Purana 3.2.9-31.

43. Prophet, Mark, and Elizabeth Clare Prophet. *Lords of the Seven Rays: Mirror of Consciousness*. Summit University Press, 1986.

44. Dimock, Edward C. , Buitenen, J.A.B. van , Smith, Brian K. , Narayanan, Vasudha , Doniger, Wendy , Gold, Ann G. and Basham, Arthur Llewellyn. "Hinduism". *Encyclopedia Britannica*, 30 Nov. 2020, https://www.britannica.com/topic/Hinduism.

45. Cronk, George. *On Shankara*. Thomson/Wadsworth, 2003.

46. Saraswati, Chandrasekharendra (1995), *Hindu Dharma: The Universal Way of Life*, Bhavan's Book University.

47. "Beyond the Body and Mind." *Yoga Nidra*, by Satyananda Saraswati, Yoga Publications Trust, 2013, p. 53.

48. Cronk, George. *On Shankara*. Thomson/Wadsworth, 2003.

49. Aurobindo, Sri. "The Concept of Satchitananda." *Essays Divine and Human: Writings from Manuscripts 1910-1950*, Sri Aurobindo Ashram Publication Dept., 1997, pp. 85–87.

50. "The Yoga Bearers." *American Veda: From Emerson and the Beatles to Yoga and Meditation—How Indian Spirituality Changed the West*, by Philip Goldberg, Three Rivers Press, 2013, p. 197-209.

51. "A Quiet Mind Is All You Need." *I Am That: Talks with Sri Nisargadatta Maharaj*, by Nisargadatta et al., Acorn Press, 2012,

p. 308.

52. Sri Anandamayi Ma. "Chapter III: Selected Discourses." *The Essential Srī Anandamayī Mā: Life and Teachings of a 20th Century Indian Saint*, edited by Alexander Lipski and Joseph A. Fitzgerald, World Wisdom, Bloomington, 2007, p. 142.

53. Abhedananda, Swami and Sri Ramakrishna Paramahansa. *Sayings of Ramakrishna*, by Ramakrishna, Ramakrishna Vedanta Math, 1968.

54. Abhedananda, Swami. "Introduction." *The Gospel of Ramakrishna*, The Vedanta Society, 1907, pp. 2–4.

55. "The Boyhood of Ramakrishna." *Ramakrishna and His Disciples*, by Christopher Isherwood, Vedanta Society of Southern California, 1965, pp. 28–29.

56. "Keshab Sen." *Ramakrishna and His Disciples*, by Christopher Isherwood, Vedanta Society of Southern California, 1965, pp. 166.

57. Ibid.

58. Abhedananda, Swami. "Introduction." *The Gospel of Ramakrishna*, The Vedanta Society, 1907, pp. 11-12.

59. Gupta, Mahendranath. "The Master with the Brahmo Devotees." *The Gospel of Sri Ramakrishna*, translated by Nikhilananda, Sri Ramakrishna Math, 1942.

60. LeBlanc, Pam. "'Richie Flores Found Yoga in Prison; Now He Wants to Teach Others.'" *Austin-American Statesman*, 26 Jan. 2014, www.statesman.com/article/20140126/NEWS/301269796.

61. Crair, Ben. "Prakashanand Saraswati, the Fugitive Guru of Barsana Dham." *The Daily Beast*, 21 June 2011, www.thedailybeast.com/prakashanand-saraswati-the-fugitive-guru-of-barsana-dham.

62. Vonk, Roos, and Anouk Visser. "An Exploration of Spiritual Superiority: The Paradox of Self - Enhancement." European Journal of Social Psychology, vol. 51, no. 1, 2021, pp. 152–165., doi:10.1002/ejsp.2721.

63. Thielman, Samuel B. "Reflections on the Role of Religion in the History of Psychiatry." *Handbook of Religion and Mental Health*, edited by Harold Koenig, Elsevier, 2007, pp. 2–4.

64. Freud, Sigmund. *The Ego and the Id*. W.W. Norton, 1923.

65. Breuer, Josef. "Case Histories: Fraulein Anna O." *Studies on Hysteria*, by Sigmund Freud and Josef Breuer, Hogarth Press, [1895] 1955, p. 24.

66. Dunne, Claire. *Carl Jung: Wounded Healer of the Soul*. Watkins, 2015.

67. Hull, R.F.C., translator. "The Symbolism of the Mandala" (Paragraph 126). *The Collected Works of C.G.Jung 12: Psychology and Alchemy*, by C. G. Jung, Bollingen Series, Princeton University Press, 1968, pp. 99–100.

68. Hull, R.F.C., translator. "The Philosophical Tree" (Paragraph 335). *The Collected Works of C.G.Jung 13: Alchemical Studies*, by C. G. Jung, Bollingen Series, Princeton University Press, 1970, pp. 265–266.

69. Bolte Taylor, J. (2008, February). My stroke of insight [Video]. TED Conferences. https://www.ted.com/talks/jill_bolte_taylor_my_stroke_of_insight

70. Taylor, Jill Bolte. *My Stroke of Insight: A Brain Scientist's Personal Journey*. Viking, 2006.

71. *The Diaries of a Cosmopolitan*, by Harry G. Kessler, Weidenfeld and Nicolson, 1971, p. 322.

72. Chalmers, David John. *The Conscious Mind: In Search of a Theory of Conscious Experience*. Oxford University Press, 1996.

73. Hassert, Kurt. *Allgemeine Verkehrsgeographie*. De Gruyter, 1931.

74. Pringle, Heather. "What Happens When an Archaeologist Challenges Mainstream Scientific Thinking?" *Smithsonian.com*, Smithsonian Institution, 8 Mar. 2017, www.smithsonianmag.com/science-nature/jacques-cinq-mars-bluefish-caves-scientific-progress-180962410/.

75. "EINSTEIN Believes In 'SPINOZA'S GOD'; SCIENTIST Defines His Faith in Reply, to Cablegram From Rabbi HERE. Sees a Divine Order but Says Its Ruler Is Not CONCERNED 'WITH Fates and Actions of Human Beings."." *The New York Times*, 25 Apr. 1929, www.nytimes.com/1929/04/25/archives/einstein-believes-in-spinozas-god-scientist-defines-his-faith-in.html.

76. Abhedananda, Swami and Sri Ramakrishna Paramahansa. *Sayings of Ramakrishna*, by Ramakrishna, Ramakrishna Vedanta Math, 1968.

77. Smith, Jeremy Adam, et al. "The State of Mindfulness Science." *Greater Good Magazine*, UC Berkeley's Greater Good Science Center, 5 Dec. 2017, https://greatergood.berkeley.edu/article/item/the_state_of_mindfulness_science.

78. Harrison, Olivia, and Martin Scorsese. *George Harrison: Living in the Material World*. Grove Street Pictures, HBO Films, 2011.

79. Hagelin, J. S., Orme-Johnson, D. W., Rainforth, M., Cavanaugh, K., & Alexander, C. N. (1999). Results of the National Demonstration Project to Reduce Violent Crime and Improve Governmental Effectiveness in Washington, D.C. *Social Indicators Research*, 47, 153–201.

80. "Nobel Disease." *Wikipedia,* Wikimedia Foundation, en.wikipedia.org/wiki/Nobel_disease.

81. Knox, Dilwyn, "Giordano Bruno", *The Stanford Encyclopedia of Philosophy* (Summer 2019 Edition), Edward N. Zalta (ed.). https://plato.stanford.edu/archives/sum2019/entries/bruno/

Part Three: Awareness is the Foundation

1. Walker, Ethan. *The Mystic Christ: The Light of Non-Duality and the Path of Love According to the Life and Teachings of Jesus,* Devi Press, 2003, p. 3.

2. Hertel, Howard. "From the Archives: Marilyn Monroe Dies; Pills Blamed." *Los Angeles Times,* 6 Aug. 1962, www.latimes.com/local/obituaries/archives/la-me-marilyn-monroe-19620806-story.html.

3. Greene, Joshua M. *Here Comes the Sun: George Harrison's Spiritual and Musical Journey.* Wiley, 2006.

4. "Introduction." *History of Mysticism: The Unchanging Testament,* by Swami Abhayananda, Watkins, 2002, p. 1-3.

5. "The Place of Science." *Forgotten Truth: The Common Vision of the World's Religions,* by Huston Smith, Harper San Francisco, 1992, p. 110.

6. "VIII. Ecstasy and Rapture." *Mysticism: A Study in the Nature and Development of Man's Spiritual Consciousness,* by Evelyn Underhill, Methuen & Co. Ltd., London, 1911.

7. "After Nag Hammadi I: Categories and Origins." *What Is Gnosticism?*, by Karen L. King, The Belknap Press of Harvard University Press, 2005, p. 155.

8. "The Formation of the Canon of the New Testament." *The New Testament: Its Background, Growth, and Context,* by Bruce Manning Metzger, Lutterworth Press, 1969, p. 316.

9. Kim, David W. "Is the Gospel of Thomas Gnostic?" *The Gnostic World,* 2018, pp. 170–179., doi:10.4324/9781315561608-15.

10. "Definitions of Sufism." *The Elements of Sufism,* by Shaykh Fadhlalla Haeri, Element Books, 1990.

11. "The Principles of Tawhid." *Sufism: Meaning, Knowledge, and Unity*, by Nūrbakhsh Javād, Khaniqahi-Nimatullahi, p. 76.

12. Mason, Herbert W. "Preface." *The Death of Al-Hallaj: A Dramatic Narrative*, Univ. of Notre Dame Press, 1979, p. xiv.

13. "Kabbalah: The Term and Its Meanings." *Kabbalah: A Very Short Introduction*, by Joseph Dan, Oxford University Press, 2007.

14. "The Ideas and Practices of Kabbalah." *Kabbalah and the Spiritual Quest: The Kabbalah Centre in America*, by Jody Elizabeth Myers, Praeger, 2007, p. 10.

15. *Major Trends in Jewish Mysticism*, by Gershom Scholem, Schocken, 1941, p. 27.

16. "Buddhism: The Secret of the Flower." *The World's Religions*, by Huston Smith, HarperOne, 2009, p. 128-131.

17. Ibid.

18. Fujita, Issho. "Zazen Is Not the Same as Meditation." BuddhistInquiry.org. "The Lived-Body Experience in Buddhist Meditation", Mar. 2002, Barre, Massachusetts, USA, Barre Center for Buddhist Studies, www.buddhistinquiry.org/article/zazen-is-not-the-same-as-meditation/.

19. "June 17th, 1970." *I AM THAT: Part I*, by Maharaj Nisargadatta, Chetana, 1973, p. 296.

20. Melton, J. Gordon. "New Age Movement." *Encyclopædia Britannica*, Encyclopædia Britannica, Inc., 10 Nov. 2000, www.britannica.com/topic/New-Age-movement.

21. Krishnamurti, Jiddu. "Dissolution Speech: 'Truth Is a Pathless Land.'" The Order of the Star in the East (The Theosophical Society). 3 Aug. 1929, Ommen, Holland, Star Camp.

22. "Edgar Cayce's Life: The Sleeping Prophet: Psychic: Edgar Cayce's A.R.E." Edgar Cayce's Life | The Sleeping Prophet | Psychic | *Edgar Cayce's A.R.E.*, www.edgarcayce.org/edgar-cayce/his-life/.

23. Sutcliffe, Steven J., and John P. Willmett. "'The Work': The Teachings of G. I. Gurdjieff and P. D. Ouspensky in Russia and Beyond." *The Oxford Handbook of Russian Religious Thought*, 2020, pp. 542–561., doi:10.1093/oxfordhb/9780198796442.013.14.

24. Goldberg, Philip. *American Veda: From Emerson and the Beatles to Yoga and Meditation—How Indian Spirituality Changed the West.* Three Rivers Press, 2013.

25. Goleman, Daniel, and Richard Davidson. *Altered Traits: Science*

Reveals How Meditation Changes Your Mind, Brain, and Body. Penguin USA, 2018.

26. Davidson, Richard J., and Antoine Lutz. "Buddha's Brain: Neuroplasticity and Meditation [In The Spotlight]." *IEEE Signal Processing Magazine,* vol. 25, no. 1, 2008, pp. 176–174., doi:10.1109/msp.2008.4431873.

27. "Science of the Heart." *HeartMath Institute,* 20 Dec. 2020, www.heartmath.org/research/science-of-the-heart/.

28. Godman, David. "Bhagavan's Death Experience." *Arunachala and Ramana Maharshi,* 7 May 2008, sri-ramana-maharshi.blogspot.com/2008/05/bhagavans-death-experience.html.

29. Godman, David. "An Introduction to Sri Ramana's Life and Teachings." DavidGodman.org, 12 July 2019, www.davidgodman.org/an-introduction-to-sri-ramanas-life-and-teachings/.

30. Dedieu, Jean-Raphael. *JNANI - The Silent Sage of Arunachala.* YouTube, CINEFX Productions, 25 May 2018, www.youtube.com/watch?v=hVYv9ktilQw.

31. Godman, David. "An Introduction to Sri Ramana's Life and Teachings - Page 4 of 5." *DavidGodman.org,* 12 July 2019, www.davidgodman.org/an-introduction-to-sri-ramanas-life-and-teachings/4/.

32. Katie, Byron, and Stephen Mitchell. "Introduction." *Loving What Is: Four Questions That Can Change Your Life,* Harmony Books, 2002, pp. x-xi.

33. Katie, Byron. *Raising Children.* YouTube, ByronKatie.com, 26 June 2017, www.youtube.com/watch?v=VLPOXcIfb4g.

Part Four: Turning Them into Us

1. "Karma." *The Shambhala Encyclopedia of Yoga,* by Georg Feuerstein, Shambhala, 2000, pp. 149–150.

2. Ibid.

3. Rai Bahadur Srisa Chandra Vasu. "Chapter II (Knowledge): Verses 39-44." *The Siva Samhita,* The Yoga Sastra ed., XV, Subhindranatha Vasu, The Panini Office, Bhuvaneswari Asrama, 1914. The Sacred Books of the Hindus.

4. "Who's Helping?" *How Can I Help?: Stories and Reflections on Service,* by Ram Dass and Paul Gorman, Alfred A. Knopf, 1985, p. 20.

5. Peck, Bob, director. *The Blazing Heart | A Portrait of the Hindu Saint, Amma Sri Karunamayi*. Mind Heart Lens Channel, Mind Heart Lens Films, 2016, https://www.youtube.com/watch?v=CUK4G2AuHKA.

6. May Peace Prevail On Earth. "Prayerful Launch to the 2015 UN Commission on the Status of Women, March 9 at the Church Center for the United Nations-USA." *May Peace Prevail On Earth International*, 19 May 2015, www.worldpeace.org/2015/05/prayerful-launch-to-the-2015-un-commission-on-the-status-of-womenmarch-9-at-the-church-center-for-the-united-nations-usa/.

7. Andrews, Karen. "Women in Theravada Buddhism." *Alliance for Bhikkhunis*, Institute of Buddhist Studies, Berkeley, CA, 8 June 2019, www.bhikkhuni.net/women-in-theravada-buddhism/.

8. Austin, Shoshan Victoria. "The True Human Body". In Carney, Eido Frances (ed.) *Receiving the Marrow*. Temple Ground Press, 2012. p. 148.

9. King, Martin Luther. "'The Chief Characteristics and Doctrines of Mahayana Buddhism' (April 1950)." *The Papers of Martin Luther King, Jr. Volume I: Called to Serve, January 1929-June 1951*, edited by Clayborne Carson et al., by Martin Luther King, University of California Press, 1992.

10. Radhakrishnan, S. "Chapter X. Buddhism As A Religion." *Indian Philosophy*, London: George Allen & Unwin Ltd., 1923, p. 589.

11. Goodman, Charles, "Ethics in Indian and Tibetan Buddhism", *The Stanford Encyclopedia of Philosophy* (Summer 2021 Edition), Edward N. Zalta (ed.), https://plato.stanford.edu/archives/sum2021/entries/ethics-indian-buddhism.

12. Mark, Joshua J. "A Short History of the Buddhist Schools." *Ancient History Encyclopedia*, 29 Sept. 2020, www.ancient.eu/article/492/a-short-history-of-the-buddhist-schools/.

13. Ibid.

14. Thích Nhất Hạnh. "Cultivating Our Bodhisattva Qualities." Dharma Talk. 15 Jan. 1998, Loubès-Bernac, France, Plum Village Monastery. https://www.mindfulnessbell.org/archive/2016/01/dharma-talk-cultivating-our-bodhisattva-qualities-2.

15. Thích Nhất Hạnh. "'They Call You A Bodhisattva': Thích Nhất Hạnh's Friendship with Dr. King." Plum Village, plumvillage.org/thich-nhat-hanhs-friendship-with-dr-king/.

Excerpted from *At Home in the World: Stories from a Monk's Life*, Thích Nhất Hạnh (2016) pp.72-73

16. David, Ariel. "For You Were (Not) Slaves in Egypt: The Ancient Memories behind the Exodus Myth." *Haaretz.com*, Haaretz, 19 Apr. 2019, www.haaretz.com/archaeology/.premium.MAGAZINE-for-you-were-not-slaves-in-egypt-the-memories-behind-the-exodus-myth-1.7138961.

17. Pearce, Laurie E. "New Evidence for Judeans in Babylonia." *Judah and the Judeans in the Persian Period*, by Oded Lipschitz and Manfred Oeming, Eisenbrauns, 2014.

18. "Expulsions and Exoduses of Jews." *Wikipedia*, Wikimedia Foundation, 17 Sept. 2021, en.wikipedia.org/wiki/Expulsions_and_exoduses_of_Jews. Source: Melton, J. Gordon (15 January 2014). *Faiths Across Time: 5,000 Years of Religious History*. pp. 967–. ISBN 978-1-61069-026-3.

19. "The 'Final Solution': Estimated Number of Jews Killed." Estimated Number of Jews Killed in the Final Solution, *Jewish Virtual Library: U.S. Holocaust Memorial Museum*, www.jewishvirtuallibrary.org/estimated-number-of-jews-killed-in-the-final-solution.

20. Mietkiewicz, Mark. "Nobel Prize and the Jews." *The Canadian Jewish News*, 11 Dec. 2018, www.cjnews.com/living-jewish/nobel-prize-and-the-jews.

21. Angel, Arielle. "Jewish Americans Are at a Turning Point with Israel." *The Guardian*, Guardian News and Media, 22 May 2021, www.theguardian.com/commentisfree/2021/may/22/jewish-americans-israel-palestine-arielle-angel.

22. King, Shaun. "Why Bernie Sanders's History of Racial Justice Activism Matters." *Jacobin*, www.jacobinmag.com/2018/06/bernie-sanders-civil-rights-movement-activism.

23. "The Crèche at Greccio, the Stigmata, the Death of Francis." *Saint Francis of Assisi, 1182-1226*, by Cristiani Léon, St. Paul Editions, 1983, pp. 146–148.

24. Snodgrass, Klyne. "Jesus and Money—No Place to Hide and No Easy Answers." *Word & World*, vol. 30, no. 2, 2010, p. 137.

25. Jones, Jeffrey M. "U.S. Church Membership Falls Below Majority for First Time." *Gallup.com*, Gallup, 13 Aug. 2021, news.gallup.com/poll/341963/church-membership-falls-below-majority-first-time.aspx.

26. "Parables About Money." *Stories with Intent: A Comprehensive Guide to the Parables of Jesus*, by Klyne Snodgrass, Eerdmans Publishing Co., 2018, p. 400.

27. Johari, Harish. "Introduction." *Chakras: Energy Centers of Transformation*, Inner Traditions India, 1987.

28. "The Ancient and Modern Mystery." *Wheels of Light: Chakras, Auras, and the Healing Energy of the Body*, by Rosalyn L. Bruyere, Fireside Book, 1994, pp. 24–25.

29. "Discovering Your Chakras." *The Power of Chakras: Unlock Your 7 Energy Centers for Healing, Happiness, and Transformation*, by Susan G. Shumsky, Career Press, 2014, pp. 104–105.

30. "Chakra Centers." *The Only Dance There Is; Talks Given at the Menninger Foundation, Topeka, Kansas, 1970, and at Spring Grove Hospital, Spring Grove, Maryland, 1972*, by Ram Dass, Anchor Press, 1974, p. 29.

31. Yogananda, Paramahansa. "Chapter IV: The Supreme Science of Knowing God." *The Bhagavad Gita: God Talks with Arjuna: Royal Science of God-Realization*, Self-Realization Fellowship, Los Angeles, 1995, p. 438.

32. Vigh, B, et al. "Nonvisual Photoreceptors of the Deep Brain, Pineal Organs and Retina." *Histol Histopathol*, 17 Apr. 2002, pp. 555–90., https://doi.org/10.14670/HH-17.555.

33. "The Force-Centres." *The Chakras*, by C. W. Leadbeater, Quest Books/ Theosophical Publishing House, 1927, pp. 14–15.

34. Sivananda, Swami. *Kundalini Yoga*. The Divine Life Society, 1980.

35. Krishna, Gopi, and James Hillman. "Introduction." *Kundalini: The Evolutionary Energy in Man*, Shambala Publications, Inc., 1971, pp. 12–13.

36. Peck, Bob, director. *Asanas in the Yard*. Mind Heart Lens Channel, Mind Heart Lens Films, 2016, https://www.youtube.com/watch?v=sxksLgKU5sU.

37. Agenyi, Jeremiah. "Recidivism in the United States – An Overview." *Atlas Corps*, 31 May 2017, atlascorps.org/recidivism-united-states-overview/.

38. Raab, Diana. "What Is Spiritual Bypassing?" *Psychology Today*, Sussex Publishers, 23 Jan. 2019, www.psychologytoday.com/us/blog/the-empowerment-diary/201901/what-is-spiritual-bypassing.

39. "Volume 1: Lectures & Discourses - Krishna." *The Complete Works of Swami Vivekananda*, by Swami Vivekananda, Advaita

Ashrama, 2016, pp. 475–476.

40. Lemle, Mickey, director. Ram Dass, Fierce Grace. Lemle Pictures, Inc., 2001, www.lemlepictures.com/film_RD.html.

41. Goleman, Daniel, and Richard J. Davidson. *Altered Traits: Science Reveals How Meditation Changes Your Mind, Brain, and Body.* Penguin USA, 2018.

42. "Content to Be." *Polishing the Mirror: How to Live from Your Spiritual Heart*, by Ram Dass and Rameshwar Das, Sounds True, 2014, pp. 205–206.

43. Dass, Ram. "Journey: The Transformation — Dr. Richard Alpert, Ph.D into Baba Ram Dass." *Be Here Now,* Lama Foundation, 1971.

44. Ibid.

45. Hiatt, Nathaniel. "A Trip Down Memory Lane: LSD at Harvard." *The Harvard Crimson,* 23 May 2016, www.thecrimson.com/article/2016/5/23/trip-down-memory-lane/.

46. Ram Dass. "Transformation of a Man - WBAI Radio Talks Part 2 of 7." *YouTube,* Baba Ram Dass Channel, 19 May 2014, www.youtube.com/watch?v=uxrsMptVF2s%3Flist.

47. Ibid.

48. Dass, Ram. "Bhagwan Dass." *Be Here Now,* Lama Foundation, 1971.

49. Ibid.

50. Dass, Ram, and Rameshwar Das. "Fast Foreword." *Polishing the Mirror: How to Live from Your Spiritual Heart,* Sounds True, 2014.

51. Dass, Ram. "About Anger and Love." *Miracle of Love: Stories about Neem Karoli Baba,* E.P. Dutton New York, 1979, p. 258.

52. "Simple Truth." *Polishing the Mirror: How to Live from Your Spiritual Heart,* by Ram Dass and Rameshwar Das, Sounds True, 2014, p. 31.

53. Dass, Ram. "Faith… No Fear." *Miracle of Love: Stories about Neem Karoli Baba,* E.P. Dutton New York, 1979, p. 90.

54. "It's All Perfect." *Polishing the Mirror: How to Live from Your Spiritual Heart,* by Ram Dass and Rameshwar Das, Sounds True, 2014, p. 191.

Part Five: We are not the body: We are Spirit

1. Thurman, Robert. "Expanding Your Circle of Compassion." *TED*, Chautauqua Institution, Oct. 2009, www.ted.com/talks/robert_thurman_expanding_your_circle_of_compassion.

2. "The Place of Science." *Forgotten Truth: The Common Vision of the World's Religions*, by Huston Smith, Harper San Francisco, 1992, p. 111.

3. Yogananda, Paramahansa. *Journey to Self-Realization: Collected Talks and Essay on Realizing God in Daily Life*. Self-Realization Fellowship, 2012.

4. Faggin, Federico. "Consciousness Is Fundamental." *Wall Street International*, 11 Dec. 2020, https://wsimag.com/science-and-technology/63569-consciousness-is-fundamental.

5. "Founder: Dr. Ian Stevenson." *Division of Perceptual Studies*, University of Virginia | School of Medicine, 4 Mar. 2021, med.virginia.edu/perceptual-studies/who-we-are/history-of-dops/dr-ian-stevenson/. Source: Stevenson's Obituary, written by Emily Williams Kelly, Ph.D.

6. Stevenson, Ian. "Chapter 1: An Introduction to the Study of Reincarnation." *Children Who Remember Previous Lives: A Question of Reincarnation*, McFarland, Jefferson, NC, 2001, p. 12.

7. Stevenson, Ian. "Some of My Journeys in Medicine." The Flora Levy Lecture in the Humanities. 1989, Lafayette, Louisiana, The University of Southwestern Louisiana. https://med.virginia.edu/perceptual-studies/wp-content/uploads/sites/360/2015/11/some-of-my-journeys-in-medicine.pdf.

8. Tucker, Jim (2000), 'A scale to measure the strength and weakness of children's claims of previous lives: Methodology and initial findings', *Journal of Scientific Exploration*, 14 (4), pp 571–81.

9. Bernet, William, and Jonathan Edelmann. "Setting Criteria for Ideal Reincarnation Research." *Journal of Consciousness Studies*, vol. 14, no. 12, 2007, pp. 92–101.

10. Hardo, Trutz. "The Three-Year-Old Who Convicted His Murder." *Children Who Have Lived Before: Reincarnation Today*, Random House, London, 1988, pp. 26–29.

11. Semkiw, Walter. "Reincarnation Case of an Israeli Child Who Recalled Being Killed with an Axe & Identifies His Past Life Murderer, Who Confesses." *Reincarnation Research*, 12 Sept. 2019, https://www.reincarnationresearch.com/reincarnation-case-of-an-israeli-child-who-recalled-being-killed-with-an-ax-identifies-his-past-life-murderer-who-confesses/.

12. Yogananda, Paramahansa. "Do Souls Reincarnate?" *The Divine Romance*, Self-Realization Fellowship, Los Angeles, 2000, pp. 277–278.

13. Harris, Dan, and Ely Brown. "'Nightline' 'Face-Off': Does God Have a Future?" *ABC News*, ABC News Network, 22 Mar. 2010, https://abcnews.go.com/Nightline/FaceOff/nightline-face-off-god-future/story?id=10170505.

14. Das, Surya. "The Sage, the Lady, and the Fish." *The Snow Lion's Turquoise Mane*, HarperOne, New York, 2009, pp. 177–178.

15. McKenna, Terence. Food of the Gods: The Search for the Original Tree of Knowledge. Bantam Books, 1992.

16. Sloat, Sarah. "In 'Stoned Ape' Theory, Consciousness Has Roots in Psilocybin." *Inverse*, 14 July 2017, https://www.inverse.com/article/34186-stoned-ape-hypothesis.

17. Mishlove, Jeffrey. "Terence McKenna: Hallucinogens & Culture." *YouTube*, Thinking Allowed with Jeffrey Mishlove, 24 Jan. 2011, https://www.youtube.com/watch?v=u8y-khMKIbU.

18. Space Time Continuum. "Archaic Revival." *Alien Dreamtime with Terence McKenna*, Jonah Sharp, San Francisco, CA, 1993.

19. Laufer, Berthold. "Origin of the Word Shaman." *American Anthropologist*, vol. 19, no. 3, 1917, pp. 361–371., https://doi.org/10.1525/aa.1917.19.3.02a00020.

20. Belcourt, Billy-Ray. "Fatal Naming Rituals." *Hazlitt*, 31 July 2018, https://hazlitt.net/feature/fatal-naming-rituals.

21. "SHAMAN." *Lexico Dictionaries | English*, Oxford Dictionary, https://www.lexico.com/definition/shaman.

22. McKenna, Terence K. *The Archaic Revival: Speculations on Psychedelic Mushrooms, the Amazon, Virtual Reality, UFOs, Evolution, Shamanism, the Rebirth of the Goddess, and the End of History*, HarperSanFrancisco, San Francisco, CA, 1992, p. 2.

23. "Mushroom Laws by State 2021." *World Population Review*, https://worldpopulationreview.com/state-rankings/mushroom-laws-by-state.

24. Pollan, Michael. "The Trip Treatment: Psychedelics in Psychotherapy." *How to Change Your Mind: What the New Science of Psychedelics Teaches Us About Consciousness, Dying, Addiction, Depression, and Transcendence*, Penguin Press, New York, 2019, pp. 331–396.

25. "Understanding the Epidemic." *CDC.gov*, Centers for Disease

Control and Prevention, National Center for Injury Prevention and Control, 17 Mar. 2021, https://www.cdc.gov/opioids/basics/epidemic.html.

26. Passie, Torsten, et al. "The Pharmacology of Psilocybin." Addiction Biology, vol. 7, no. 4, 2002, pp. 357–364., https://doi.org/10.1080/1355621021000005937.

27. Raspolich, Joseph. "Can You Overdose on Mushrooms?" Arete Recovery, 8 Sept. 2021, https://areterecovery.com/psilocybin/overdose/.

28. Dasgupta, Amitava. "Abuse of Magic Mushroom, Peyote Cactus, LSD, Khat, and Volatiles." *Critical Issues in Alcohol and Drugs of Abuse Testing*, 2019, pp. 477–494., https://doi.org/10.1016/b978-0-12-815607-0.00033-2.

29. Pollan, Michael. "How to Change Your Mind." *Talks at Google*. 19 June 2018, https://www.youtube.com/watch?v=KuhmZSFvhL0.

30. Leary, T. 1969. The effects of consciousness-expanding drugs on prisoner rehabilitation, *Psychedelic Review* Vol.10: 32-38.

31. "Come Together." The Beatles Bible, 12 Jan. 2021, https://www.beatlesbible.com/songs/come-together/.

32. Leary, T. 1969. The effects of consciousness-expanding drugs on prisoner rehabilitation, *Psychedelic Review* Vol.10: 30-31.

33. Doblin, Rick. "Dr. Leary's Concord Prison Experiment: A 34-Year Follow-Up Study." *Journal of Psychoactive Drugs*, vol. 30, no. 4, 1998, pp. 419–426., https://doi.org/10.1080/02791072.1998.10399715.

34. Ibid.

35. Ibid.

36. "The Psychedelic Evidence." *Forgotten Truth: The Common Vision of the World's Religions*, by Huston Smith, Harper San Francisco, 1992, p. 155.

37. Dass, Ram. "Journey: The Transformation — Dr. Richard Alpert, Ph.D into Baba Ram Dass." *Be Here Now*, Lama Foundation, 1971.

38. Ram Dass. "Transformation of a Man - WBAI Radio Talks Part 3 of 7." *YouTube*, Baba Ram Dass Channel, 19 May 2014, https://www.youtube.com/watch?v=mD2G8DMBAXk.

39. Dass, Ram. "Journey: The Transformation — Dr. Richard Alpert, Ph.D into Baba Ram Dass." *Be Here Now*, Lama Foundation, 1971.

40. Horgan, John. "Baba Ram Dass and the Tale of The Acid-Gobbling Guru." *Scientific American Blog Network*, Scientific American, 24 Dec. 2019, https://blogs.scientificamerican.com/cross-check/baba-ram-dass-and-the-tale-of-the-acid-gobbling-guru/.

41. Dass, Ram. "About Drugs." *Miracle of Love: Stories about Neem Karoli Baba*, E.P. Dutton New York, 1979, p. 229-231.

42. Ibid.

43. Yogananda, Paramahansa. *Metaphysical Meditations: Universal Prayers, Affirmations, and Visualizations.* Self-Realization Fellowship, 1964.

44. Sliney, D H. "What Is Light? The Visible Spectrum and Beyond." *Eye*, vol. 30, no. 2, 2016, pp. 222–229., https://doi.org/10.1038/eye.2015.252.

45. Dalrymple, William. "Jesus the Prophet | Review: 'The Muslim Jesus' by Tarif Khalidi." *The Guardian*, Guardian News and Media, 22 Dec. 2001, https://www.theguardian.com/books/2001/dec/22/history books.islam.

46. Rinpoche, Dilgo Khyentse. "Part One: The Preparation." *The Heart of Compassion: The Thirty-Seven Verses on the Practice of a Bodhisattva: A Commentary*, translated by Mattieu Ricard, Shambhala Publications, Inc, Boston, 2007, p. 60.

Part Six: The Love of Our Creator is Inescapable

1. "40 Years Since Publishing ACIM • Foundation for Inner Peace: Publisher of A Course in Miracles (ACIM)." *Foundation for Inner Peace: Publisher of A Course in Miracles (ACIM)*, 21 June 2016, https://acim.org/40-years-since-publishing-acim/.

2. Schucman, Helen. "What It Is." *Autobiography of Helen Schucman*, Foundation for Inner Peace, 1990, p. 43.

3. "A Course in Miracles (How It Came, What It Is, What It Says)." *Foundation for A Course in Miracles ®*, 2 Dec. 2020, https://facim.org/foundation-course-miracles/what-is-acim/.

4. Howe, Carol M. "Part I: Childhood through Retirement." *Never Forget to Laugh: Personal Recollections of Bill Thetford, Co-Scribe of A Course in Miracles*, Carol Howe, 2009.

5. ACIM Study Group. "Bill Thetford Talks about His Life & A Course in Miracles (3/3)." *YouTube*, 5 Feb. 2011, https://www.youtube.com/watch?v=IaysZ4Po9FU.

6. "A Course in Miracles (How It Came, What It Is, What It Says)." *Foundation for A Course in Miracles ®*, 2 Dec. 2020, https://facim.org/foundation-course-miracles/what-is-acim/.

7. Keohane, Steve. "A Course in Miracles - Satanically Inspired?" *Bible Probe*, http://www.bibleprobe.com/miraclecourse.htm.

8. "A New Realities Interview with William N. Thetford, Ph.D. (1984)." *Foundation for Inner Peace: Publisher of A Course in Miracles (ACIM)*, 23 Apr. 2021, https://acim.org/archives/a-new-realities-interview-with-william-n-thetford/.

9. "Clarification of Quotes and Terms in the Bible as Presented in "A Course in Miracles"." *A Course in Miracles Urtext Manuscripts*, Miracles in Action Press, (Urtext). https://jcim.net/Images/Clarification-of-Bible-Quotes.pdf.

10. Mundy, Jon. "Chapter 1: There Must Be Another Way (How It Came To Be)." *Living A Course in Miracles: An Essential Guide to the Classic Text*, Sterling, New York, 2013, pp. 22-23.

11. Perry, Robert. "Iambic Pentameter in the Course." *Circle of Atonement*, https://circleofa.org/library/iambic-pentameter-in-the-course/.

12. Muruganar, and Ramana Maharshi. "Investigation into Truth." *Guru Vachaka Kovai (The Garland of the Guru's Sayings)*, edited by David Godman, Arunachalaramana Book Trust, Tiruvannamalai, 2008.

13. Ibid.

14. Goldhill, Olivia. "Neuroscience Backs up the Buddhist Belief That 'the Self' Isn't Constant, but Ever-Changing." *Quartz*, 20 Sept. 2015, https://qz.com/506229/neuroscience-backs-up-the-buddhist-belief-that-the-self-isnt-constant-but-ever-changing/.

15. "Baba Ram Dass, Spiritual Guru and LSD Proponent, Dies at 88." AP NEWS, Associated Press, 23 Dec. 2019, https://apnews.com/article/hi-state-wire-hawaii-timothy-leary-us-news-ap-top-news-9a69b5c29572667db80296a00633390f.

16. Mishlove, Jeffrey. "Ram Dass: Compassion In Action." *YouTube*, Thinking Allowed with Jeffrey Mishlove, 3 June. 2011, https://www.youtube.com/watch?v=_skjT_uOzyo.

17. Yogananda, Paramahansa. "An Experience in Cosmic Consciousness." *Autobiography of a Yogi*, Self-Realization Fellowship, Los Angeles, California. Reprinted with permission.

18. Moffitt, Phillip. "31 Flavors of Craving." *Tricycle*, 22 Jan. 2016, https://tricycle.org/magazine/31-flavors-craving/.

19. Abhedananda, Swami and Sri Ramakrishna Paramahansa. "Conquest of Desires." *Sayings of Ramakrishna*, by Ramakrishna, Ramakrishna Vedanta Math, 1968, p. 122.

20. "Glossary: Holy Spirit." *Foundation for A Course in Miracles®*, 4 Mar. 2018, https://facim.org/glossary/holy-spirit/.

21. Gill, N.S. "The Myth of Er from the Republic of Plato." *ThoughtCo*, 3 Apr. 2019, https://www.thoughtco.com/the-myth-of-er-120332.

22. Macurdy, Grace Harriet. "Traces of the Influence of Plato's Eschatological Myths in Parts of the Book of Revelation and the Book of Enoch." Transactions and Proceedings of the American Philological Association, vol. 41, 1910, pp. 65–67., https://doi.org/10.2307/282716.

23. Bauckham, Richard. "Cosmic Tours and Tours of Hell." *The Fate of the Dead: Studies on the Jewish and Christian Apocalypses*, Society of Biblical Literature, Atlanta, 2008, p. 71.

24. Macurdy, Grace Harriet. "Traces of the Influence of Plato's Eschatological Myths in Parts of the Book of Revelation and the Book of Enoch." Transactions and Proceedings of the American Philological Association, vol. 41, 1910, pp. 65–67., https://doi.org/10.2307/282716.

25. Pearson, Fred B. "Sheol and Hades in Old and New Testament." *Review & Expositor*, vol. 35, no. 3, 1938, pp. 304–314., https://doi.org/10.1177/003463733803500304.

26. Lundell, Peter. "Hell and Gehenna." *Peter Lundell | Live by God's Word and Spirit*, https://www.peterlundell.com/online-library/entries/to-hades-with-hell/hell-gehenna/.

27. Roos, Dave. "A Short History of Hell." *HowStuffWorks*, 27 Apr. 2020, https://people.howstuffworks.com/hell.htm.

28. Pate, W.E. "Hell in the Gospels: Mark, Luke, and John." Deconversion Blog, 23 Feb. 2021, https://deconversionblog.com/2021/02/23/hell-in-the-gospels-mark-luke-and-john/.

29. Paul, John. "General Audience: 28 July 1999 - Pope John Paul II." *The Holy See*, Libreria Editrice Vaticana, 28 July 1999, https://www.vatican.va/content/john-paul-ii/en/audiences/1999/documents/hf_jp-ii_aud_28071999.html.

30. Haygood, Lisa. "The Battle To Authenticate 'The Gospel of Thomas'." *LUX*, vol. 3, no. 1, 2013, pp. 1–31.,

doi:10.5642/lux.201303.06.

31. Viljoen, Francois. "The Matthean Community within a Jewish Religious Society." *HTS Teologiese Studies / Theological Studies*, vol. 72, no. 4, 2016, https://doi.org/10.4102/hts.v72i4.3418.

32. Plato. "Book VII: The World of Shadows and of Realities." *Plato's The Republic*, translated by B. Jowett, Vintage Books: A Division of Random House, New York, 1888, pp. 253–261.

33. Ibid.

34. Ferguson, A. S. "Plato's Simile of Light (Continued). Part II. the Allegory of the Cave." *The Classical Quarterly*, vol. 16, no. 1, 1922, pp. 17., https://doi.org/10.1017/s0009838800001956.

35. Filonik, Jakub. (2014). Athenian Impiety Trials: A Reappraisal. https://doi.org/10.5281/zenodo.896899.

36. "When We Understand the Text: Sin Means to Miss the Mark?" Christian Podcast Central, *Patheos*, 26 Nov. 2016, https://www.patheos.com/blogs/e2medianetwork/2016/11/wwutt-sin-means-to-miss-the-mark/.

37. Renard, Gary R. *The Disappearance of the Universe: Straight Talk about Illusions, Past Lives, Religion, Sex, Politics, and the Miracles of Forgiveness*, Hay House, London, 2005, pp. 9–13.

38. Valea, Ernest. "The Parable of the Prodigal Son in Christianity and Buddhism." ComparativeReligion.com, https://www.comparativereligion.com/prodigal.html.

39. O'Grady, Maggie. "Mistake of the Intellect: 'Pragyapradh'." *Medium*, Space for Insight, 16 Feb. 2021, https://mogrady.medium.com/mistake-of-the-intellect-pragyapradh-78cdc3ea3b4.

40. Godman, David. "Swami Siddheswarananda's Views on Bhagavan's Teachings on Creation." Arunachala and Ramana Maharshi, 1 Jan. 1970, http://sri-ramana-maharshi.blogspot.com/2010/04/swami-siddheswaranandas-views-on.html.

41. Thích Nhất Hạnh. "The Wave and the Water." *Buddha Mind, Buddha Body*, Parallax Press, Berkeley, CA, 2007.

42. Maharaj, Nisargadatta, and Maurice Frydman. "11. Awareness and Consciousness." *I Am That: Conversations with Sri Nisargadatta Maharaj*, Chetana, Bombay, 1978.

43. Sri Anandamayi Ma. "Chapter III: Selected Discourses." *The Essential Srī Anandamayī Mā: Life and Teachings of a 20th Century Indian Saint*, edited by Alexander Lipski and Joseph A. Fitzgerald, World Wisdom, Bloomington, 2007, p. 180.

44. Yogananda, Paramahansa. "The Resurrection of Sri Yukteswar." *Autobiography of a Yogi*, Self-Realization Fellowship, Los Angeles, California. Reprinted with permission.

45. Rowe, Harry T. "Yogananda's Mortuary Report." Received by Self-Realization Fellowship, Forest Lawn Memorial-Park, 16 May 1952, Los Angeles, California. http://oaks.nvg.org/yogananda_mortuary_report.pdf.

46. Wilber, Ken. "The Secret Impulse." *A Brief History of Everything*, Shambhala Publications, Inc., Boston, 2000, pp. 42–43.

47. Johnson, Robin. "Byron Katie." *Great Mystery*, 6 Sept. 2019, https://greatmystery.org/byron-katie-2/.

48. Holmes, Pete. "You Made It Weird with Pete Holmes." Guest, Byron Katie, Apple Podcasts, August 19, 2020. http://youmadeitweird.nerdistind.libsynpro.com/.

49. Thích Nhất Hạnh. "The Six Paramitas." *The Heart of the Buddha's Teaching Transforming Suffering Into Peace, Joy & Liberation : the Four Noble Truths, the Noble Eightfold Path, and Other Basic Buddhist Teachings*, Parallax Press, Berkeley, CA, 1998, p. 196.

50. Ortiz, Erik, and Daniel Arkin. "Dylann Roof 'Almost Didn't Go Through' With Charleston Church Shooting." *NBCNews.com*, NBCUniversal News Group, 20 June 2015, https://www.nbcnews.com/storyline/charleston-church-shooting/dylann-roof-almost-didnt-go-through-charleston-church-shooting-n378341.

51. "Charleston Church Shooting: What Victims' Families Said to Dylann Roof." *BBC News*, BBC, 19 June 2015, https://www.bbc.co.uk/news/world-us-canada-33185848.

52. King, Martin Luther. "'Loving Your Enemies," Sermon Delivered at Dexter Avenue Baptist Church." *The Martin Luther King, Jr. Research and Education Institute*, Stanford University, 10 Sept. 2021, Delivered at Dexter Avenue Baptist Church, November 17, 1957. https://kinginstitute.stanford.edu/king-papers/documents/loving-your-enemies-sermon-delivered-dexter-avenue-baptist-church

Epilogue

1. Hoffmeister, David. "Truth and Self-Realization." A Course in Miracles Audio. Straight Talk on Truth and Self-Realization ACIM Gathering. https://a-course-in-miracles.org/mp3-recordings/straight-talk-truth/

2. Vivekananda, Swami. "Concentration: Its Practice." Volume 1:

Raja Yoga. *The Complete Works of Swami Vivekananda,* 1896, London.

Gratitude

My initial feeling of gratitude goes directly to the Infinite Creator. At its purest intention, this entire book is devoted to the Rootless Root of All. The Cosmic Mystery. Mother-Father-God. To us mystics, everything we do is a ritual. Everything we say is a prayer. So it's all for The All—what else is there anyway?

Secondarily, to the liberated ones: the saints who overcame the wheel of samsara. I've mentioned many of those whom I admire most in these pages. I extend sincere thankfulness for showing the rest of us that their way of seeing the world is not only attainable, but inevitable.

More directly, to the people who encouraged me to write this book... I will never be able to express the depths of gratitude I feel for your contributions in eliminating my relentless hesitations.

To my wife: Melissa, thank you for being my mirror; true love reveals both the blemishes on the surface and the underlying beauty within. I have absolutely no conception of who I would be in this incarnation without you in my life for all this time.

To my family: my mom Rhonda, my dad Bob, my stepmom Joan, and my sister Haley, I'm a motionless sailboat without your encouraging gales. I understand now how important an environment of love is to a developing human being.

To Richard the Apache medicine man: thank you for your guidance to me and your patience with me, and for the tireless, connected work you've done for so many.

To the Gonzalez family: thank you all for listening to me blabber on endlessly about historical Bible scholarship and those crazy mystics; and for your support of me being *that* member of the extended family.

To the *Be Where How?* family: Scott, Ryan, Melena, and Maggie, your continued affirmations that this material has value is a vital reason why it made it to this current manifestation in form. Extreme brotherhood shoutout to Scott Standley who offered hundreds of suggestions on readability to improve the thing. It was a hefty block of wood before you got it.

To my most personally influential professors: Dr. White, Dr. Phillips, Dr. Buckley, your exhaustive passions for examining dusty old ancient literature is noble and beneficial for modern society.

To my close friends who sat through so many late nights of "Bob's Church" ... my proselytizing post-happy hour "sermons" as I worked through this material, this is only the beginning.

To my boy, Bobby V, you don't know it yet but mapping out my ventures into comparative religion and the perennial philosophy for the next generation was a primary motivation... ultimately, I'm only here to be truly helpful. You already are Love; may this information help you navigate the rest.

And lastly, thank *you* for holding this book and reading these words.

What felt like countless hours went into its creation and I want you to feel my gratitude for being on the reciprocating end of what were unmanifested thoughts for many years. If my humble discoveries offer you even the slightest, fleeting glimpse of Real Peace, it was all worth it.

—Bob

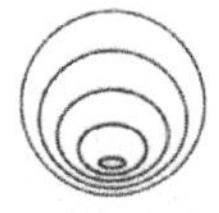

Stay Connected

(To Your Inner Being, But Also To Me)

If you're interested in more from me, keep reading this book over and over again.

Or head to originalsinisalie.com where you can find the audio version of this book, podcast appearances, TikToks, and my ongoing presence on Medium.com.

I'm also a co-host of the *Be Where How? Show*, a lighthearted spiritual podcast on mindfulness, creativity and the perennial philosophy. Check us out at bewherehow.com.

And lastly, I am one of the co-founders of *The Awareness & Compassion Project*. We have online courses on mindfulness, philosophy and more: awarenessandcompassion.org.

May all beings be at peace.

Printed in Great Britain
by Amazon